Quality in Academic Libraries

Quality in Academic Libraries

Ramesh Jabnoor

ABD PUBLISHERS
Jaipur ■ New Delhi

ABD PUBLISHERS

Regd. Off. "Bony Residency", Gate No. 2
Opp. Tilak Public School, Vishweswariya Nagar,
Gopalpura Road, Jaipur - 302018, India
Ph: 0141 - 2761280, Telefax: 2761381
Email: abdpublishersjpr@gmail.com

Delhi Office: 102, 1st Floor, Satyam House,
4327/3, Ansari Road, Darya Ganj,
New Delhi - 110002, India
Ph: 011-45652440

visit us: www.oxfordbookcompany.com

Distributed By
KEYA INTERNATIONAL PRESS LLP
E-mail: keyainternationalpressllp@gmail.com

Published in India, 2025

ISBN: 9788183768962

Typeset by Shivangi Computer, Jaipur

Printed and bound in India by Thomson Press Ltd.,
New Delhi

This book dedicated to
My Father
Late Shri Gaibanna Jabnoor,
Mangalgi.

Contents

Preface

The present era, which is a age of technology and information, the libraries are now not a store of books or journals but a source of latest information. In this book all the latest methods/tools concerned with a modern academic library has been discussed in detail. How to use a modern library, what are latest technologies, how to use e-book, e-journal, e-mail etc. has been explained in a lucid and simplified manner such that even a layman can understand all the process in technologies with ease. However, with the collection of media other than books for storing information, many libraries are now also repositories and access points for maps, prints, or other documents and various storage media such as microform (microfilm/microfiche), audio tapes, CDs, cassettes, videotapes, and DVDs. Libraries may also provide public facilities to access CD-ROMs, subscription databases, and the Internet.

Thus, modern libraries are increasingly being redefined as places to get unrestricted access to information in many formats and from many sources. In addition to providing materials, they also provide the services of specialists, librarians, who are experts at finding and organizing information and at interpreting information needs. Organization of a modern library, library network and allied subjects has been also discussed. The book is of immense use not only to trained librarians but also to students and general reader.

— Ramesh Jabnoor

CHAPTER 1

Library and User Education

The Library is a collection of information, sources, resources, books, and services, and the structure in which it is housed: it is organized for use and maintained by a public body, an institution, or a private individual. In the more traditional sense, a library is a collection of books. The term can mean the collection, the building that houses such a collection, or both. Public and institutional collections and services may be intended for use by people who choose not to—or cannot afford to—purchase an extensive collection themselves, who need material no individual can reasonably be expected to have, or who require professional assistance with their research. However, with the collection of media other than books for storing information, many libraries are now also repositories and access points for maps, prints, or other documents and various storage media such as microform (microfilm/microfiche), audio tapes, CDs, cassettes, videotapes, and DVDs. Libraries may also provide public facilities to access CD-ROMs, subscription databases, and the Internet. Thus, modern libraries are increasingly being redefined as places to get unrestricted access to information in many formats and from many sources. In addition to providing materials, they also provide the services of specialists, librarians, who are experts at finding and organizing information and at interpreting information needs. More recently, libraries are understood as extending beyond the physical walls of a building, by including material accessible by electronic means, and by providing the assistance of librarians in navigating and analysing tremendous amounts of knowledge with a variety of digital tools.

The term "library" has itself acquired a secondary meaning: "a collection of useful material for common use," and in this sense is used in fields such as computer science, mathematics and statistics, electronics and biology.

Early History

Antiquity: The first two libraries were composed for the most part, of published records, a particular type of library called archives. Archaeological findings from the ancient city-states of Sumer have revealed temple rooms full of clay tablets in cuneiform script. These archives were made up almost completely of the records of commercial transactions or inventories, with only a few documents touching theological matters, historical records or legends. Things were much the same in the government and temple records on papyrus of Ancient Egypt.

The earliest discovered private archives were kept at Ugarit; besides correspondence and inventories, texts of myths may have been standardized practice-texts for teaching new scribes. There is also evidence of libraries at Nippur about 1900 BC and those at Nineveh about 700 BC showing a library classification system.

Over 30,000 clay tablets from the Library of Ashurbanipal have been discovered at Ninevah, providing archaeologists with an amazing wealth of Mesopotamian literary, religious and administrative work. Among the findings were the Enuma Elish, also known as *the Epic of Creation,* which depicts a traditional Babylonian view of creation, the Epic of Gilgamesh, a large selection of "omen texts" including *Enuma Anu Enlil* which "contained omens dealing with the moon, its visibility, eclipses, and conjunction with planets and fixed stars, the sun, its corona, spots, and eclipses, the weather, namely lightning, thunder, and clouds, and the planets and their visibility, appearance, and stations.", and astronomic/astrological texts, as well as standard lists used by scribes and scholars such as word lists, bilingual vocabularies, lists of signs and synonyms, and lists of medical diagnoses.

Libraries in Persian Empire

During the Achaemenid Persian Empire (558–330 BC) the religious and scientific books of Persia since Zoroaster, were archived in the libraries of "Ganj-i-hapigan" in Takht-i-Suleiman and "Dez-i-Napesht" in Persepolis. These books were probably in the fields of philosophy, astronomy, alchemy and medical sciences, the fields in which Magus of Persia were master in. After the invasion of Persia by Alexander the Great all these books were burned. It has been mentioned in the book Arda Viraf that:

> *"He came to Persia with severe cruelty and war and devastation... and destroyed the metropolis and empire, and made them desolate... all the*

avesta and zand, written upon prepared cow-skins and with gold ink, was deposited in the archives... he burned them up."

Libraries in the Hellenic World and Rome

Private or personal libraries made up of non-fiction and fiction books (as opposed to the state or institutional records kept in archives) appeared in classical Greece in the 5th century BC. The celebrated book collectors of Hellenistic Antiquity were listed in the late second century in *Deipnosophistae:*

Polycrates of Samos and Pisistratus who was tyrant of Athens, and Euclides who was himself also an Athenian and Nicorrates of Samos and even the kings of Pergamos, and Euripides the poet and Aristotle the philosopher, and Nelius his librarian; from whom they say our countryman Ptolemæus, surnamed Philadelphus, bought them all, and transported them, with all those which he had collected at Athens and at Rhodes to his own beautiful Alexandria.

All these libraries were Greek; the cultivated Hellenized diners in *Deipnosophistae* pass over the libraries of Rome in silence. By the time of Augustus there were public libraries near the forums of Rome: there were libraries in the Porticus Octaviae near the Theatre of Marcellus, in the temple of Apollo Palatinus, and in the Biblioteca Ulpiana in the Forum of Trajan. The state archives were kept in a structure on the slope between the Roman Forum and the Capitoline Hill.

Private libraries appeared during the late republic: Seneca inveighed against libraries fitted out for show by non-reading owners who scarcely read their titles in the course of a lifetime, but displayed the scrolls in bookcases (*armaria*) of citrus wood inlaid with ivory that ran right to the ceiling: "by now, like bathrooms and hot water, a library is got up as standard equipment for a fine house (*domus*). Libraries were amenities suited to a villa, such as Cicero's at Tusculum, Maecenas's several villas, or Livy the Younger's, all described in surving letters.

At the Villa of the Papyri at Herculaneum, apparently the villa of Caesar's father-in-law, the Greek library has been partly preserved in volcanic ash; archaeologists speculate that a Latin library, kept separate from the Greek one, may await discovery at the site.

In the West, the first public libraries were established under the Roman Empire as each succeeding emperor strove to open one or many which outshone that of his predecessor. Unlike the Greek libraries, readers had direct access to the scrolls, which were kept on shelves built into the walls of a large room. Reading or copying was normally done in the room itself. The surviving records give only a few instances of lending features. As a rule Roman public libraries were bilingual: they had a Latin room and a Greek room. Most of the large Roman baths were also cultural centres, built from the start with a library, with the usual two room arrangement for Greek and Latin texts.

Libraries were filled with parchment scrolls as at Library of Pergamum and on papyrus scrolls as at Alexandria: export of prepared writing materials was a staple of commerce. There were a few institutional or royal libraries which were open to an educated public (like the Library of Alexandria, once the largest library in the ancient world), but on the whole collections were private. In those rare cases where it was possible for a scholar to consult library books there seems to have been no direct access to the stacks. In all recorded cases the books were kept in a relatively small room where the staff went to get them for the readers, who had to consult them in an adjoining hall or covered walkway.

In the sixth century, at the very close of the Classical period, the great libraries of the Mediterranean world remained those of Constantinople and Alexandria. Cassiodorus, minister to Theodoric, established a monastery at Vivarium in the heel of Italy with a library where he attempted to bring Greek learning to Latin readers and preserve texts both sacred and secular for future generations. As its unofficial librarian, Cassiodorus not only collected as many manuscripts as he could, he also wrote treatises aimed at instructing his monks in the proper uses of reading and methods for copying texts accurately. In the end, however, the library at Vivarium was dispersed and lost within a century.

Through Origen and especially the scholarly presbyter Pamphilus of Caesarea, an avid collector of books of Scripture, the theological school of Caesarea won a reputation for having the most extensive ecclesiastical library of the time, containing more than 30,000 manuscripts: Gregory Nazianzus, Basil the Great, Jerome and others came to study there.

With education firmly in Christian hands, however, many of the works of classical antiquity were no longer considered useful. Old texts were washed off the valuable parchment and papyrus, which were reused, forming palimpsests. As scrolls gave way to the new book-form, the codex, which was universally used for Christian literature, old manuscript scrolls were cut apart and used to stiffen leather bindings.

Ancient Chinese Libraries

Little is known about early Chinese libraries, save what is written about the imperial library which began with the Qin Dynasty. One of the curators of the imperial library in the Han Dynasty is believed to have been the first to establish a library classification system and the first book notation system. At this time the library catalog was written on scrolls of fine silk and stored in silk bags.

Islamic Libraries

In Persia many libraries were established by the Zoroastrian elite and the Persian kings. Among the first ones was a royal library in Isfahan. One of the most important public libraries established around AD 667 in south-western Iran was the Library of Gundishapur. It was a part of a bigger scientific complex located at the Academy of Gundishapur. Upon the rise of Islam, libraries in newly Islamic lands knew a brief period of expansion in the Middle East, North Africa, Sicily and Spain. Like the Christian libraries, they mostly contained books which were made of paper, and took a codex or modern form instead of scrolls; they could be found in mosques, private homes, and universities. In Aleppo, for example the largest and probably the oldest mosque library, the Sufiya, located at the city's Grand Umayyad Mosque, contained a large book collection of which 10,000 volumes were reportedly bequeathed by the city's most famous ruler, Prince Sayf al-Dawla. Some mosques sponsored public libraries. Ibn al-Nadim's bibliography *Fihrist* demonstrates the devotion of medieval Muslim scholars to books and reliable sources; it contains a description of thousands of books circulating in the Islamic world circa 1000, including an entire section for books about the doctrines of other religions. Unfortunately, modern Islamic libraries for the most part do not hold these antique books; many were lost, destroyed by Mongols, or removed to European libraries and museums during the colonial period.

By the 8th century first Iranians and then Arabs had imported the craft of papermaking from China, with a paper mill already at work in Baghdad in 794. By the 9th century completely public libraries started to appear in many Islamic cities. They were called "halls of Science" or *dar al-'ilm*. They were each endowed by Islamic sects with the purpose of representing their tenets as well as promoting the dissemination of secular knowledge.

The 9th century Abbasid Caliph al-Mutawakkil of Iraq, even ordered the construction of a 'zawiyat qurra *literally an enclosure for readers which was 'lavishly furnished and equipped.'* In Shiraz Adhud al-Daula (d. 983) set up a library, described by the medieval historian, al-Muqaddasi, as *'a complex of buildings surrounded by gardens with lakes and waterways. The buildings were topped with domes, and comprised an upper and a lower story with a total, according to the chief official, of 360 rooms.... In each department, catalogues were placed on a shelf... the rooms were furnished with carpets...'.* The libraries often employed translators and copyists in large numbers, in order to render into Arabic the bulk of the available Persian, Greek, Roman and Sanskrit non-fiction and the classics of literature. This flowering of Islamic learning ceased centuries later when learning began declining in the Islamic world, after many of these libraries were destroyed by Mongol invasions. Others were victim of wars and religious strife in the Islamic world. However, a few examples of these medieval libraries, such as the libraries of Chinguetti in West Africa, remain intact and relatively unchanged even today. Another ancient library from this period which is still operational and expanding is the Central Library of Astan Quds Razavi in the Iranian city of Mashhad, which has been operating for more than six centuries.

A number of distinct features of the modern library were introduced in the Islamic world, where libraries not only served as a collection of manuscripts as was the case in ancient libraries, but also as a public library and lending library, a centre for the instruction and spread of sciences and ideas, a place for meetings and discussions, and sometimes as a lodging for scholars or boarding school for pupils. The concept of the library catalogue was also introduced in medieval Islamic libraries, where books were organized into specific genres and categories.

The contents of these Islamic libraries were copied by Christian monks in Muslim/Christian border areas, particularly Spain and Sicily. From there they eventually made their way into other parts of Christian Europe. These copies joined works that had been preserved directly by Christian monks from Greek and Roman originals, as well as copies Western Christian monks made of Byzantine works. The resulting conglomerate libraries are the basis of every modern library today.

Medieval Christian Libraries

With the retrenchment of literacy in the Roman west during the fourth and fifth centuries, fewer private libraries were maintained, and those in unfortified villas proved to be among their most combustible contents.

In the early Middle Ages, after the fall of the Western Roman Empire and before the rise of the large Western Christian monastery libraries beginning at Montecassino, libraries were found in scattered places in the Christian Middle East.

Medieval library design reflected the fact that these manuscripts —created via the labour-intensive process of hand copying— were valuable possessions.

Library architecture developed in response to the need for security. Librarians often chained books to lecterns, armaria (wooden chests), or shelves, in well-lit rooms. Despite this protectiveness, many libraries were willing to lend their books if provided with security deposits (usually money or a book of equal value). Monastic libraries lent and borrowed books from each other frequently and lending policy was often theologically grounded. For example, the Franciscan monasteries loaned books to each other without a security deposit since according to their vow of poverty only the entire order could own property. In 1212 the council of Paris condemned those monasteries that still forbade loaning books, reminding them that lending is "one of the chief works of mercy".

Lending meant more than just having another work to read to librarians; while the work was in their possession, it could be copied, thus enriching the library's own collecion. The book lent as a counter effort was often copied in the same way, so both libraries ended up having an additional title. The early libraries located in monastic cloisters and associated with scriptoria were collections of lecterns with books chained to them.

Shelves built above and between back-to-back lecterns were the beginning of bookpresses. The chain was attached at the fore-edge of a book rather than to its spine. Book presses came to be arranged in carrels (perpendicular to the walls and therefore to the windows) in order to maximize lighting, with low bookcases in front of the windows. This *stall system* (fixed bookcases perpendicular to exterior walls pierced by closely spaced windows) was characteristic of English institutional libraries. In Continental libraries, bookcases were arranged parallel to and against the walls. This *wall system* was first introduced on a large scale in Spain's El Escorial.

Early Modern Libraries

Johannes Gutenberg's movable type innovation in the 1400s revolutionized bookmaking. From the 15th century in central and northern Italy, the assiduously assembled libraries of humanists and their enlightened patrons provided a nucleus around which an "academy" of scholars congregated in each Italian city of consequence. Cosimo de Medici in Florence established his own collection, which formed the basis of the Laurentian Library. In Rome, the papal collections were brought together by Pope Nicholas V, in separate Greek and Latin libraries, and housed by Pope Sixtus IV, who consigned the Bibliotheca Apostolica Vaticana to the care of his librarian, the humanist Bartolomeo Platina in February 1475.

In the 16th century Sixtus V bisected Bramante's Cortile del Belvedere with a cross-wing to house the Apostolic Library in suitable magnificence. The sixteenth and seventeenth centuries saw other privately-endowed libraries assembled in Rome: the Vallicelliana, formed from the books of Saint Filippo Neri, with other distinguished libraries such as that of Cesare Baronio, the Biblioteca Angelica founded by the Augustinian Angelo Rocca, which was the only truly public library in Counter-Reformation Rome; the Biblioteca Alessandrina with which Pope Alexander VII endowed the University of Rome; the Biblioteca Casanatense of the Cardinal Girolamo Casanate; and finally the Biblioteca Corsiniana founded by the bibliophile Clement XII Corsini and his nephew Cardinal Neri Corsini, still housed in Palazzo Corsini in via della Lungara.

A lot of factors combined to create a "golden age of libraries" between 1600 and 1700: The quantity of books had gone up, as the cost had gone down, there was a renewal in the interest of classical literature and culture, nationalism was encouraging nations to build great libraries, universities were playing a more prominent role in education, and renaissance thinkers and writers were producing great works. Some of the more important libraries include the Bodleian Library at Oxford, the Library of the British Museum, the Mazarine Library in Paris, and the National Central Library in Italy, the Prussian State Library, the M.E. Saltykov-Shchedrin State Public Library of St. Petersburg, and many more.

Public Libraries

The earliest example in England of a library to be endowed for the benefit of users who were not members of an institution such as a cathedral or college was the Francis Trigge Chained Library in Grantham, Lincolnshire, established in 1598. The library still exists and can justifiably claim to be the forerunner of later public library systems.The beginning of the modern, free, open access libraries really got its start in the UK in 1847.

Parliament appointed a committee, led by William Ewart, on Public Libraries to consider the necessity of establishing libraries through the nation: In 1849 their report noted the poor condition of library service, it recommended the establishment of free public libraries all over the country, and it led to the Public Libraries Act in 1850, which allowed all cities with populations exceeding 10,000 to levy taxes for the support of public libraries. Another important act was the 1870 Public School Law, which increased literacy, thereby the demand for libraries, so by 1877, more than 75 cities had established free libraries, and by 1900 the number had reached 300. This finally marks the start of the public library as we know it. And these acts led to similar laws in other countries, most notably the US.

1876 is a well known year in the history of librarianship. The American Library Association was formed, as well as The American Library Journal, Melvil Dewey published his decimal based system of classification, and the United States Bureau of Education published its report, "Public libraries in the United States of America; their history, condition, and management".

The American Library Association continues to play a major role in libraries to this day, and Dewey's classification system, although under heavy criticism of late, still remains as the prevailing method of classification used in the United States.

As the number of books in libraries increased, so did the need for compact storage and access with adequate lighting, giving birth to the *stack system*, which involved keeping a library's collection of books in a space separate from the reading room, an arrangement which arose in the 19th century. Book stacks quickly evolved into a fairly standard form in which the cast iron and steel frameworks supporting the bookshelves also supported the floors, which often were built of translucent blocks to permit the passage of light (but were not transparent, for reasons of modesty).

With the introduction of electrical lighting, it had a huge impact on how the library operated. Also, the use of glass floors was largely discontinued, though floors were still often composed of metal grating to allow air to circulate in multi-story stacks. Ultimately, even more space was needed, and a method of moving shelves on tracks (compact shelving) was introduced to cut down on otherwise wasted aisle space.

Library 2.0, a term coined in 2005, is the library's response to the challenge of Google and an attempt to meet the changing needs and wants of the users by using web 2.0 technology. Some of the aspects of Library 2.0 include, commenting, tagging, bookmarking, discussions, using social software, plug-ins, and widgets. Inspired by web 2.0, it is an attempt to make the library a more user driven institution.

A Working Definition of Digital Library [1998]

For DLF partners effectively to "federate" digital libraries, they must share a comon understanding of what a digital library is. Here is their working definition.

"Digital libraries are organizations that provide the resources, including the specialized staff, to select, structure, offer intellectual access to, interpret, distribute, preserve the integrity of, and ensure the persistence over time of collections of digital works so that they are readily and economically available for use by a defined community or set of communities."

Of course, the concept of digital library has multiple senses that one might invoke in various contexts. For example, the concept may refer simply to the notion of collection without reference to organization, intellectual accessibility or service attributes. This extended sense seems to be in play, for example, when we hear the World Wide Web described as a digital library.

The concept might also refer to the organization underlying the collection, or even more specifically to the computer-based system in which the collection resides. The latter sense seems to be most operative in the NSF digital library initiative programme. See, for example, C.L. Borgman, et al. *Social Aspects of Digital Libraries.* Digital *libraries* might also be distinguished from digital *archives* to emphasize the nature of the works collected or, as in *Preserving Digital Information: Report of the Task Force on the Archiving of Digital Information*, to stress the preservation function.

One could, of course, revise, refine, and otherwise improve this comprehensive definition. However, it is meant here mainly to suggest that there is a set of attributes that gives coherence to the concept of digital libraries. These attributes include functions of collection, organization, preservation, access and economy. A programme for the development of "federated" digital libraries needs to be defined and measured in terms of the development of these attributes.

However, the proposed definition also emphasizes that "digital libraries" need to be defined and measured in relation to the communities they serve. Thus, the DLF programme aims to situate the development of digital libraries in a larger context of service. Given the complexity and costs of developing digital libraries, DLF efforts and investments need to be conscious of and strategically designed to address the larger institutional and social goals of its participants.

USER EDUCATION IN ACADEMIC LIBRARIES

Developments in computers, microelectronics, and communication technologies have radically changed the library and information environment. Gone are the days of stand-alone libraries, in which a library was judged less by the quality of its resources and services than by the number of documents it had available. Traditional libraries were dominated by print publications and the access mechanisms were also by-and-large manual. The paradigm shift from stand-alone libraries to library and information networks, available via the Internet, can provide end-users with a seamless connection to Internet-based services. Moreover, we are surrounded by automated, digital, and virtual libraries as well as by networked data, specialized networks, and library networks. Multimedia and the Internet have further made the job of library and information professionals more challenging.

The development of new technology makes direct access to information easier for users, and, while information skills are required to collect and present that information, in the future there is likely to be less of a role for information workers as intermediaries between users and information sources.

In fact, there is a paradigm shift from a parent-child relationship between information provider and user to an "adult-adult" relationship. While new formats and mechanisms are being developed to cope with this rapidly changing environment, the existing gap between the generation and use of information is further widening in the present situation. A major aim of user education is therefore to widen the use of a range of library resources, which will enable academics to improve their teaching and research, and students to learn more and achieve better results in their work.

In the print-based environment we spoke of library instruction, bibliographic instruction, and user education programmes. Initiation of users, lectures to library users, library tours, pamphlets and brochures, audio-visual aids, and, in a few cases, user education programmes were the main tools and techniques for enabling patrons to make good use of the library. These tools and techniques must now be supplemented. End-user training should now be the focus of user education.

The Need for End-user Education

User education is essential. It helps publicize library services. It improves the image of the library. Above all, user education and training are the best ways to implement Ranganathan's five laws of library science. User education and training are often fee-based, because developing the infrastructure for the network environment is very costly.

The Challenge in Information Services

Information has become more complex and expensive. The traditional services, such as reference service, current awareness services, and selective dissemination of information need be supplemented by "Selective *Elimination* of Information," the evaluation of information to separate quality information from junk. In this context, the basic challenge is to convince and convert traditional users into users of Internet-based resources and services. Information literacy can contribute to developing information technology

(IT) related competencies among end-users as it includes basic computer and network literacy. The aim of information literacy is to make information users capable of locating, retrieving, and using information.

Planning Strategies

Traditionally, librarians instructed the end-users in the use of print publications, but a balance between print and digital documents will be a basic norm in the near future. In this context, training and retraining the end-users in the use of IT-based resources and services, such as e-mail, ftp, telnet, www, browsers, search engines, opacs, databases, system software, application software, electronic journals, computer conferences, scholarly discussion lists, mailing lists, Usenet newsgroups, websites, CDs, and DVDs should become an integral part of a library's user education programme. This is where strategic planning comes in, in order to develop a comprehensive user-education and training programme at the national level.

The University Grants Commission (UGC), the National Information system for Science and Technology (NISSAT), National Social Science Documentation Centre (NASSDOC), Indian National Scientific Doumentation Centre (INSDOC), Defence Scientific Information & Documentation Centre (DESIDOC), university libraries, library associations, library and information science departments can play a pivotal role in this direction. Such national programmes can be customized at the local level to suit institutional needs.

The Changing Academic Library

During the recent economic recession, money for education and libraries in India became very tight, requiring cuts in serial subscriptions and book purchases for academic libraries. At the same time, subscription prices were soaring, as were the costs and number of databases and journals available. Library planning is now essential in order to maximize available resources and take advantage of emerging technologies. A Library Planning and Action Initiative (LPAI) should now be implemented by academic libraries in India.

To accomplish the goals of the LPAI, a planning team should be established in every academic library. An advisory task force must be formed to work closely with the planning team. The advisory task force members could be chancellors, vice-chancellors, other academic administrators, academic librarians, a representative from the Librarian's Association, information technologists, and other faculty including representation from faculty governance bodies.

The LPAI task force should use the following strategies to guide the academic library's transition to the digital future:

Seek Innovative and Cost-effective Means to Strengthen Resource Sharing: Resource sharing should extend throughout academic libraries (and other important libraries) as a strategy to maximize the resources available for print collections that meet the needs of students and faculty for information needed in teaching and research.

Create Digital Libraries: The Academic Digital Library (ADL) should provide new services and extend existing ones to guide libraries in the successful integration of traditional and digital formats. The programmes of the ADL should support information access and delivery via electronic communications; information preservation, storage, and retrieval; information management consultation and training; new forms of scholarly and scientific communication; and development of the knowledge network of the university.

Mutually Beneficial Collaboration of Academic Libraries with Libraries, Museums and Industry: Collaboration is a strategy to extend library access, share the costs of library collections and services, and develop an academically and economically sustainable model of scholarly communication.

Information Infrastructure that Supports the Dissemination of and Access to Scholarly and Scientific Information in a Networked Environment: A sophisticated and robust technological infrastructure is required to disseminate and access digital information. Academic libraries must invest in technology to support the delivery of digital collections and be tightly integrated into information management and technology planning at all levels.

Organize an Environment of Continuous Planning and Innovation: The environment for scholarly information is expected to be highly fluid for at least the next decade, as universities attempt to meet the challenges of scholarly and scientific communication in the 21st century. The academic library should develop a planning process that will support our libraries as they continue to engage in innovation and the development of organizational, technical, policy, and financial structures needed to make the transition to integrated print and digital collections. Planning structures should also encourage and support strategies to enhance the transmission of scholarly and scientific communication in a digital environment.

INTERNATIONAL LIBRARIANSHIP

A FIELD DOMINATED BY ANTHOLOGIES

If you search in bibliographic databases using the search term "International librarianship", you will find a fair number of monographs that include these words in their titles. In a review of Carroll and Harvey's *International Librarianship: Cooperation and Collaboration* (Carroll and Harvey, 2001), W.V. Jackson (Jackson, 2003), not to be confused with Miles Jackson, made the following observation:Although the literature of comparative and international librarianship has not flourished in recent years, one type of work seems to recur periodically.

This is the anthology of articles... by various authors: such compilations generally include pieces both geographical (that is, about a country or region) or topical (for example, about cooperation, buildings and so on) in nature (Jackson, 2003).

I concur with Jackson's observation. Most books on "international librarianship" are compilations of chapters by various authors, describing library conditions in particular foreign countries or regions, along the lines of the following (real) examples:

- The standardisation of Chinese bibliography
- University libraries in West Africa
- Public libraries in Nigeria
- Library and information services in Bermuda
- Indonesian university libraries and their reference services

In these volumes we also find chapters on international library cooperation, the work of international agencies in the field of librarianship, and relations between countries in the field of librarianship. More real examples:

- Colonialism and the development of libraries and archives in French Indochina
- IFLA and international librarianship
- Anglo-Nordic library relationships
- International cultural exchange through libraries
- International influences in Thailand

The second group of examples come closer to what I understand by international librarianship, as I shall discuss shortly, but what has generally been missing is attempts to systematise or develop a conceptual framework for international librarianship. In most cases the introduction or preface to the compilation is extremely brief and provides only the most cursory attempt at defining what is meant by "international librarianship".

For example, Miles Jackson's impressive volume of well over 600 pages offers no attempt to provide a systematic introduction or conceptual framework. The 1985 Festschift for William J Welsh (Price and Price, 1985) is an example of a book with the words "international librarianship" in its title, but which does not say anything about international librarianship as such.

Presumably the title, *International Librarianship Today and Tomorrow*, was chosen because Welsh, at that time Deputy Librarian of Congress, was well-known in international circles and participated actively in forums such as IFLA and the Conference of Directors of National Libraries.

There is a striking exception to the general trend in books on international librarianship, the book *World Librarianship: A Comparative Study*, by Richard Krzys and Gaston Litton (1983). This is an ambitious attempt to create a "world librarianship", defined as "the abstraction referring to the status of the profession in all parts of the world during a specified period of time" and its scientific investigation, which they call "world study in librarianship". Under this they subsume "international library science" and "comparative library science" (Krzys & Litton, 1982:3). Their work does not appear to have attracted followers; certainly the terminology they attempted to introduce has not been adopted by later writers. Generally, the field remains dominated by anthologies.

If you're not American you must be international. It has struck me that the way we understand "international librarianship" may be related to the different ways in which the word "international" is used in American and British English. In the USA the word "international" is commonly used to mean "from another country". Thus an "international student" or an "international visitor" in most cases is just a student or visitor from another country. In British English we would call them *foreign* students or *foreign* visitors. In British English the expression "international scholar" would be used only for a foreign scholar who enjoys international renown.

This analysis suggests that the multilateral or multinational (many to many) connotation of the word "international" is lost in American English and replaced by a one to many connotation (American to other). What is not

American is "international". This is illustrated by Stephen K. Bailey's 1966 definition of "international education" as "...non-American substance of school and university curriculums in the United States", cited by Carroll (1970:175).

It is debatable whether the semantic shift of "international" from British to American English can be explained by the parochialism or isolationism so often attributed to Americans. This is also unkind. It is more likely (and charitable) to assume that "international" is simply used in the USA as a euphemism to avoid labelling other people as "foreign". Be that as it may, it would be interesting to determine whether the meaning given to the word "international" in the USA has had any effect on the conceptualization of international librarianship, and whether this is different from the way international librarianship has been conceptualized in Britain.

For now, in my view, the term "international librarianship" should not be used in the titles of books merely containing a collection of chapters about libraries in various countries. Something more is needed. In this lecture I will try to explore what that may be. Before I do that, however, I need to say that for the purposes of this lecture I interpret "librarianship" broadly to encompass the study of processes, systems and theories relating to not only libraries but also other allied information agencies. I also need to undertake a little excursus on international and comparative librarianship.

International and Comparative Librarianship

Louis Shores (1966) defined comparative librarianship as follows:

> *...the study and comparison of library theory and practice in all of the different countries of the world for the purpose of broadening and deepening our understanding of professional problems and solutions. (Cited in Appendix I, Definitions) of (Carroll, 1970).*

Here comparative librarianship is clearly international. Comparisons within countries (between cities, states or library types, for example) are excluded.

In the preface to his 1981 book, referred to earlier, Miles Jackson distinguishes international librarianship from comparative librarianship:

> *...the terms "international" and "comparative librarianship" are regarded as having different meanings but both are of importance in understanding world librarianship. International librarianship is limited strictly to those activities that involve librarianship and all its aspects across national boundaries. It would thereby exclude comparative analysis, but include*

such activities as exchange of librarians, books, ideas, and the study of library systems in different countries. On the other hand, comparative librarianship should lean on the tradition of comparative studies found in other fields such as political, government and legal studies (Jackson, 1981).

Relating international librarianship to "activities that involve librarianship and all its aspects across national boundaries" is a good beginning, but I find the exclusion of comparative analysis unsatisfactory. It would be much simpler to use the words "international" and "comparative" as overlapping and not mutually exclusive, as in the following Venn diagram:

This suggests that comparative librarianship may be conducted at both national and international levels. After all, we can compare library systems or conditions between countries or within countries. It also suggests that international librarianship may or may not have a comparative dimension.

From Exoticism to Understanding

If this seems like splitting hairs, bear with me for a little longer. Comparison is a step up from mere description. This implies that we consider the aims or teleology of this intellectual activity. I would like to look briefly at the motives or rationales of those who have written about international librarianship, and how these relate to the results achieved. I suggest that authors who have contributed to what is broadly known as international librarianship have been variously motivated by the following, or combinations thereof:

- Exoticism
- Philanthropy
- Influence
- Internationalism
- Cooperation
- Innovation
- Understanding

Exoticism

The first cluster of motives can be placed under the label of exoticism. It includes curiosity about how things are done in foreign countries, a love of travel and adventure, and the prestige that comes from having been where others have not. Writings motivated by exoticism tend to be anecdotal and descriptive.

Philanthropy

The second motive is philanthropy, love of our fellow humans. Here we have accounts by librarians and students who have travelled to other countries to assist in library development there. Accounts of their experiences also tend to be anecdotal and descriptive, with occasional analytical and evaluative elements.

Influence

Often interwoven with the previous motive is, thirdly, cultural or economic influence through foreign aid for library development, the intention being to extend or strengthen the influence of the country providing the assistance. Accounts in this genre tend to be descriptive or promotional, but insufficiently evaluative.

In this context it is interesting to consider Frances Laverne Carroll's systematic attempt, in a doctoral dissertation submitted in 1970, to analyse the goals of international education and to apply them to international librarianship in US library schools (Carroll, 1970). Carroll constructed an instrument for the evaluation of "internationalism in education for librarianship in the United States" (p.34).

As part of her research, Carroll analysed the schools' calendars ("catalogues") to see whether they contained any references to "internationalism". The results were somewhat meagre. The most cogent statement of the goals of internationalism in library education was found in the calendar of the Graduate Library School of the Pratt Institute, Brooklyn: "The post-war expansion of American education has created a need for librarians with the special skills necessary to acquire and process overseas and foreign language materials to support the multiplying number of language and area study programmes. As an aside, it would be interesting to determine to what extent interest in international librarianship in the USA correlates with the development of area studies and teaching of foreign languages. A further question that arises is whether the apparent decline in international librarianship (in terms of literature and the teaching thereof in LIS schools) could be a result of declining interest in area studies and foreign language teaching.

Given the lack of explicit goals in the library school calendars, Carroll used the goals of international education as her point of departure. She undertook a detailed analysis to determine whether the goals found in the literature were major or minor goals or activities. The goals were then related to the goals of internationalism in library education (pp.42-43). Without going into the details, the goals found in the literature (as discussed on pp. 43-55) can be summarized as follows:

- *International Understanding:* This has three dimensions:
  - Attitude (an affective dimension concerned with feelings of friendliness and willingness to cooperate).
  - Knowledge (a cognitive dimension concerned with understanding the behaviour of other people).
  - Strategic knowledge (another cognitive dimension concerned with understanding the intentions of others with a view to decision-making, *e.g.* in foreign policy).
- *Advancement of Knowledge:* This can be divided into two dimensions:
  - Diffusion or transmission of existing knowledge, *e.g.* through primary, secondary and undergraduate education.
  - Discovery or production of new knowledge, including synthesis through research and scholarship.
- Technical assistance.
- To advance the objectives of US foreign policy (including the combating of communism and the strengthening of relations with the allies of the USA).
- To promote international understanding and appreciation of the United States.
- To gain perspective on one's own values and traditions.

In view of her objective of developing a checklist, Carroll eliminated the last four as minor goals, leaving only the first two goals as appropriate goal statements for library science. Her analysis highlights some of the ambivalence in inherent in international studies, particularly at the height of the Cold War. Do we study librarianship in other countries with altruistic or self-centred motives? Some goals are clearly subordinated to national policy interests. Others too, may not be as altruistic or idealistic as they look.

Internationalism

In the context of international librarianship, and especially in the context of international library cooperation, internationalism frequently features as a shared value. This appears to be an idealistic motive: librarians engaged in international cooperation are described by Harrison (1989:xv) as "citizens of the world with a strong faith that what they are supporting is really worthwhile and that both short-term and long-term good will come from it". In the USA internationalism has had a strong protagonist in Frances Laverne Carroll, who devoted much research to the internationalisation of library and information science education. Internationalisation is defined by Carroll and Harvey (1987) as "the process by which a nationalistic library school topic, an entire curriculum, or an entire school is changed into one with a significant and varied international thrust, the process whereby it is permeated with international policies, viewpoints, ideas and facts"(p.x).

Cooperation

Librarians have a long and honourable tradition of cooperation. Peter Havard-Williams goes so far as to make cooperation the central theme of international librarianship. He wrote: "I define international librarianship as cooperative activity in the field of librarianship done for the benefit of the individual librarian in the whole of the world, and done frequently by the likes of you and me" (Havard-Williams, 1972:170). International cooperation in respect of document supply, bibliographic standards, preservation and other technical areas will undoubtedly remain an important motivation. But rapid developments in information and communications technologies and the accompanying phenomena of globalization and disintermediation, efficient cooperation among librarians worldwide is needed for us to participate effectively in the global forums. These are forums such as the World Intellectual Property Organisation (WIPO), the World Trade Organisation (WTO) and the World Summit on the Information Society (WSIS), where far-reaching decisions are made that affect free and fair access to information resources in libraries serving the peoples of the world (cf. Schleihagen, 2004).

Innovation

A fifth motive is innovation. As K. C. Harrison (1989:xii) has put it: "...librarians with weather-eyes on professional practices in other countries have been able to adopt, adapt and apply many of these to their own library situations." Such transplanting has occurred particularly in technical library processes. This has led to writings of a technical and evaluative nature.

Understanding

Finally, there is the quest for understanding. Earlier I cited Louis Shores's statement of the purpose of what he calls comparative librarianship:

"broadening and deepening our understanding of professional problems and solutions" (Shores 1970).

In his Foreword (Asheim, 1989) to Harrison's *International librarianship* (Harrison, 1989), Lester Asheim points to the value of "learning-through-participation... not only through actual practice as a librarian in some other country, but also through the mutual exchange of ideas and viewpoints made possible through international associations... Both of these... provide the librarian with the opportunity to have direct contact with the practice and philosophy of library service in varying circumstances and at different levels of societal development, and from this insight, to identify and appreciate the many factors outside of librarianship itself that shape and define the nature of a library's services and its social role" (p.vii).

Asheim goes on to list a number of factors outside of librarianship that determine who uses libraries, how and why, and what barriers inhibit their use. Such factors operate everywhere, "...but somehow we can see and understand this much more clearly in a foreign setting than we can when we are looking at a phenomenon with which we feel comfortably "at home"(p.viii). What I find significant about this motive is that is concerned with self-understanding, which represents considerable progress from the starting point of exoticism. (It can be said that self-understanding, achieved by seeing the self in relation to others, is the ultimate goal of travel.) A more recent statement of this motive is found in the introduction to a new column, "International perspectives on academic libraries" in the *Journal of Academic Librarianship*. The editors of the column, Philip J Calvert and Rowena Cullen, wrote:

> *It is hoped that this column will help broaden the journal's perspective outside North America; raise issues faced by academic librarians in the developing as well as the developed world; and identify issues that are common to all academic libraries, but to which the solutions must sometimes be modified to suit particular countries, cultures or economic environments. It should also be remembered that, although North America academic libraries are the drivingforce behind much innovation in the LIS field and are the source of much new thinking in the discipline, librarians in other countries have sometimes to deal with certain issues before they become critical in the United States or Canada; hence there will be times that the flow of information will travel in the other direction (Calvert & Cullen, 2001).*

This statement raises interesting questions about the notion of librarians in different countries learning from one another.

Conclusion

At the end of the 20th century, college and university libraries face enormous challenges and opportunities. As campuses move into the information age, the mission and role of the library is being redefined. While the amount of information libraries need to acquire continues to increase, the resources available to do so are insufficient. Moreover, administrators need to assess the relationship between the library and the computer center, as both fight for limited resources.

The growing universe of print-based publications and digital documents on the one hand, and the declining universe of library budgets on the other, can be handled confidently by adopting certain strategies, such as by developing critical thinking skills, as well as promoting information literacy at large In the near future, uses should expect timely access to quality information.

This information must be accurate, relevant, comprehensive, and engaging. This can be done successfully by incorporating end-user education and training components, in the academic libraries developing continuing professional education and training programmes for the library and information professionals, as well as the end-users will have to develop learning attitude and network related competence to us by the information and communication technologies.

CHAPTER 2

Information Sources

INFORMATION

Information as a concept has a diversity of meanings, from everyday usage to technical settings. Generally speaking, the concept of information is closely related to notions of constraint, communication, control, data, form, instruction, knowledge, meaning, mental stimulus, pattern, perception, and representation.

Many people speak about the Information Age as the advent of the Knowledge Ageor knowledge society, the information society, the Information revolution, and information technologies, and even though informatics, information science and computer science are often in the spotlight, the word "information" is often used without careful consideration of the various meanings it has acquired.

Etymology

According to the Oxford English Dictionary, the first known historical meaning of the word *information* in English was the act of *informing*, or giving form or shape to the mind, as in education, instruction, or training. A quote from 1387: "Five books come down from heaven for information of mankind." It was also used for an *item* of training, *e.g.* a particular instruction. "Melibee had heard the great skills and reasons of Dame Prudence, and her wise information and techniques."

The English word was apparently derived by adding the common "noun of action" ending "*-ation*" (descended through French from Latin "*-tio*") to the earlier verb *to inform*, in the sense of to give form to the mind, to discipline, instruct, teach: "Men so wise should go and inform their kings." (1330) *Inform* itself comes (via French) from the Latin verb *informare*, to give form to, to form an idea of. Furthermore, Latin itself already even contained the word *informatio* meaning concept or idea, but the extent to which this may have influenced the development of the word *information* in English is unclear.

As a final note, the ancient Greek word for *form* was "ìïñöÞ" (morf-> morphe, Morph) and also *åßäïò* eidos (kind, idea, shape, set), the later word was famously used in a technical philosophical sense by Plato (and later Aristotle) to denote the ideal identity or essence of something (see Theory of forms). "Eidos" can also be associated with thought, proposition or even concept.

As a Message

Information is a term with many meanings depending on context, but is as a rule closely related to such concepts as meaning, knowledge, instruction, communication, representation, and mental stimulus. Simply stated, information is a message received and understood. In terms of data, it can be defined as a collection of facts from which conclusions may be drawn. There are many other aspects of information since it is the knowledge acquired through study or experience or instruction. But overall, information is the result of processing, manipulating and organizing data in a way that adds to the knowledge of the person receiving it.

Information is the state of a system of interest. Message is the information materialized.

Information is a quality of a message from a sender to one or more receivers. Information is always *about* something (size of a parameter, occurrence of an event, value, ethics, etc.). Viewed in this manner, information does not have to be accurate; it may be a truth or a lie, or just the sound of a falling tree. Even a disruptive noise used to inhibit the flow of communication and create misunderstanding would in this view be a form of information. However, generally speaking, if the *amount* of information in the received message increases, the message is more accurate.

This model assumes there is a definite sender and at least one receiver. Many refinements of the model assume the existence of a common language understood by the sender and at least one of the receivers. An important variation identifies information as that which would be communicated by a message if it were sent from a sender to a receiver capable of understanding the message. In another variation, it is not required that the sender be capable of understanding the message, or even cognizant that there is a message, making information something that can be extracted from an environment, e.g., through observation, reading or measurement.

Communication theory provides a numerical measure of the uncertainty of an outcome. For example, we can say that "the signal contained thousands of bits of information". Communication theory tends to use the concept of information entropy, generally attributed to Claude Shannon, see below.

Another form of information is Fisher information, a concept of R.A. Fisher. This is used in application of statistics to estimation theory and to science in general. Fisher information is thought of as the amount of information that a message carries about an unobservable parameter. It can be computed from knowledge of the likelihood function defining the system. For example, with a normal likelihood function, the Fisher information is the reciprocal of the variance of the law. In the absence of knowledge of the likelihood law, the Fisher information may be computed from normally distributed score data as the reciprocal of their second moment.

Even though information and data are often used interchangeably, they are actually very different. Data is a set of unrelated information, and as such is of no use until it is properly evaluated. Upon evaluation, once there is some significant relation between data, and they show some relevance, then they are converted into information. Now this same data can be used for different purposes. Thus, till the data convey some information, they are not useful and therefore not information.

Measuring Information Entropy

The view of information as a message came into prominence with the publication in 1948 of an influential paper by Claude Shannon, "A Mathematical Theory of Communication." This paper provides the foundations of information theory and endows the word *information* not only with a technical meaning but also a measure. If the sending device is equally likely to send any one of a set of N messages, then the preferred measure of "the information produced when one message is chosen from the set" is the base two logarithm of N (This measure is called *self-information*). In this paper, Shannon continues:

> *The choice of a logarithmic base corresponds to the choice of a unit for measuring information. If the base 2 is used the resulting units may be called binary digits, or more briefly bits, a word suggested by J. W. Tukey. A device with two stable positions, such as a relay or a flip-flop circuit, can store one bit of information. N such devices can store N bits...*

A complementary way of measuring information is provided by

algorithmic information theory. In brief, this measures the information content of a list of symbols based on how predictable they are, or more specifically how easy it is to compute the list through a programme: the information content of a sequence is the number of bits of the shortest programme that computes it. The sequence below would have a very low algorithmic information measurement since it is a very predictable pattern, and as the pattern continues the measurement would not change. Shannon information would give the same information measurement for each symbol, since they are statistically random, and each new symbol would increase the measurement.

It is important to recognize the limitations of traditional information theory and algorithmic information theory from the perspective of human meaning. For example, when referring to the meaning content of a message Shannon noted "Frequently the messages have *meaning*... these semantic aspects of communication are irrelevant to the engineering problem. The significant aspect is that the actual message is one selected *from a set of possible messages*" (emphasis in original).

In information theory signals are part of a process, not a substance; they do something, they do not contain any specific meaning. Combining algorithmic information theory and information theory we can conclude that the most random signal contains the most information as it can be interpreted in any way and cannot be compressed. Michael Reddy noted that "'signals' of the mathematical theory are 'patterns that can be exchanged'. There is no message contained in the signal, the signals convey the ability to select from a set of possible messages." In information theory "the system must be designed to operate for each possible selection, not just the one which will actually be chosen since this is unknown at the time of design".

As a Pattern

Information is any represented pattern. This view assumes neither accuracy nor directly communicating parties, but instead assumes a separation between an object and its representation. Consider the following example: economic statistics represent an economy, however inaccurately. What are commonly referred to as data in computing, statistics, and other fields, are forms of information in this sense. The electro-magnetic patterns in a computer network and connected devices are related to something other than the pattern itself, such as text characters to be displayed and keyboard input. Signals, signs, and symbols are also in this category.

On the other hand, according to semiotics, data is symbols with certain syntax and information is data with a certain semantic. Painting and drawing contain information to the extent that they represent something such as an assortment of objects on a table, a profile, or a landscape. In other words, when a pattern of something is transposed to a pattern of something else, the latter is information. This would be the case whether or not there was anyone to perceive it.

But if information can be defined merely as a pattern, does that mean that neither utility nor meaning are necessary components of information? Arguably a distinction must be made between raw unprocessed data and information which possesses utility, value or some quantum of meaning. On this view, information may indeed be characterized as a pattern; but this is a necessary condition, not a sufficient one.

An individual entry in a telephone book, which follows a specific pattern formed by name, address and telephone number, does not become "informative" in some sense unless and until it possesses some degree of utility, value or meaning. For example, someone might look up a girlfriend's number, might order a take away etc. The vast majority of numbers will never be construed as "information" in any meaningful sense. The gap between data and information is only closed by a behavioral bridge whereby some value, utility or meaning is added to transform mere data or pattern into information.

When one constructs a representation of an object, one can selectively extract from the object (sampling) or use a system of signs to replace (encoding), or both. The sampling and encoding result in representation. An example of the former is a "sample" of a product; an example of the latter is "verbal description" of a product. Both contain information of the product, however inaccurate.

When one interprets representation, one can predict a broader pattern from a limited number of observations (inference) or understand the relation between patterns of two different things (decoding). One example of the former is to sip a soup to know if it is spoiled; an example of the latter is examining footprints to determine the animal and its condition. In both cases, information sources are not constructed or presented by some "sender" of information. Regardless, information is dependent upon, but usually unrelated to and separate from, the medium or media used to express it.

In other words, the position of a theoretical series of bits, or even the output once interpreted by a computer or similar device, is unimportant, except when someone or something is present to interpret the information.

Therefore, a quantity of information is totally distinct from its medium.

WEB LEARNING SOURCES

What is the Internet?

The Internet is an international computer network made up of smaller networks. Originally designed as a way for government and academic researchers to share information, the net now connects universities, schools, corporations, non-profit organizations, and individuals. Unlike most networks, the Internet remains usable even if one or more of its network connections should fail. Therefore the Internet is a very robust tool both for sharing information and, more recently, for conducting electronic commerce.

What is the World Wide Web?

The term "World Wide Web" refers to the Internet's ability to display and link files containing text, images, and a variety of other information. For example, a person creates a web site containing a series of pages that describes a science project. These files can also contain links to other files located anywhere in the world. The links are typically based on content related to the page containing the reference. The result is an ability to continually branch from a single starting point to any number of pages of related content located at sites all over the world.

What is the Difference between a Website and a Web Page?

A website is made up of a web page(s).

A website is similar to a file folder. A folder contains and organizes information and documents. These documents are similar to web pages.

For example-www.teachersfirst.com is the main page of the TeachersFirst website. The links from this page are separate web pages. All of these pages together make up the website.

Many personal websites consist of a single page. On the other hand, the site created by IBM for the 1998 Winter Olympics contained over 30,000 pages.

For consistency, we will refer to information placed on the Web as websites since these encompass web pages as well.

What can I Find on the Web?

Content on the Web is as diverse as the people and cultures of the world. Web content covers an array of subjects that makes it more extensive than even the largest bookstore. The originality of the Web has no comparison and thousands of new websites and information is added to the Internet every day.

Websites are created by individuals and companies and contain the variety of information one would expect from such organizations. While the Web was originally conceived as a way to share academic information, today it contains far more. There remains a wealth of academic content for all levels, as well as a huge amount of corporate information that range from sites seeking to sell or advertise everything from computers to real estate. There are also promotional and informational sites operated by non-profit, political, and a variety of other organizations. In many respects, the Web is an international library, almanac, yellow pages, and flea market all rolled into one. Unfortunately, the Web contains a fair amount of material which is unsuitable for children and young adults. So while it is a powerful teaching tool, it is a tool which should be used with deliberate caution.

An important thing to remember is that the Internet is huge; it is unstructured, and it is growing rapidly. Therefore, if you can not find the information you want today, it may be available next week. Keep looking!

Why Use the Web?

The World Wide Web is an invaluable tool in today's teaching environment. You can find a seemingly endless amount of information on the Web: teaching materials, pictures, videos, sound clips, exercises, games and so much more to enhance your instructional materials. Keeping students motivated and interested in learning is the goal of all teachers. TeachersFirst links can help you do that.

What is Wrong with All Caps?

You should not use ALL CAPS when using Internet applications. This is important! If you use all caps you are YELLING at someone, not emphasizing a point. Unless you really are upset and wish to yell at someone, use normal sentence case. Internet users can be very touchy about this. They will know you are a newbie and if they are in a bad mood they may send you a nasty reply (flame) or get others to spam you.

What is a Browser?

A browser is a software programme/application which allows users to view and navigate the content of the World Wide Web. The two most popular browser programmes are Netscape's Navigator and Communicator, and Microsoft's Internet Explorer. Basic versions of these programmes can be downloaded free from their publishers website, or you can click on the icons in the TeachersFirst Toolbox to download either programme. TeachersFirst has a complete browser tutorial, but the following paragraphs should give enough information to get you started.

Browsers do not have precisely the same features, but their basic capabilities are very similar. If you are a typical user, you'll probably find that 80 per cent of your time on the Web is spent using 20 per cent of your browser's capabilities. These capabilities are:

1. *Viewing and Navigating the Web*: A browser displays websites. As you move from one site to another you have the option to go back to the previous page as well as going forward to a page you just viewed if you have used the back key. These keys are very useful when viewing a website that has not placed links to different pages on their site.
2. *Marking Favourite Pages:* Browsers can store a list of sites to which you want to return. Netscape calls these "bookmarks," and Explorer calls them "favorite places." Remember that these are links to web sites and are not stored copies of the files themselves. This means that when you click on a bookmark/favorite place, your browser will load the most recent version of that website.
3. *Saving Pages:* Your browser has the ability to save the contents of a page to your computer. It is important to remember that a single web page may contain numerous pictures and graphic files. Each of these files must be saved separately. You must also have software applications that are capable of viewing those images or you are saving them for nothing.

What is a URL?

The acronym URL stands for "uniform resource locator," a fancy term for the unique location of a particular web file on the Internet. A typical URL looks like this:

http://www.TeachersFirst.com/history/ushistory.htm

Why is this important? If you know what a URL means, you can tell a lot about the source of the pages you are viewing. THIS IS IMPORTANT. Let's begin by breaking the URL into its component parts.

http:// is the protocol (a set of operating rules) by which computers on the Internet send files back and forth. The protocol for the Web "http" is called " hypertext transfer protocol."

www.TeachersFirst.com is the domain name. The domain name is the unique name for the network which contains the web site you are viewing.

/history/ is the pathname. A pathname is the location within the website where a specific web page is located. This is similar to a subfolder or a folder within a folder. Also, this is not always part of a URL. Pathnames can be called anything that the web sites creator came up with. In most cases, the use of a tilde "~" in a pathname indicates a website reserved for a given individual's personal use.

Ushistory.htm is the file name. It is the name of a single hypertext file, web page, located on the Internet.

All Internet addresses contain these components in varying combinations.

Go to URL Anatomy Tutorial

What is html?

HTML stands for Hyptertext Markup Language. This is the code that creates the page format (layout, font, size, colour, pictures, etc.) of a web page. HTML was developed in order to have a standard to ease communication across the Internet. Since all browser applications read HTML, it eliminates the necessity to convert files or data so that all users can read them. The HTML standard is responsible for the ease in access and ultimately, the growth of the Internet.

How do I begin?

There are only three requirements to begin using the World Wide Web.

1. a computer
2. Internet access
3. browser software

Since you are viewing this page you have these items or are borrowing them from someone.

The World Wide Web's greatest frustration is locating the information you need. That's why we created TeachersFirst – to provide content which concentrates entirely on the needs of K-12 teachers. This site is designed to save you time and facilitate finding useful information for your teaching and your students.

If this is your first experience with the World Wide Web, we suggest the following:

1. Work through the browser tutorial to learn how to use your browser

software. Navigating the Web is a lot easier once you master a few simple commands and how to use them.

2. Take a look at the "URL Anatomy" tutorial. It will help you understand those long web addresses to which we constantly refer.
3. Browse through the TeachersFirst contents, especially the "Classroom Materials" section.

E-BOOK

An e-book (short for electronic book, also written eBook or ebook) is an e-text that forms the digital media equivalent of a conventional printed book, often protected with a digital rights management system. e-books are usually read on personal computers or smart phones, or on dedicated hardware devices known as e-book readers or e-book devices. Many mobile phones can also be used to read e-books.

History

Early e-books were generally written for specialty areas and a limited audience, meant to be read only by small and devoted interest groups. The scope of the subject matter of these e-books included technical manuals for hardware, manufacturing techniques, and other subjects.

Numerous e-book formats emerged and proliferated, some supported by major software companies such as Adobe's PDF format, and others supported by independent and open-source programmers. Multiple readers naturally followed multiple formats, most of them specializing in only one format, and thereby fragmenting the e-book market even more. Due to exclusiveness and limited readerships of e-books, the fractured market of independents and specialty authors lacked consensus regarding a standard for packaging and selling e-books.

e-books continued to gain in their own underground markets. Many e-book publishers began distributing books that were in the public domain. At the same time, authors with books that were not accepted by publishers offered their works online so they could be seen by others. Unofficial (and occasionally unauthorized) catalogs of books became available over the web, and sites devoted to e-books began disseminating information about e-books to the public.

As of 2008, new marketing models for e-books were being developed and dedicated reading hardware was produced. e-books (as opposed to ebook readers) have yet to achieve global distribution. Only two e-book readers dominate the market, Amazon's Kindle model or Sony's PRS-500. However, not all authors have endorsed the concept of electronic publishing. J.K Rowling, author of the Harry Potter series, has stated that there will be no e-versions of the books.

- 1971: Michael S. Hart launch the *Gutenberg Project.*
- 1993: Zahur develops the first software to read digital books. Digital Book v.1 and the first e-book is published *On Murder Considered as one of the Fine Arts* (Thomas de Quincey).
- 1993: Digital Book offers the first 50 e-books in floppy disk with Digital Book Format (DBF).
- 1993: Hugo Award for Best Novel nominee texts published on CD-ROM by Brad Templeton.
- 1993: Bibliobytes, a project of free digital books online in Internet.
- 1995: Amazon starts to sell physical books in Internet.
- 1996: The Project Gutemberg reachs the 1,000 titles. The target is 1,000,000
- 1998: Launched the first e-book Readers: Rocket e-book and Softbook.
- 1998-1999: Websites selling e-books in English, like *eReader.com* and *eReads.com.*
- 2000: Stephen King offers his book "Riding Bullet" in digital file, it only can be read in computer.
- 2001: Open 'Todoebook.com' the first website selling ebooks in Spanish.
- 2002: Random House and HarperCollins start to sell digital versions of their titles in English.
- 2005: Amazon bought Mobipocket like a strategic positioning.
- 2006: Sony presents the *Sony Reader* with e-ink.
- 2006: LibreDigital Launched BookBrowse as an online reader for publisher content.
- 2007: Amazon launched Kindle in US.
- 2008: Adobe and Sony agreeded to share their technologies (Reader and DRM).
- 2008: Sony sells the *PRS-505* in UK and France
- 2008: Amazon launched Kindle2 in US.

Formats

Comparison of e-books with printed books:

Advantages

- Text can be searched automatically and cross-referenced using hyperlinks.
- A single e-book reader containing several books is easier to carry around (less weight and volume) than the same books (or sometimes even a single book) in printed form. Even hundreds or thousands of books may be stored on the same device. Using removable media even more can be carried around easily.
- Also at a fixed place such as at home it can be an advantage that an e-book collection requires very little space.
- Mobile availability of e-books may be provided for users with a mobile data connection, so that these e-books need not be carried around.
- e-books can allow non-permanent highlighting and annotation.
- Font size and font face can be adjusted.
- e-books may allow animated images or multimedia clips to be embedded.
- e-books allow for greater fidelity in colour reproduction compared to CMYK colour printing (although some e-book readers have only monochrome displays).
- Depending on the device an e-book may be readable in low light or even total darkness.
- An e-book can automatically open at the last read page.
- While an e-book reader costs much more than one book, the electronic texts are generally cheaper. Moreover, a great share of books are available for free, without any charge at all. For example, all fiction from before the year 1900 is in the public domain.
- Text-to-speech software can be used to convert e-books to audio books automatically.
- An e-book can be offered indefinitely, without ever going "out of print".
- Depending on possible digital rights management, it may be easy and cheap to produce a back-up for the case that the e-book is lost or damaged, and/or it may be possible to get a free new copy if that happens.

- It is easier for authors to self-publish e-books.
- A free e-book can stimulate the sales of the printed version.
- The production of e-books does not consume paper, ink, etc.

Disadvantages

- Reading e-books requires an electronic device and software. Even in the case of reading it on a personal computer one already has, it may require additional software.
- A small book is easier to carry around than a typical e-book reader.
- e-book readers require electrical power; in the case of mobile use, the battery can get exhausted.
- e-book readers are more fragile than paper books and more susceptible to physical damage.
- e-book readers can malfunction and e-books can be damaged due to faults in hardware or software.
- e-book readers are more likely to be stolen than paper books.
- Depending on the device an e-book may be difficult to read in bright sunlight.
- Most publishers do not produce the e-book equivalent of their printed books. In other cases the product quality is lower or it is released later.
- e-books can be easily hacked through the use of hardware or software modifications and widely disseminated on the Internet and/or other e-book readers, without approval from the author or publisher (piracy). This is a disadvantage for publishers, but at the same time an advantage for readers, since they do not have to pay for reading a book.
- If an e-book device is stolen, lost, or broken beyond repair, all e-books stored on the device may be lost. This can be avoided by backup either on another device or by the e-book provider.
- There is a loss of tactility and aesthetics of book-bindings. Also lost is the ability to very quickly riffle through the pages to search for a particular section or to get a sense of the book merely by sight.
- Screen resolution of reading devices may be lower than actual paper.
- Due to the digital rights management reselling or lending out an e-book may have complications.

- Some books available as e-book cannot be read on some e-book readers because they are not supplied in a format those readers allow.
- While printed books remain readable for ages, changing technologies and less durable electronic storage media require e-books to be copied to a new carrier after some years.
- e-book readers require various substances to produce, and are an environmental hazard as they're non-biodegradable.
- Piracy is also a serious issue. It is difficult to make an illegal copy of a printed book where as e-books can easily be copied. Most proprietary software come with anti-piracy codes etc., but soon pirated copies were widely available. The same could be said of the e-book as well.

Digital Rights Management

Anti-circumvention techniques may be used to restrict what the user may do with an e-book. For instance, it may not be possible to transfer ownership of an e-book to another person, though such a transaction is common with physical books. Some devices can phone home to track readers and reading habits, restrict printing, or arbitrarily modify reading material. This includes restricting the copying and distribution of works in the public domain through the use of "click-wrap" licensing, effectively limiting the rights of the public to distribute, sell or use texts in the public domain freely.

Most e-book publishers do not warn their customers about the possible implications of the digital rights management tied to their products. Generally they claim that digital rights management is meant to prevent copying of the e-book. However in many cases it is also possible that digital rights management will result in the complete denial of access by the purchaser to the e-book. With some formats of DRM, the e-book is tied to a specific computer or device. In these cases the DRM will usually let the purchaser move the book a limited number of times after which he cannot use it on any additional devices. If the purchaser upgrades or replaces their devices eventually they may lose access to their purchase. Some forms of digital rights management depend on the existence of online services to authenticate the purchasers. When the company that provides the service goes out of business or decides to stop providing the service, the purchaser will no longer be able to access the e-book.

As with digital rights management in other media, e-books are more like rental or leasing than purchase. The restricted book comes with a number of restrictions, and eventually access to the purchase can be removed by a number of different parties involved. These include the publisher of the book, the provider of the DRM scheme, and the publisher of the reader software. These are all things that are significantly different from the realm of experiences anyone has had with a physical copy of the book.

E-JOURNAL

This module is a powerful production publishing system. It allows you to create and control your own electronic (and possibly printed) journals in Drupal—you can set up as many journals as you want, add authors and editors. Module gives you issue management, basic user and access control, vocabularies and archives. This module was inspired by Open Journal System which is an open-source online submission and manuscript tracking system. The Drupal platform is more flexible though, it gives you many ways to extend your publishing system.

Currently, the module is made of the following packages (needless to say, you can combine them with other modules):

ejournal-the core functionality of an publications/issue management

ejournalaccess-for setting access to different group of users

ejournalauthors-use Drupal taxonomy as user profiles links

ejournalcitation-construct citation reference beneath published articles

ejournalshortly-for publication of short messages along side with the main content

E-LEARNING

Electronic learning (or e-Learning or eLearning) is a type of Technology supported education/learning (TSL) where the medium of instruction is through computer technology, particularly involving digital technologies. E-learning has been defined as "pedagogy empowered by digital technology". In some instances, no face-to-face interaction takes place. E-learning is used interchangeably in a wide variety of contexts. In companies, it refers to the strategies that use the company network to deliver training courses to employees. In the United States, it is defined as a planned teaching/learning experience that uses a wide spectrum of technologies, mainly Internet or computer-based, to reach learners. Lately in most Universities, e-learning is used to define a specific mode to attend a course or programmes of study where the students rarely, if ever, attend face-to-face for on-campus access to educational facilities, because they study online.

Market

The worldwide e-learning industry is estimated to be worth over thirty-eight billion Euros according to conservative estimates, although in the European Union only about 20 per cent of e-learning products are produced within the common market. Developments in internet and multimedia technologies are the basic enabler of e-learning, with content, technologies and services being identified as the three key sectors of the e-learning industry. eLearning is a catch-all term that covers a wide range of instructional material that can be delivered on a CD-ROM or DVD, over a local area network (LAN), or on the Internet.

Growth of e-learning

By 2006, nearly 3.5 million students were participating in on-line learning at institutions of higher education in the United States. Many higher education, for-profit institutions, now offer on-line classes. By contrast, only about half of private, non-profit schools offer them. The Sloan report, based on a poll of academic leaders, says that students generally appear to be at least as satisfied with their on-line classes as they are with traditional ones. Private institutions may become more involved with on-line presentations as the cost of instituting such a system decreases. Properly trained staff must also be hired to work with students on-line. These staff members need to understand the content area, and also be highly trained in the use of the computer and Internet. Online education is rapidly increasing, and online doctoral programmes have even developed at leading research universities..

Technology

As early as 1993, Graziadei, W. D. described an online computer-delivered lecture, tutorial and assessment project using electronic mail, two VAX Notes conferences and Gopher/Lynx together with several software programmes that allowed students and instructor to create a Virtual Instructional Classroom Environment in Science (VICES) in Research, Education, Service & Teaching (REST). In 1997 Graziadei, W.D. et al., published an article entitled "Building Asynchronous and Synchronous Teaching-Learning Environments: Exploring a Course/Classroom Management System Solution". They described a process at the State University of New York (SUNY) of evaluating products and developing an overall strategy for technology-based course development and management in teaching-learning. The product(s) had to be easy to use and maintain, portable, replicable, scalable, and immediately affordable, and they had to have a high probability of success with long-term cost-effectiveness. Today many technologies can be, and are, used in e-Learning, from blogs to collaborative software, ePortfolios, and virtual classrooms. Most eLearning situations use combinations of these techniques.

Along with the terms *learning technology*, *instructional technology*, and educational technology, the term is generally used to refer to the use of technology in learning in a much broader sense than the computer-based training or *Computer Aided Instruction* of the 1980s. It is also broader than the terms *Online Learning* or *Online Education* which generally refer to purely web-based learning. In cases where mobile technologies are used, the term M-learning has become more common. e-learning, however, also has implications beyond just the technology and refers to the actual learning that takes place using these systems.

e-learning is naturally suited to distance learning and flexible learning, but can also be used in conjunction with face-to-face teaching, in which case the term Blended learning is commonly used. e-Learning pioneer Bernard Luskin argues that the "E" must be understood to have broad meaning if e-Learning is to be effective. Luskin says that the "e" should be interpreted to mean exciting, energetic, enthusiastic, emotional, extended, excellent, and educational in addition to "electronic" that is a traditional national interpretation. This broader interpretation allows for 21st century applications and brings learning and media psychology into the equation.

In higher education especially, the increasing tendency is to create a Virtual Learning Environment (VLE) (which is sometimes combined with a Management Information System (MIS) to create a Managed Learning Environment) in which all aspects of a course are handled through a consistent user interface standard throughout the institution. A growing number of physical universities, as well as newer online–only colleges, have begun to offer a select set of academic degree and certificate programmes via the Internet at a wide range of levels and in a wide range of disciplines. While some programmes require students to attend some campus classes or orientations, many are delivered completely online. In addition, several universities offer online student support services, such as online advising and registration, e-counselling, online textbook purchase, student governments and student newspapers.

e-Learning can also refer to educational web sites such as those offering learning scenarios, worksheets and interactive exercises for children. The term is also used extensively in the business sector where it generally refers to cost-effective online training.

The recent trend in the e-Learning sector is screencasting. There are many screencasting tools available but the latest buzz is all about the web based screencasting tools which allow the users to create screencasts directly from their browser and make the video available online so that the viewers can stream the video directly. The advantage of such tools is that it gives the presenter the ability to show his ideas and flow of thoughts rather than simply explain them, which may be more confusing when delivered via simple text instructions. With the combination of video and audio, the expert can mimic the one on one experience of the classroom and deliver clear, complete instructions. From the learners point of view this provides the ability to pause and rewind and gives the learner the advantage to move at their own pace, something a classroom cannot always offer. One such example of e-Learning platform based on screencasts is YoHelpOnline.

Services

e-learning services have evolved since computers were first used in education. There is a trend to move toward blended learning services, where computer-based activities are integrated with practical or classroom-based situations.

Goals of E-learning

E-Learning lessons are generally designed to guide students through information or to help students perform in specific tasks. Information based e-Learning content communicates information to the student. Examples include content that distributes the history or facts related to a service, company, or product. In information-based content, there is no specific skill to be learned. In performance-based content, the lessons build off of a procedural skill in which the student is expected to increase proficiency.

Computer-based Learning

Computer-based learning, sometimes abbreviated to CBL, refers to the use of computers as a key component of the educational environment. While this can refer to the use of computers in a classroom, the term more broadly refers to a structured environment in which computers are used for teaching purposes. The concept is generally seen as being distinct from the use of computers in ways where learning is at least a peripheral element of the experience (e.g. computer games and web browsing).

Computer-based Training

Computer-based training (CBT) services are where a student learns by executing special training programmes on a computer relating to their occupation. CBT is especially effective for training people to use computer applications because the CBT programme can be integrated with the applications so that students can practice using the application as they learn. Historically, CBTs growth has been hampered by the enormous resources required: human resources to create a CBT programme, and hardware resources needed to run it.

However, the increase in PC computing power, and especially the growing prevalence of computers equipped with CD-ROMs, is making CBT a more viable option for corporations and individuals alike. Many PC applications now come with some modest form of CBT, often called a tutorial. Web-based training (WBT) is a type of training that is similar to CBT; however, it is delivered over the Internet using a web browser.

Web-based training frequently includes interactive methods, such as bulletin boards, chat rooms, instant messaging, videoconferencing, and discussion threads. Web based training is usually a self-paced learning medium though some systems allow for online testing and evaluation at specific times. Recent years have seen an explosion in online training for educators by content providers such as Knowledge Delivery Systems, Atomic Learning, PBS Teacherline, and more.

Computer-Supported Collaborative Learning (CSCL)

"Computer-supported collaborative learning (CSCL) is one of the most promising innovations to improve teaching and learning with the help of modern information and communication technology. Collaborative or group learning refers to instructional methods whereby students are encouraged or required to work together on learning tasks. It is widely agreed to distinguish collaborative learning from the traditional 'direct transfer' model in which the instructor is assumed to be the distributor of knowledge and skills" Lehtinen et al.

Pedagogical Elements

Pedagogical elements are an attempt to define structures or units of educational material. For example, this could be a lesson, an assignment, a multiple choice question, a quiz, a discussion group or a case study. These units should be format independent, so although it may be implemented in any of the following methods, pedagogical structures would not include a textbook, a web page, a video conference or Podcast.

When beginning to create e-Learning content, the pedagogical approaches need to be evaluated. Simple pedagogical approaches make it easy to create content, but lack flexibility, richness and downstream functionality.

On the other hand, complex pedagogical approaches can be difficult to set up and slow to develop, though they have the potential to provide more engaging learning experiences for students. Somewhere between these extremes is an ideal pedagogy that allows a particular educator to effectively create educational materials while simultaneously providing the most engaging educational experiences for students.

REFERENCE SERVICES

Reference Desk

General reference services are provided from the Library's Reference Desks at the Murdoch, Rockingham and Peel campuses. The librarians can help you make effective use of the Library's resources by advising you on the use of the catalogue and website and suggesting appropriate databases for your subject area.

Ask a Librarian

Ask a Librarian is an e-mail reference service provided for Murdoch University students and staff. Send us your question and we will respond by the next working day.

Online Librarian

Online Librarian lets you get answers to your basic reference questions in real-time using chat.

Specialised Reference Services

The subject and liaison librarians provide specialized reference services and research skills training programmes from their offices. They also provide a subject request service for eligible external students. Forms for this service are available online. Online searching of databases on behalf of clients is also available. Contact the relevant subject librarian for further information and costs.

LEARNING RESOURCE CENTRE

Since 2004, with the help of Learning for Life (LFL), SIDH has been able to construct a new campus-our Learning Resource Center, or LRC, on two acres of land near the existing Bodhigram campus.

ONLINE COMPUTER LIBRARY CENTRE

On-line Computer Library Centre OCLC was founded in 1967 and originally named the Ohio College Library Centre. It is a non-profit, membership, computer library service and research organization dedicated to the public purpose of furthering access to the world's information and reducing information costs. More than 60,000 libraries in 112 countries and territories around the world use OCLC services to locate, acquire, catalogue, lend and preserve library materials. The organization was founded by Fred Kilgour, and its offices are located in Dublin, Ohio.

OCLC acquired Net Library, the largest eContent provider, in 2002 and owns 100% of the shares of OCLC PICA, a library automation systems and services company, which has its headquarters in Leiden in the Netherlands, which was renamed into "OCLC" at the end of 2007. In June 2006, the Research Libraries Group (RLG) merged into OCLC. On January 11, 2008, OCLC announced that they have purchased EZproxy.

HOW IT WORKS?

Researchers, students, faculty, scholars, professional librarians and other information seekers use OCLC services to obtain bibliographic, abstract and full-text information when and where they need it.

OCLC and its member libraries cooperatively produce and maintain WorldCat—the OCLC On-line Union Catalogue, the largest On-line Public Access Catalogue (OPAC) in the world. WorldCat contains holding records from most public and private libraries worldwide. WorldCat is available through many libraries and university computer networks.

The Open WorldCat programme makes records of library-owned materials in OCLC's WorldCat database available to Web users on popular Internet search, bibliographic and bookselling sites. OCLC member libraries' catalogues are more accessible from the sites where many people start their search for information.

Open WorldCat records may be accessed through Google or Yahoo's advanced search features, by simply limiting the scope of a search to the site or domain "worldcatlibraries.org." In the fall of 2004, the Open WorldCat collection was expanded to include information about *all* WorldCat records.

In October 2005, the OCLC technical staff began a wiki-like project that allows readers and librarians to add commentary, and structured-field information, associated with any WorldCat record.

OCLC owns a preservation microfilm and digitization operation called the OCLC Preservation Service Centre, with its principal office in Bethlehem, Pennsylvania. Libraries, museums, historical societies, colleges and universities utilize the OCLC Preservation Services to preserve printed works, books, maps, manuscripts, newspapers, etc. in microfilm format for future generations due to its 500-year life expectancy. In addition OCLC Preservation Services converts print and microfilm to digital objects for computer access.

ON-LINE DATABASE

OCLC maintains a database for cataloguing and searching purposes which is used by librarians and the public. OCLC Passport was one of the computer programmes used. Connexion was introduced in 2001 and replaced Passport when it was phased out in May of 2005.

This database contains records in Machine Readable Cataloguing (MARC) format contributed by library cataloguers worldwide who use OCLC as a cataloguing tool. These MARC format records are then downloaded into the libraries local catalogue systems to drive their on-line catalogues. This allows libraries worldwide to find and download records for materials they want to add to their local catalogue without having to go through the lengthy process of cataloguing them each individually.

As of February 2007, their database contains over 1.1 billion catalogued items. It remains the world's largest bibliographic database. Connexion is available to professional librarians both as a computer programme or on the web at connexion.oclc.org.

WorldCat is also available to the public for searching through a web-based service called First Search, as well as through the Open WorldCat programme.

Dewey Decimal System

The On-line Computer Library Centre acquired the trademark and copyrights associated with the Dewey Decimal Classification System when it bought Forest Press in 1988.

Web Junction

Web Junction is a division of OCLC funded by a grant from the Bill and Melinda Gates Foundation.

Question Point

Question point reference management service provides libraries with tools to communicate with users in multiple ways. This around-the-clock reference service is provided by a cooperative of participating global libraries.

WorldCat

WorldCat is a union catalogue which itemizes the collections of the more than 50,000 libraries which participate in the OCLC global cooperative. It is built and maintained collectively by the participating libraries from more than ninety countries. Created in 1971, it contains more than 90 million different records pointing to over 1.2 billion physical and digital assets in more than 360 languages, as of November 2007. It is the world's largest bibliographic database. WorldCat itself is not directly purchased by libraries, but serves as the foundation for many other fee-based OCLC services (such as resource sharing and collection management).

How to Access WorldCat?

The entire WorldCat database may be searched through the websites of libraries that subscribe to OCLC's First Search reference service. Often, access to WorldCat requires only an authenticated logon associated with a user's library account. WorldCat records can also be found on major Web search engines as well as selected bibliographic and bookselling sites, as part of the "Open WorldCat" programme (below).

Open WorldCat

In 2003, OCLC began the "Open WorldCat" pilot programme, making abbreviated records from a subset of WorldCat available to partner Web sites such as Yahoo!, Google and various booksellers, to increase the accessibility of its member libraries' collections. On the general search sites, a user can limit their search to Open WorldCat records by adding the phrase "find in a library" (with quotes included) to their search string. In 2004, this functionality became a permanent feature of WorldCat, and the entire database was made available for search-engine harvesting.

Starting in 2005, it is possible to make direct links to Open WorldCat records, allowing immediate access to all libraries holding a given book. Instructions can be found at the basic structure for linking to items is:

- **ISBN:** worldcatlibraries.org/isbn/(ISBN)
- **ISSN:** worldcatlibraries.org/issn/(ISSN number)
- **OCLC Number:** worldcatlibraries.org/oclc/(OCLC number)

Examples:

- **ISBN** - The Da Vinci code
- **ISSN** - Newsweek
- **OCLC Number** - Dictionary of American naval fighting ships

The easiest way to obtain an OCLC number is to go to a statewide union catalogue, like California's and search for the desired book. The OCLC number will appear towards the bottom of any given record.

Once in an Open WorldCat record, a user is asked to type in his zip code and the nearest libraries that own the book are displayed. If his library is an OCLC member, then available library services will appear on the right hand of the page.

WorldCat.org

In August 2006, it became possible to search WorldCat directly through a central Web page at worldcat.org or through a downloadable search box. Anyone can download the WorldCat search box and add it to a blog or Web site through a WorldCat Affiliate programme.

Watch WorldCat grow

As of November 2007, WorldCat has 1.2 billion holdings in its catalogue. OCLC has made a Watch WorldCat Grow page that updates every 8 seconds and tells you the bibliographic information for the most recently added entry.

WorldCat Identities

Prototyped as of February 2007, WorldCat Identities provides pages for 20 million 'identities' (predominantly authors and persons who are the subjects of published titles).

Internet Archive

The Internet Archive (IA) is a non-profit organization dedicated to maintaining an on-line library and archive of Web and multimedia resources. Located at the Presidio in San Francisco, California, this archive includes "snapshots of the World Wide Web" (archived copies of pages, taken at various points in time), software, movies, books, and audio recordings. To ensure the stability and endurance of the archive, IA is mirrored at the Bibliotheca Alexandrina in Egypt, the only library in the world with a mirror. The IA makes the collections available at no cost to researchers, historians, and scholars. It is a member of the American Library Association and is officially recognized by the State of California as a library.

History

The Internet Archive was founded by Brewster Kahle in 1996.

According to its website:

> *Most societies place importance on preserving artifacts of their culture and heritage. Without such artifacts, civilization has no memory and no mechanism to learn from its successes and failures. Our culture now produces more and more artifacts in digital form. The Archive's mission is to help preserve those artifacts and create an Internet library for researchers, historians, and scholars. The Archive collaborates with institutions including the Library of Congress and the Smithsonian.*

Because of its goal of preserving human knowledge and artifacts, and making its collection available to all, proponents of the Internet Archive have likened it to the Library of Alexandria.

Wayback Machine

The Wayback Machine is the Internet Archive's archive of snapshots of the Web, and is maintained with content from Alexa Internet. This service allows users to see archived versions of web pages across time—what the Archive calls a "three dimensional index."

Snapshots become available 6 to 12 months after they are archived. The frequency of snapshots is variable, so not all updates to tracked web sites are recorded, and intervals of several weeks sometimes occur. Newsweek.com snapshots for 2001

As of 2006 the Wayback Machine contained almost 2 petabytes of data and was growing at a rate of 20 terabytes per month, a two-thirds increase over the 12 terabytes/month growth rate reported in 2003. Its growth rate eclipses the amount of text contained in the world's largest libraries, including the Library of Congress. The data is stored on Petabox rack systems manufactured by Capricorn Technologies.

The name *Wayback Machine* is a reference to a segment from *The Rocky and Bullwinkle Show* in which Mr. Peabody, a bow tie-wearing dog with a professorial air, and his human "pet boy" assistant Sherman use a time machine called the "WABAC machine" to witness, participate in, and more often than not alter famous events in history.

Archive-It

Users who want to permanently archive material and immediately cite an archived version can use the Archive-It system, a for-fee subscription service, instead. Data collected with Archive—It is periodically indexed into the general Wayback Machine. As of December 2007, Archive—It had created over 230 million URLs for 466 public collections, including government bodies, universities, and cultural institutions. Some of the organizations participating in Archive—It include the Electronic Literature Organization, the State Archives of North Carolina, the Texas State Library and Archives Commission, Stanford University, the National Library of Australia, the Research Libraries Group (RLG), and many others.

Media Collections

In addition to web archives, the Internet Archive maintains extensive collections of digital media that are either public domain or licensed under a license that allows redistribution, such as the Creative Commons License. The media are organized into collections by media type (moving images, audio, text, *etc.*), and into sub-collections by various criteria. Each of main collection includes an "Open Source" sub-collection where general contributions by the public can be stored.

MOVING IMAGE COLLECTION

Aside from feature films, IA's Moving Image collection includes: newsreels; classic cartoons; pro- and anti-war propaganda; Skip Elsheimer's "A.V. Geeks" collection; and ephemeral material from Prelinger Archives, such as advertising, educational and industrial films and amateur and home movie collections.

IA's *Brick Films* collection contains stop-motion animation filmed with LEGO bricks, some of which are 'remakes' of feature films. The *Election 2004* collection is a non-partisan public resource for sharing video materials related to the 2004 United States Presidential Election. The *Independent News* collection includes sub-collections such as the Internet Archive's *World At War competition from 2001*, in which contestants created short films demonstrating "why access to history matters." Among their most-downloaded video files are eyewitness recordings of the devastating 2004 Indian Ocean earthquake. The September 11th Television Archive contains archival footage from the world's major television networks as the attacks of September 11th, 2001 unfolded on live television.

CHAPTER 3

Organization of Information

COLLECTION DEVELOPMENT POLICY OF INFORMATION RESOURCES FOR TEACHER EDUCATION INSTITUTION LIBRARIES

In her recently published book, *Fundamentals of Collection Development and Management*, Peggy Johnson provided a definition of a 'collection development policy' that would probably be broadly acceptable to most in the library and information profession:

> *A formal written statement of the principles guiding a library's selection of books and other materials, including the criteria used in selection, de-selection, and acceptance of gifts. It may also address intellectual freedom, future goals, and special areas of attention (2004: 311).*

But if there are few who would be unwilling to accept this definition, there would probably also be few who were excited by it or felt that it related to a particularly dynamic branch of information provision. Collection development policies have been with us for a long time: Johnson (2004: 73) herself suggests that they were becoming prominent in United States libraries by the 1950s and 1960s. While their 'golden age' was probably later than this, at least in Australia where they attracted most attention in the late 1980s and early 1990s, there can be no doubt that in the early years of the twenty-first century they are not a burning issue.

One possible reason for this may suggest itself from looking at the wording of Johnson's definition. It will be noticed that it mentions 'books' but does not explicitly mention digital materials. This is not of course because Johnson is unaware of such material: she in fact devotes a section of her book to a discussion of what might appear in a policy document devoted to 'e-resources'

(2004: 80, 83). There has been considerable discussion in the literature of what should appear in collection development policies devoted to digital resources, and of whether it is more appropriate to have a separate policy for such resources or a policy document that combines consideration of both print and digital resources.

The website *Electronic Collections Development* (2002) provides numerous examples of collection development policies largely or entirely devoted to digital resources. Notwithstanding this, however, Peter Clayton and Gary Gorman were able to observe in a book published as recently as 2001 that "Most existing collection development policies are strong on their approach to traditional print materials but weak on electronic materials—if, indeed, they are covered at all".

If this is true, and collection development policies are closely linked to print materials in the minds of librarians, it is hardly surprising that collection development policies are not a major focus of attention in the library and information profession at the beginning of the twenty-first century. For many professionals and paraprofessionals today, in particular those working in major academic and research libraries, it is digital resources that are of primary importance, and it is digital resources that their clients seem most to want and need.

These digital resources may come in many different forms, including computer-mediated materials like CD-ROMs brought into the library and owned by it, and others not owned by the library but accessed remotely when needed from terminals either within the library or linked to the library from the homes and offices of the library's clients. Familiar examples include websites on the World Wide Web and digital versions of serials. Increasingly there are available digital counterparts of all the familiar kinds of print and audiovisual materials-some straightforward machine-readable counterparts of items that may have been created decades or centuries before the advent of computerisation, and others digital editions of such materials which exploit the possibilities of hypertext—as well as items which exist only in digital form and indeed would be inconceivable employing technology such as print.

Libraries today often see themselves as 'hybrid' institutions, making available both print and digital resources, and many observers see this as a transitional stage on the way to the digital library, defined by Oppenheim and Smithson as "an information service in which all the information resources are available in computer-processable form, and the functions of acquisition, storage, preservation, retrieval, access and display are carried out through the use of digital technologies" (1999: 97). A visit to a large university library today is not likely to convince anyone that this prediction is fanciful: typically the bays of print materials are areas of largely undisturbed tranquillity, while crowds, queues, and frantic keyboard activity identify where the computer terminals linked to electronic resources are to be found.

Even in this environment there may be few ready to commit themselves in print to the view that written collection development policies are 'Wasted words' (Snow, 1996), or willing to join Hazen in stating that:

> *Collection development policies as traditionally conceived are static, reactive, and of little practical utility. They have outlived their purpose (1995: 29).*

The recent collection management texts of Evans and Zarnosky (2000), Clayton and Gorman (2001), and Johnson (2004) all devote considerable space to such policy documents. But clearly many practitioners have 'voted with their feet' (or at least the allocation of their time). Despite exceptions such as the State Library of New South Wales, which published on the internet the first part of a new two-part collection development policy, completed in 2002, part two of which is yet to appear (State Library of New South Wales, 2004), creating new collection development policies, or revising those now several years old, is not a major activity in the profession now focusing ever more intently on digital resources.

Of course, the reason for this neglect of such policies among practitioners is not merely that they are associated with print materials and other resources that the library purchases in a tangible form for in-house processing and eventual location on its shelves. It is not merely that they have come to seem old-fashioned. The very concept of collecting has been called into question as a primary activity of libraries. When increasingly the resources that the library makes available are ones which are not physically collected and brought within its walls but to which it provides access if and when they are needed, it would hardly be surprising if some came to regard a document that seeks to guide its collecting activities as of diminishing relevance.

Furthermore, now that it is an easy task to explore online the records of the holdings of almost all major libraries and many lesser ones in the developed world, the question might arise as to whether the traditional role of collection development policies in communicating to interested parties the collecting strengths and collecting intentions of libraries is as important as it was when discovering 'who held what' meant consulting cumbersome print or microform catalogues, or even long journeys by land, sea, and air.

Collecting in a Digital Environment

The idea that in a digital environment libraries no longer collect does not really stand up to closer scrutiny, however. They may increasingly not collect physical objects that can be admired in serried rows on the shelves, and they may only to a limited extent collect files that occupy server storage in computers under the direct control of the library. But they do assemble virtual collections of materials to which they have access.

However strong a library's commitment to relying on digital resources accessed remotely when needed, it is most unlikely not to identify the resources that it considers to be of particular interest to its clients, and to conclude agreements with the vendors of these items to make them available. Often this will in fact be the only way to ensure prompt access to the resources in question: electronic publishers and vendors frequently insist on a contract or licence before making their products such as digital versions of scholarly journals available if and when needed. In some circumstances such 'anticipatory' arrangements may not be strictly necessary-access to an item on a fee per individual use may be possible. But such 'pay-as-you-go' access is likely to be clumsy to operate in a busy library and significantly less economic than prior purchase of access if the resource in question is one likely to be used frequently by library clients.

Though recent years have seen some resources, such as digital versions of newspapers, move from being available free of charge on the internet to being available only for a fee, it remains true that many useful resources (as well as immense dross) are available free of charge to the user on the internet. Few information professionals, however, would take the view that if they provide computer terminals and access to Google their duty to the clients of their library in respect to such material has been fully discharged. Most professionals see as part of the library's role the identification of what is worthwhile and of particular relevance to their clients amidst the bewildering overabundance of the anarchic internet, and the bringing of this material to the attention of clients by establishing links to it from the library's web pages or its OPAC.

What this means is that in a very real sense libraries continue to collect in a digital environment. They select from the universe of digital publications those that to some extent they bring under their control, by paying fees to ensure access to them or by establishing well-defined pathways to them. The control may be more intangible and impermanent than that which exists over printed items sitting on the library shelves; it may even vanish overnight when a subscription is not renewed or an internet site disappears. The content of the collection may be more fluid than it ever was in any print collection subject to the ravages of theft and physical deterioration. But the fact of collecting seems beyond dispute.

Traditional Collection Development Policy Functions in a New Context

If collecting occurs there is a need for management of the process. In any organisation accountable for the funding it receives, collecting obviously needs to be systematic. Decisions need to be made as to what should be collected to serve the purposes for which the library exists within the limitations set by the funding available to it. For digital resources, as for traditional print ones, the available funding will provide access to only a fraction of what has been 'published' (and probably of what clients would like to have available to them), so there need to be principles to guide the act of selection in individual cases, with a view to ensuring that funds are optimally spent to serve the needs of the clientele. More is involved than just payments to publishers and vendors: the library needs to ensure that the time of its staff is used wisely, rather than on mater ial not likely to be of value to the users of the library. Consideration also needs to be given to the fact that what finds its way into the digital collection does not necessarily have a justification for remaining there indefinitely: the digital library may not have to worry about its shelves being cluttered by material that is outmoded, no longer relevant, dirty, or torn, but it does need to concern itself about paying for access to what is no longer of value, and about the cluttering of catalogues and web pages with links that lead to outmoded material if indeed they lead anywhere at all.

The collection development policy for digital resources is an essential planning device in a way broadly similar to the policy for print resources. It should also fulfil a broadly similar communication function for, unlike a good collection development policy, digital access to the catalogues of a library indicates the individual items it holds or makes available, not the principles and policies which inform the work of those building and maintaining its collection. As in the case of print resources a collection development policy can provide some protection for library staff in the legitimate performance of their selection duties by laying down the principles governing selection that have the sanction of the library's parent body. This protection is at least as important in a digital environment as in a print one, since, for example, potentially offensive sites displayed by clients of the library on the screens of its computer terminals in public areas are more likely to cause outrage than material less obtrusively retained with the covers of a printed volume.

New and Enhanced Functions

Such considerations suggest that a collection development policy for digital resources is as important as one for print resources. The reality, however, is that the policy is more important in the case of digital resources than it ever was in the case of print.

Partly this is because of the nature of digital resources. In the 'pre-digital' era libraries did acquire materials such as audio disks and microforms that required equipment to access the data they contained, and there was of course the 'time bomb' of the slow physical deterioration of most twentieth century paper-based materials. But most collections were predominantly print and most libraries most of the time were able to operate without giving much consideration to these problems. In general, materials once acquired and placed on the shelves, could be expected to be readily available several decades later. Digital materials, in contrast to paper-based ones, require computer hardware and if they are to be used, the library must ensure that the appropriate kinds of hardware and software are available in sufficient quantities. In the case of material not owned but accessed remotely the problem may usually be minor, as vendors will normally ensure their material operates on standard software; but digital resources that the library purchases outright and maintains on its own electronic systems pose a potentially far greater problem. Finding that changes in information technology, including rapid obsolescence may make it difficult or impossible to access a resource created several years earlier is quite a common experience. This means that the selection decision becomes more complicated, because it involves what are in effect new and possibly unpredictable factors to be considered. In the words of Ellis Weinberger, "The institution will need to determine the possibility and cost of preserving the object before obtaining it" (2000: 68). Collection development policies must include consideration of both the equipment to use and the preservation implications of the digital materials to which they refer.

The complexities of collecting digital resources also stem partly from the ways in which such resources are made available to libraries. Publishers of digital materials, a cynic might say, have avoided many of the mistakes made by print publishers, who allowed a situation to develop in which libraries purchasing examples of their products were free to make them available to whomsoever they choose, including casual visitors to the library and even individuals in other libraries who sought access to the items through an interlibrary loan service. In the case of digital resources publishers' interests are typically protected by licensing conditions that they impose, or attempt to impose, on libraries seeking to purchase access to their products.

The library may find itself confronted with extremely restrictive conditions attempting to govern to whom and under what conditions it may make the digital resource in question available, and further, imposing on it legal liability for any breaches of these conditions by people who access the resource through the library. Consideration of licensing conditions needs to form part of the selection or acquisition procedures for digital resources. Negotiation may well be necessary, for in extreme cases the licensing conditions proposed, if taken literally, would make library use of the resources impossible. The library may have its own conditions which it wishes to insist on writing into the licence agreement, such as a requirement that digital resources provide a satisfactory level of use statistics (Johnson, 2004: 83). The services of legal advisers may even be needed. A digital resources collection development policy should probably not be a detailed negotiator's manual, but if it is to be an effective planning device it will need to outline the procedures to be followed in dealing with the complexities of licensing.

In many cases the library will not be acting alone. Some digital resources are very expensive, and libraries band together in purchasing consortia to obtain access to them. Such consortia inevitably restrict to some extent the library's collecting autonomy, and modern collection development policies need to make provision for the possibility of the library's entering into consortia agreements that convey both advantages and obligations on it. It is not merely in relation to other members of a consortium that a library may find its autonomy somewhat circumscribed in a digital environment. In concerning itself with digital resources the library is entering territory to which the parent organisation's computer centre might lay claim, since the centre might well argue that matters relating to computer hardware, computer software, and even data files are its area of expertise. The matter may be dealt with, if not always resolved, by amalgamating the library and the computer centre, but whether or not this happens, an important role of the collection development policy may be staking out the claim of the library to be the collecting agency for files collected for their information content rather than as tools required in the conduct of the organisation's operations.

A different kind of demarcation is involved when, as is usually still the case, the library actively collects print materials despite its emphasis on digital resources. When does the library purchase only the digital version, when only the print version, and when both? Increasingly academic and research libraries appear to be resolving this issue by declaring that digital versions are preferred, and print versions will be acquired only when digital ones are not available. But this may not always be a desirable option, particularly for public libraries, and a collection development policy may need to address the issue. (This, of course, is an important argument for not having completely separate print and digital policy documents: if a library does collect in both formats, efficient use of its budget requires the coordination of development of the two.)

The hybrid or the digital library does need a collection development policy, and it needs a policy prepared with as much care and consultation as was devoted to the creation of print policies when creating them was a 'fashionable' library activity. In fact, the further the library ventures into the rich variety and complexity of different kinds of digital resources, with the challenges of licensing and consortia negotiations, the greater the need for a collection development policy is likely to be. Clearly too, the rapid and constant transformation of the world of digital resources and information technology make revision of the policy at regular and reasonably frequent intervals more important than the often-neglected revision of the print policy ever was. The content of the policy will indeed need to be somewhat different from that of policies of earlier decades to take account of new problems and new complexities such as those outlined above.

There may even be a case for abandoning the word 'collection' as being too redolent of a bygone age when libraries boasted of the number of volumes that sat ready for use on their shelves. But arguably the case for retaining it and emphasising that today collecting activity includes acquiring access to resources in digital format, is even stronger, since it is essential to keep in mind that even in an entirely digital environment, libraries are still in a vital sense collecting institutions.

Library Collection Development Policy

Purpose of Policy Statement: This collection development policy for the Brooks Library is intended for the use and guidance of librarians and faculty responsible for the building of collections that strongly support the learning and instructional needs and programmes of Central Washington University. The collections also seek to support the general cultural and intellectual formation of students and the work of staff engaged in university business. A library collection should have both the resource depth and breadth to serve institutional goals and objectives for learning, teaching, and other mission activities. Funding, staffing, and services to support materials acquisition, processing, and maintenance must be provided in suitable and adequate measure.

In order to meet the immediate needs and future goals of the university, the acquisition and maintenance of library resources and materials require constant attention. These activities are guided by a policy that sets priorities and distributes decision-making among the Collection Management Librarian, Library Liaisons, and Library Representatives. The policy also stands as a means of communicating the library's collection policy to the university community and other users. The Collection Development Policy of Brooks Library outlines the broad perimeters of collection development activities within the library. It is accompanied by the document titled "Collection Development Procedures and Information For Department Representatives and Library Liaisons" and the Materials Withdrawal Guidelines to provide a complete account of collection management efforts related to the Circulating, Reference and Serials Collections. Government Documents and Special Collections have individual policies not contained in this document.

Brooks Library Mission Statement: According to the Brooks Library Mission, the library "provide[s] resources and services to stimulate intellectual curiosity and to facilitate learning and research within the academic community." To that end, this policy will clearly define the types of resources collected. It considers the presence of electronic formats, university centers, and the cooperative efforts of the Orbis-Cascade Alliance and their effects on materials acquisition.

The primary mission of the Brooks Library is to support the mission and goals of Central Washington University, particularly in its commitment to teaching as the means to facilitate learning. The library supports a relationship between teacher and student that makes both partners in learning, scholarship, research, creative expression, and the application of knowledge to solve human and societal problems.

The library presents information services and collections of materials that directly support quality education to students and foster the physical, intellectual, social, and ethical development of each student. Assistance in the preparation of students for meaningful and productive careers and the development of independent, life-long learning are central goals. Our information resources and services show students how to locate, use and evaluate information and help students become conscious of their role as members of a pluralistic society through emphasis on the collection and presentation of multicultural resources.

With firm commitment to responsibilities as a resource to the local community and region as well as the university community, the library shares its resources with other institutions and with the citizens of Washington.

A guiding vision of the Brooks Library is the development of a completely integrated information resources center in which all users will find the best available materials regardless of the format or media in which it occurs. The library must continue to act as a regional presence for preserving locally produced knowledge. The library is committed to providing access and delivery of services utilizing the best available technologies as well as anticipating changes within the information technology marketplace.

Collection Development Objectives:

- Advance the missions of the university and library through the implementation of relevant activities and programmes
- Build a collection that meets the instruction, research and information needs of students, faculty and the university community
- Coordinate collection development activities with library liaisons and department representatives, with special emphasis in promoting involvement of teaching faculty
- Recommend and implement collection development policy
- Modify collection development policy and programmes in response to changes in the curriculum
- Spend the materials budget allocation to achieve the greatest benefit possible
- Manage the collection so as to accommodate budget changes, space needs and new trends in curriculum and research
- Maintain the fiscal accounting and bibliographic systems used to administer collection development activities
- Conduct periodic evaluations of the various collections and correct deficiencies, including weeding the collection, purchasing materials to fill gaps, and replacing missing materials as needed
- Pursue cooperative and coordinated collection development with the Orbis-Cascade Alliance libraries

General Policies

Selection Priorities: Acquisitions are financed chiefly by appropriations from the university budget. Library funds from the university appropriation are allocated to academic departments and certain library units for the purchase of materials.

Contingent on library funding, the following priorities shall be observed in the allocation of collection development funds for library materials and electronic resources:

- Support for student learning in, and faculty preparation for, existing prerequisites, major/minor courses, and graduate majors are given the highest level of priority
- Support for student learning in, and faculty preparation for, general education courses and electives.
- Support for non-curriculum related but mandated government programmes, such as maintaining our government document depository and regional public services of the documents library and cooperative library projects adopted by the Orbis-Cascade Alliance.
- Support for new majors and new graduate programmes consistent with clearly formulated and approved departmental, college, and university strategic plans, to the extent of the availability of additional funds provided for these new programmes by the state legislature and the university.
- Non-course related intellectual development of students and the general information needs of students, faculty, and other university personnel.
- Library materials and electronic resources for faculty research and development consistent with clearly formulated and approved departmental, college, and university strategic plans. These activities shall be supported by the library to the extent of the availability of funds provided for these programmes by the state legislature, the university, or from grant monies intended by granting agencies for the support of university infrastructure.
- Library materials and electronic resources for supporting the public services functions of Central Washington University in the local community and in Central Washington when funds are made available by the state and the university.

Resource Sharing

The Central Washington University Interlibrary Loan Programme provides access to material from many other educational institutions in Washington, the Northwest states and throughout the nation. Access is also provided to our materials to other institutions of higher education for borrowing purposes. Some shared collection development activity has been coordinated through the Collection Development and Management Committee of the Orbis-Cascade Alliance.

Intellectual Freedom

The Brooks Library is committed to providing a balanced collection that represents a diversity of perspectives on issues and ideas. Material is primarily selected to meet the teaching, research, and service needs of the University community. The library adheres to the principles of intellectual freedom as outlined in the Library Bill of Rights of the American Library Association. Article 1 of the Library Bill of Rights states "Books and other library resources should be provided for the interest, information, and enlightenment of all people of the community the library serves". "Materials should not be excluded because of the origin, background, or views of those contributing to their creation." Article 2 says "Libraries should provide materials and information presenting all points of view on current and historical issues. Materials should not be proscribed or removed because of partisan or doctrinal disapproval." Academic Freedom is also protected by the Central Washington University Faculty Code. Any individual or group questioning the appropriateness of material within the collection will be referred to the Library's Challenged Materials Policy.

Current versus Retrospective Selection

Primary emphasis is on the selection and acquisition of current (recently published, in-print) materials. The library will attempt to obtain retrospective materials as determined by systematic collection analysis when funds permit. Librarians and faculty are encouraged to use any and all information sources available to identify materials for selection and acquisition within their subject areas. Contact with the faculty of the academic units is vital, especially through Departmental Library Representatives. The use of Choice cards and the approval slips from book vendors aid both librarians and faculty in this process.

Collection Evaluation and Deselection

Librarians will conduct periodic evaluations of the collection to ensure that it reflects the changing and growing needs of the university community. The "Materials Withdrawal Guidelines" address these activities.

Collection Scope

The primary consideration of the Brooks Library collections is to provide books contributive to and supportive of the undergraduate curriculum of Central Washington University. As the university's curriculum grows, adapts, and otherwise changes in relation to the world and human knowledge, so the monograph collection must evolve. Collections related to the undergraduate curriculum should be as broad and deep as the monographic budget allows. Of secondary importance are the graduate curriculum, faculty research areas, and the larger body of published knowledge that has no direct connection to the university's instructional programmes. Purchases in these areas will be highly selective.

Format of materials is chosen based on the consideration of permanence, utility, accessibility, and appropriateness to content. Formats collected include:

- monographs
- serials
- videotapes
- digital video discs
- scores
- compact discs
- electronic databases
- electronic journals
- electronic books

Monograph Collection Development

The Library primarily selects single editions of cloth or paperbound books/monographs.

Textbooks, workbooks, study guides, etc., are generally not collected. Possible exceptions would be textbooks that are considered important in their field or if they are the best source of information on a certain topic.

The Summit catalogue and the collections it represents provide an immensely valuable body of literature to consider alongside local collections. Availability of materials in Summit does impact acquisition behaviour in Brooks Library, though with limited effect. Materials represented in Summit may nevertheless be purchased for the local collection if deemed necessary, or their accessibility through Summit may be considered adequate.

Library Liaisons are encouraged to write specific collection development policies for the subject areas for which they are responsible.

Recognition of Teacher Education Institutions

Recognition of institutions offering course or training in teacher education.

(1) Every institution offering or intending to offer a course or training in

teacher education on or after the appointed day, may, for grant of recognition under this Act, make an application to the Regional Committee concerned in such form and in such manner as may be determined by regulations:

Provided that an institution offering a course or training in teacher education immediately before the appointed day, shall be entitled to continue such course or training for a period of six months, if it has made an application for recognition within the said period and until the disposal of the application by the Regional Committee.

(2) The fee to be paid along with the application under sub-section (1) shall be such as may be prescribed.

(3) On receipt of an application by the Regional Committee from any institution under sub-section (1), and after obtaining from the institution concerned such other particulars as it may consider necessary, it shall—

(a) if it is satisfied that such institution has adequate financial resources, accommodation, library, qualified staff, laboratory and that it fulfils such other conditions required for proper functioning of the institution for a course or training in teacher education, as may be determined by regulations, pass an order granting recognition to such institution, subject to such conditions as may be determined by re-gulations;or

(b) if it is of the opinion that such institution does not fulfil the requirements laid down in sub-clause (a), pass an order refusing recognition to such institution for reasons to, be recorded in writing:

Provided that before passing an order under sub-clause (b), the Regional Committee shall provide a reasonable opportunity to the concerned institution for making a written representation.

(4) Every order granting or refusing recognition to an institution for a course or training in teacher education under sub-section (3) shall be published in the Official Gazette and communicated in writing for appropriate action to such institution and to the concerned examining body, the local authority or the state government and the central government.

(5) Every institution, in respect of which recognition has been refused shall discontinue the course or training in teacher education from the end of the academic session next following the date of receipt of

the order refusing recognition passed under clause (b) of sub-section (3).

The Gazette of India Extraordinary

(6) Every examining body shall, on receipt of the order under sub-section (4):

(a) grant affiliation to the institution, where recognition has been granted; or

(b) cancel the affiliation of the institution, where recognition has been refused.

Permission for a New Course on Training by Recognised Institution

(1) Where any recognized institution intends to start any new course or training in teacher education, it may make an application to seek permission therefor to the Regional Committee concerned in such, form and in such manner as may be determined by regulations.

(2) The fees to be paid along with the application under sub-section (1) shall be such as may be prescribed.

(3) On receipt of an application from an institution under sub-section (1), and after obtaining from the recognized institution such other particulars as may be considered necessary, the Regional Committee shall-

(a) if it is satisfied that such recognized institution has adequate financial resources, accommodation, library, qualified staff, laboratory, and that it fulfils such other conditions required for proper conduct of the new course or training in teacher education, as may be determined by regulations, pass an order granting permission, subject to such conditions as may be determined by regulation; or

(b) if it is of the opinion that such institution does not fulfil the requirements laid down in sub-clause (a), pass an order refusing permission to such institution, for reasons to be recorded in writing:

Provided that before passing an order refusing permission under sub-clause (b), the Regional Committee shall provide a reasonable opportunity to the institution concerned for making a written re-presentation.

(4) Every order granting or refusing permission to a recognized institution for a new course or training in teacher education under

sub-section (3), shall be published in the Official Gazette and communicated in writing for appropriate action to such recognized institution and to the concerned examining body, the local authority, the state government and the central government.

Affiliating Body to Grant Affiliation after Recognition or Permission by the Council

Notwithstanding anything contained in any other law for the time being in force, no examining body shall, on or after the appointed day,-

(a) grant affiliation, whether provisional or otherwise, to any institution; or

(b) hold examination, whether provisional or otherwise, for a course or training conducted by a recognised institution, unless the institution concerned has obtained recognition from the Regional Committee concerned, under section 14 or permission for a course or training under section 15.

The Gazette of India Extraordinary [Part II]

Contravention of provisions of the Act and consequences thereof.

(1) Where the Regional Committee is, on its own motion or on any representation received from any person, satisfied that a recognised institution has contravened any of the provisions of this Act, or the rules, regulations, orders made or issued thereunder, or any condition subject to which recognition under sub-section (3) of section 14 or permission under sub-section (3) of section 15 was granted, it may withdraw recognition of such recognised institution, for reasons to be recorded in writing:

Provided that no such order against the recognized institution shall be passed unless a reasonable opportunity of making representation against the proposed order has been given to such recognized institution:

Provided further that the order, withdrawing or refusing recognition passed by the Regional Committee shall come into force only with effect from the end of the academic session next following the date of communication of such order.

(2) A copy of every order passed by the Regional Committee under sub-section (1):

(a) shall be communicated to the recognized institution concerned and a copy thereof shall also be forwarded simultaneously to the university or the examining body to which such institution was affiliated for cancelling affiliation; and

(b) shall be published in the Official Gazette for general information.

(3) Once the recognition of a recognised institution is withdrawn under subsection (1), such institution shall discontinue the course or training in teacher education, and the concerned university or the examining body shall cancel affiliation of the institution in accordance with the order passed under sub-section (1), with effect from the end of the academic session next following the date of communication of the said order.

(4) If an institution offers any course or training in teacher education after the coming into force of the order withdrawing recognition under sub-section (1), or where an institution offering a course or training in teacher education immediately before the appointed day fails or neglects to obtain recognition or permission under this Act, the qualification in teacher education obtained pursuant to such course or training or after undertaking a course or training in such institution, shall not be treated as a valid qualification for purposes of employment under the central government, any state government or university, or in any school, college or other educational body aided by the central government or any state government.

DOCUMENT SELECTION

Library always tries to select and purchase the most valuable document in the fields of interest to fulfil the requirements of its members.

Frequently book selection bulletin is sent through e-mail to the members to receive their recommendations for books.

Apart from this, members are always welcome to suggest titles of documents to be purchased by filling up the Purchase Request Form. The final decision will be taken by the Library Committee.

A member who suggests a document would be informed, if the document is acquired and the document will be automatically reserved for him/her, after display for a week.

No document shall be issued before it is processed and put on display.

A Finer Measure of Benefit in Document Selection?

If it makes sense to use a finer unit of measurement from the next lower level in our hierarchy for library selection, why not do the same in document selection? Might it not also, by the same argument, be excessively simple to judge documents as simply relevant or not relevant? Again, how ``relevant" does it have to be---or how much of it has to be relevant---for the whole document to be deemed relevant? By the reasoning we applied in our discussion of libraries, it would seem better to move down a level and compare documents in terms of how much of each one is of marginal benefit.

One might say that probabilistic retrieval systems avoid the crudeness of binary relevance judgments because they generate a ranking of documents with respect to relevance, but this is not the case. What is generated are probability estimates that a document is or is not relevant, which is not the same as a measure of the relevant content of a document. Binary relevance judgments are still being used.

But comparing documents in a metric of the next lower level in our hierarchy (data) has problems. Library collections can be divided rather easily into their constituent elements, documents, but documents themselves are not so easy to subdivide with respect to relevance.

There are physical divisions (pages and lines) and there are rhetorical divisions (chapters, paragraphs, and sentences). Back of book indexing usually refers to pages, but the physical divisions are largely irrelevant to the subject matter and the rhetorical divisions are only weakly and inconsistently related to intellectual content. Some exceptions can be found: Bibliographies and encyclopedias are documents composed of recognizable, discrete elements. Other documents commonly follow standardized rhetorical forms but in a much less clearly and usefully defined way.

The advantages of dividing documents into separate conceptual units, into hypertextual nodes, was recognized in the seventeenth century and received detailed attention from Hartlib and Drury and from Leibniz. This interest was renewed when there was interest in applying modern technology to information management. Already by 1911 the German chemist Wilhelm Ostwald and his colleagues in an organization called Die Bruecke (The Bridge) were discussing the ``monographic principle," their name for the hypertextual division of documents into smaller units which could then be organized independently. They saw such a development as similar in nature and in significance to Gutenberg's introduction of movable printing type. Commenting on the ease with which bibliographies lend themselves to being subdivided and even rearranged, Paul Otlet wrote in 1918 f the need:

"...to detach what the book amalgamates, to reduce all that is complex to

its elements... This is the 'monographic principle' pushed to its ultimate conclusion. ... What is a book, in fact, if not a continuous line which has initially been cut to the length of a page and then cut again to the length of a justified line? Now this cutting up, this division, is purely mechanical; it does not correspond to any division of ideas."

Otlet foresaw "selection machines" searching among these smaller units of recorded knowledge and workstations for manipulating and processing them, but how to divide documents into conceptual pieces remains an unsolved problem. There is research in this direction and some of it explores how parts of documents might be used in various information retrieval tasks. Examples include automatic discovery of the topic structure of text, use of rhetorical boundaries (e.g. chapters, paragraphs, and sentences) to improve retrieval performance, and the automatic creation of hypertext links within documents. However, their effective use outside the laboratory may still be some way off.

ACCESSING THE DOCUMENT

To access the Manage Document Libraries page, the user should meet one of the following criteria:

- Member of Content Administrators group, which is set to wpsContentAdministrators user group by default

  OR

- Manager authority on the Manage Document Libraries portlet plus user authority on the portal content page and at least one document library

Configuring Library Management

Before you Begin: To configure the settings for the Manage Document Libraries portlet, the user should meet one of the following criteria:

- Member of the Content Administrators group, which is set to wpsContentAdministrators user group by default

  OR

- Manager authority on the Manage Document Libraries portlet plus user authority on the portal content page and at least one document library

The Manage Document Libraries portlet requires some additional configuration by the administrator. The configuration settings you select determine the options that administrators see when managing their document libraries. When you configure the settings for Manage Document Libraries, your changes affect that portlet instance, which means that other administrators use the options that you specified for the portlet. For example, if the administrator disables the browser plug-in, other users of the Manage Document Libraries portlet will not be able to import documents from their local machines using the import feature—the Import documents icon will be disabled. Also, if the plug-in is disabled, other users will not see the plug-in section in edit mode, so they will not be able to enable or disable the browser plug-in. Follow the steps below in the Configuring the Manage Document Libraries portlet section of this topic.

Your company might have other administrators that only manage Document Manager, instead of the administering the entire Portal. These Document Manager administrators can customize their own view of the Manage Document Libraries portlet. The settings that you configure for the Manage Document Libraries portlet affect what the Document Manager administrators see. For example, if the browser plug-in is disabled on the Manage Document Libraries portlet configure page, Document Manager administrators will not see the option to enable the plug-in on the edit page. Follow the steps below in the customizing your own view of the Manage Document Libraries portlet section of this topic.

Refer to the document libraries topic for an overview of what you can do with the Manage Document Libraries portlet.

Configuring the Manage Document Libraries Portlet

Follow these steps to configure the Manage Document Libraries portlet. These settings affect the view that other administrators see when they use the Manage Document Libraries portlet.

1. Log in as an administrator.
2. Navigate to the Manage Document Libraries page.
3. Click the wrench icon in the portlet title bar.
4. Specify the following Manage Document Libraries portlet settings:
   - Number of document libraries displayed per page
   - Enable and disable the browser plug-in
5. Save your settings.

For step-by-step information about configuring the Manage Document Libraries portlet, see the online help that is available from the portlet title bar.

Customizing Your Own View of the Manage Document Libraries Portlet

Follow these steps to modify your own view of the Manage Document Libraries portlet. These settings do not affect the view that other administrators see when they use the Manage Document Libraries portlet.

1. Log in as an administrator.
2. Navigate to the Manage Document Libraries page.
3. Click the pencil icon in the portlet title bar.
4. Specify the following Manage Document Libraries portlet settings:
   - Number of document libraries displayed per page
   - Enable and disable the browser plug-in
5. Save your settings.

For step-by-step information about modifying the Manage Document Libraries portlet, see the online help that is available from the portlet title bar.

Navigating to Manage Document Libraries Page

Follow these steps to access the Manage Document Libraries page:

1. Log in as an administrator.
2. Click Administration to go to the Portal Administration page.
3. Click Portal Content.
4. Click Manage Document Libraries.

Next Steps

You have completed this step. Continue to the next step by choosing one of the topics below.

Assigning User Access

Before you Begin: To assign access and roles from the Manage Document Libraries or Document Manager page, the user should meet one of the following criteria:

- Member of the Content Administrators group, which is set to wpsContentAdministrators user group by default

  OR
- The user needs to possess the following authority or higher:
  - User authority on the Portal Content Administrative page
  - User authority on the Manage Document Libraries portlet

- — Administrator authority on the ICM_CONTENT_REPOSITORY virtual resource
- — User authority on the Resource Permission page and the Resource Permission portlet
- — Delegator authority on the User and User Groups resources. For information on setting the Delegator authority, see Setting the Delegator authority.

Setting the Delegator authority:

1. Under Portal Administration, click Access.
2. Click User and Group Permissions > Users
3. Select the user you want to give Delegator authority to and click the pencil icon.
4. Click Virtual Resources, then click the key for Users.
5. Click the box for the Delagator role.

Follow the same process for user groups, except after clicking Virtual Resources, click on User groups and choose the Delegator role.

This section gives the administrator the information necessary to assign users access to a document library by using the Manage Document Libraries portlet. Administrators should use the Manage Document Libraries portlet to restrict who can view, edit, copy, and delete document libraries. Setting such restrictions can help keep the document repository organized and can help prevent unwanted changes to document libraries. The Manage Document Libraries portlet uses the Resource Permissions portlet to assign user access.

Setting up Access for Document Manager

As part of setting up and maintaining your document management work environment, you will need to set access authority and assign roles for your users. Some Document Manager administrators may want to restrict who can view, edit, move or delete folders or files.

Setting such restrictions can help keep the document repository organized, and can help prevent unwanted changes to documents or folders. For example, an administrator may want only project managers to have authority to delete files, and only give writers the authority to open and edit files. Administrators determine user authorization for these tasks by setting access controls.

In order to create an administrator role, the user needs to have access to the Resource Permissions portlet. Adding the user to the Content Administrators user group automatically provides the user with authority on the Manage Document Libraries portlet.

The Document Manager administrator should use the Manage Document Libraries portlet to assign access. Clicking the Access icon opens the Resource Permissions Portlet. From there, administrators can grant users and groups access rights to document libraries.

After access control for groups is set for a document library, the administrator (and certain enabled users) can set access for documents and folders. Refer to the Document Manager online help for detailed instructions on setting access control.

Steps for Assigning Access to a Document Manager Resource

Follow these steps to set access to specific Document Manager resources, such as folders and documents:

1. Navigate to the Document Manager portlet instance.
2. Select the document or folder that you want to set access to.
    a. To set access to a document, click the name of the document to open the document view page, then click More Actions-> Set Access.
    b. To set access to a folder, select the check box next to the folder, then click Folder Actions-> Set Access to This Folder.

The following table displays the roles that are relevant to Document Manager:

WebSphere Portal role	Document Manager access rights
User	Read-only access to Document Manager resources. Users can see the resource, but cannot modify or contribute content of their own.
Editor	The ability to view and add new documents, folders, and views to the current resource. Editors can also modify the properties and content of existing documents and files. **Note:** The editor role **cannot** move files.
Manager	All the privileges of Editors, plus the ability to: • convert documents to another format • delete folders or documents underneath the current resource • move files
Administrator	The Administrator role can perform any operation.

The Privileged User, Delegator, or Security Administrator roles have no special meaning for Document Manager resources.

Access control gives special privileges to the owner of a resource. For instance, if a user with the Editor authority adds a document or folder, she has view, edit, delete, grant access and delegate permissions on that file or folder, even though she is only an editor.

Note: To set access on a folder or document, the user must have User authority on the Resource Permission page and the Resource Permission portlet. If the user does not have the correct level of authority, then the set access option will not be available in Document Manager.

For step-by-step instructions, see the online help that is available from the portlet title bar.

Assigning User Access and Roles for a Document Library, Documents, or Folders

Administrators set appropriate authority to users and groups to work with Document Manager. After a new document library is created, the administrator must assign permissions for that document library. After access control is set for the document library, the administrator and certain enabled users can set access for documents and folders. Refer to the Manage Document Libraries online help for detailed instructions on setting access control.

Steps for This Task: Follow these steps to assign user access to a document library.

1. Navigate to the Manage Document Libraries page.
2. Select the document library to which you want to assign access.
3. Click the **Access** icon to open the Resource Permissions page.
4. Assign the appropriate resource permissions.
5. Save your settings.

Setting up Document Management

Before you Begin: Ensure that you have created the document library that you plan to use for document management. The default working library is Document Manager, and your ability to modify its settings is limited. If you want to use a different working document library, you must create one. You have many configuration options available for the document libraries that you create. Refer to the creating, editing, and deleting document libraries topic for more information about working with document libraries.

Important: Configure document management for importing large files by increasing the inbound buffer size. By default, 10 MB is the largest single file that can be imported. If your document repository contains any file larger than 10 MB, you need to increase the buffer size.

To increase the buffer size, do the following:

1. In the administrative console of WebSphere Application Server, click Servers > Application Servers > *portal_server* > Custom Properties > New.
2. Add the protocol_http_large_data_inbound_buffer property, and specify a value in bytes that can accommodate your largest single file.
3. Save your settings.
4. Restart your portal.

Administrators can configure and modify the settings for the Document Manager portlet instance. This section is designed to give the administrator the information necessary to set up the document management environment and modify settings for a Document Manager portlet. Refer to the Document management topic for more information about what users can do with Document Manager.

Steps for This Task: The Document Manager portlet requires some additional configuration by the administrator. The settings you modify affect only that particular instance of Document Manager. For example, you might have multiple instances of Document Manager installed on one page, and each instance can be configured differently. Document Manager A might be set up to use a different document library than that of Document Manager B.

1. Navigate to the Document Manager portlet that you want to modify and click the wrench icon to configure the settings for the Document Manager portlet instance.
2. Specify the following settings:
    a. *Set the Working Document Library:* Specifies the document library in which users will work for the Document Manager instance.
    b. *Turn on New Document Indicator:* Indicates documents that are new or have been recently modified by the word New! next to them. With the indicator turned on for the Document Manager instance, the user can set the number of days for the indicator to display in the edit mode for his or her portlet instance.
    c. *Include the Document Library in the Search Center:* Makes the

document library searchable by the Search Center. Only the working document library for the portlet instance will be queried by the Search Center. With the appropriate permissions, users can access Document Manager documents that are returned by the Search Center.

d. *Enable Conversions:* Allows users to use the Productivity Components to work with documents that were originally cre ated in other file formats. See the Viewing documents in HTML topic for a list of file types that can be viewed in HTML.

e. *Enable Editors:* Allows users to work with the productivity components. Refer to the Productivity Components topic for more information.

f. *Disable the Browser Plug-in:* Disables the browser plug-in that allows users to edit documents using applications installed on their computer. With the plug-in disabled, users will only be able to create and edit documents using the Portal editors. Users will still be able to import other document types with the browser plug-in disabled. See the setting up the browser plug-in topic for more information about enabling and disabling the browser plug-in.

g. *Enable the Folder Tree:* Turns on the folder tree option. With the folder tree enabled, users will have the option to display the document library folder hierarchy vertically, starting at the document library root folder. With the folder tree disabled, users will only be able to display the table view, which lists the contents of the current document library without the tree view on the left. Users click Show folders to display the tree view along with the table view, and users click Hide folders to display only the table view. Also, if you configure the folder tree to be enabled, the option to turn on the folder tree is also displayed in edit mode.

h. *Enable Active Content Filtering:* Removes potentially harmful active content (such as JavaScript, Java, and ActiveX) from HTML prior to displaying it in a browser.

i. *Specify the SMTP Mail Server:* Provides users the ability to send e-mail links to documents and folders to other users. In order to use the Send a link feature of Document Manager, you must specify the appropriate SMTP mail server.

j. *Configure the Default Root Path for Your Portlet:* Allows the administrator to specify an existing subfolder within the current document library as the root folder for each portlet instance. Upon login, users will begin their session from this configured root folder. If you select a default root folder that has been deleted, renamed, or inaccessible to the current user, the default root path will revert to the current document library root. Users will still have the ability to navigate to any accessible folder in the document library.

Modified configuration settings take effect immediately. Be careful when modifying configuration settings while the Document Manager portlet is in use. For step-by-step information about configuring an instance of the Document Manager portlet, see the online help that is available from the portlet title bar.

Set Preview Size

You can also adjust the size of the document preview. Documents that exceed the set size will not be displayed. To modify the document preview size, follow these steps:

1. Log in as administrator and click on Administration > Portlet Management > Portlets > Document Manager > Configure portlet.
2. Add the property previewSizeThreshold to the list and set the preview size.
   - The preview size must be a valid number of bytes such as 1024 (1KB) or 1048576 (1MB).
   - The default preview size for documents is 10485760 bytes, which is 10MB.
   - If you do not want a preview of the selected document to appear at all, you can set the previewSizeThreshold parameter to 0 (zero).
3. Click **Save** to save the changes.
4. Log out and then log back in to Document Manager for the setting to take effect.

Setting up the Browser Plug-in

Before you Begin: Ensure that you meet the following criteria:

- The browser plug-in must be enabled for users to use desktop applications. Refer to Setting up document libraries for more information.

- The browser must be configured for ActiveX and scripting in order to use desktop applications.
- *Important Note for Linux Users:* On Linux, a Java Applet is used to communicate with the client file system. This applet gives you the ability to edit files using your native editors, as well as to import multiple files and directories from the client file system. In order to run the applet, you will need to have a supported Java Runtime Environment installed on your browser. For installation instructions on Mozilla, visit http://plugindoc.mozdev.org/linux.html#Java and follow the instructions to install the Java Runtime Environment. Once the Java Runtime Environment is recognized in the browser, you should be prompted to accept an IBM certificate when you first visit the edit or administrative import pages. You should choose to always accept this certificate for the applet to be able to read and copy files from your local machine. After you accept the certificate, you might need to refresh the page. The plug-in attempts to read and write the files you are editing to the temporary directory defined in the java.io.tmpdir system property. Users need to have authority to create directories and files in that path (usually /tmp). Lastly, the plug-in requires that KDE be installed and that the kfmclient be in the path. Visit http://www.kde.org for information about installing KDE. The kfmclient exec command is used to open files with the editors registered in KDE.

The Manage Document Libraries portlet provides a browser plug-in that allows users to import their local files into a document library. Also, the Document Manager portlet provides a browser plug-in that allows users to work with documents in editing applications that are installed on their computers. Enabling the browser plug-in gives users the options to either use their preferred editing applications or the Productivity Components that are provided with the product. This section contains the information necessary to enable and disable the browser plug-in, as well as instructions for configuring a browser to automatically open a file in a certain editing application.

Note: Plug-in upgrades are not automatic if you are using a Mozilla or Firefox browser. See upgrading the Mozilla or Firefox browser plug-in for information on upgrading.

Upgrading the Mozilla or Firefox browser Plug-in

Browser upgrades are often installed automatically; however, if you require a new Mozilla or Firefox plug-in, you must manually install it.

Upgrading Plug-ins on Mozilla 1.4

In order to get new plug-ins on Mozilla 1.4, perform the following steps:

1. Be sure that you have only one version of Mozilla installed. Multiple instances of Mozilla could interfere with the plug-in installation.
2. Delete the Mozilla cache. The cache is located in c:/Documents and Settings/*your_user*/Application Data/Mozilla.
3. Delete the registry keys that bind the plug-in mime type to Document Manager by searching the registry for application/pdm-plugin under HKEY_USERS.
4. Uninstall and then reinstall Mozilla.
5. Start the Mozilla browser and navigate to the Document Manager portlet.
    - If a plug-in install window opens, follow the provided install steps.
    - If you do not see a plug-in install window, visit http://<hostname>:9081/wps/pdm/plugin/nsinstpdm.jsp?application/pdm-plugin where <hostname> is the name of your portal server.

Upgrading Plug-ins on Mozilla 1.7 and Higher

For current versions of Mozilla 1.7 and higher, perform the following steps to update the plug-in:

1. Delete the registry keys that bind the plug-in mime type to Document Manager by searching the registry for application/pdm-plugin under HKEY_USERS.
2. Delete the existing plug-in files from *Mozilla_install_dir*/plugins/*PDM*.dll and *Mozilla_install_dir*/components/nsIPDMPlugin.xpt.
3. Start the Mozilla browser and navigate to the Document Manager portlet.
    - If a plug-in install window opens, follow the provided install steps.
    - If you do not see a plug-in install window, visit http://<hostname>:9081/wps/pdm/plugin/nsinstpdm.jsp?application/pdm-plugin where <hostname> is the name of your portal server.

Upgrading Plug-ins on Firefox 1.0 and Higher

For current versions of FireFox 1.0 and higher, perform the following steps to update the plug-in:

1. Delete the existing plug-in files from *Firefox_install_dir*/plugins/ *PDM*.dll and *Firefox_install_dir*/components/ nsIPDMplugin.xpt.
2. Start the Firefox browser and navigate to the Document Manager portlet.
   - If a plug-in install window opens, follow the provided install steps.
   - If you do not see a plug-in install window, visit http:// <hostname>:9081/wps/pdm/plugin/nsinstpdm. jsp?application/pdm-plugin where <hostname> is the name of your portal server.

Setting up the Browser Plug-in

Enabling the browser plug-in allows users to create and edit documents using familiar applications that are installed on their desktop.

The browser plug-in is enabled by default, and it can be disabled for the Manage Document Libraries portlet, as well as for the Document Manager portlet. If you disable the plug-in in the Manage Document Libraries portlet, the setting for disabling the plug-in will not appear in edit mode. Also, by disabling the browser plug-in in the Manage Document Libraries portlet, the setting for disabling the plug-in will not appear in the portlet edit mode, and administrators will not be able to import documents from their local machines using the import feature.

Similarly, if you disable the plug-in in the Document Manager portlet, the setting for disabling the plug-in will not appear in edit mode, and users will not have the options to enable or disable the plug-in for that Document Manager portlet instance.

1. Follow these steps to disable the browser plug-in for the Manage Document Libraries portlet:
   a. Log in as an administrator.
   b. Click **Administration**, then click **Portal Content.**
   c. Click **Manage Document Libraries.**
   d. Click the wrench icon in the portlet title bar to see the configuration options.

   e. Select **Disable browser plug-in** to prevent users from using the plug-in.
   f. Click **OK** to save your changes.
2. Follow these steps to disable the browser plug-in for the Document Manager portlet:
   a. Log in as an administrator.
   b. Navigate to the Document Manager portlet you want to configure.
   c. Click the wrench icon in the portlet title bar to see the configuration options.
   d. Select **Disable browser plug-in** to prevent users from using the plug-in.
   e. Click **OK** to save your changes.

Setting up Draft Approvals

Before you begin:

- Ensure that you have assigned the appropriate permissions for your users:
  - Users must have access to the document library.
  - Users must have access to the Portal Content page and the Manage Document Libraries portlet.
  - Users with review responsibility must be in the Document Reviewer user group.
  - In order to override document locks, users must have at least User-level access in a user group to which the lock owner belongs. The lock owner might belong to multiple groups. As long as the user has User access in any of those groups, then the user can override the document lock.
  - In order for a reviewer to edit a document submitted for approval by an author, the reviewer must have at least User-level access in a user group to which the author belongs. The author might belong to multiple groups. As long as the reviewer has User access in any of those groups, then the reviewer can edit the document.
- Confirm that WebSphere Application Server security is enabled. The draft approvals option is only available if security is enabled on

your system. See the topic Enabling WebSphere Application Server security for WebSphere Portal for more information.

This section gives the administrator the information necessary to set up the draft approvals process for a document library.

Steps for This Task: Workflow roles are first administered through the WebSphere Portal User group administrative portlet. When the administrator configures the document library, he or she can select a user group to be the Document Reviewer group for the library's approval process. This subset is specified when the administrator elects to turn on the Document Manager approvals workflow option.

1. From the Manage Document Libraries page, select the working document library for the draft approvals process.
2. Open the Edit the document library settings page.
3. Under Approvals workflow, select Enable workflow.
4. Select the appropriate approver group.
5. Save your settings. The draft approvals process is now enabled for the document library.

For step-by-step information about working with drafts, see the online help that is available from the portlet title bar.

Once a document draft is submitted for review, the document appears in the Submitted Drafts view of the assigned reviewers. Although multiple users can have review responsibility, only one reviewer can accept or reject the document change.

Once a document change is accepted by a reviewer, it becomes visible in the Document Manager folder hierarchy. If a reviewer rejects the draft, the document returns to the Private Drafts view of the originator of the change for further modification, then a subsequent submit reactivates the approval step. Refer to the Working with drafts topic for more information.

Setting up File Type Definitions

This section describes how to set up file type definitions and enable Document Conversion Services for the Document Manager portlet, which provides users the ability to open various file types in HTML format. Documents produced by many standard applications (such as word processors or spreadsheets) can be viewed as HTML pages using the Document Conversion Services. For example, documents received as attachments to an e-mail can be viewed in a browser, even if the application that created the document is not installed. Document Conversion Services also allows documents to be searched by content. Refer to the Viewing documents in HTML topic for a list of file types that can be viewed in HTML.

Note: The document conversion process will delete previous versions of the document.

Steps for This Task: Setting up file type definitions is part of configuring Productivity Components. For details, see Configure Productivity Components. Ensure that you followed the instructions that the WebSphere Portal Customization Dialog generated for that task. One step in these instructions involves updating the content-types.properties file with the following content.

These extensions are case-sensitive.

- **Microsoft Office:**

  application/msword: \

  description=Microsoft Word;\

  file_extensions=.doc
- application/vnd.ms-excel: \

  description=Microsoft Excel;\

  file_extensions=.xls
- application/vnd.ms-powerpoint: \

  description=Microsoft PowerPoint;\

  file_extensions=.ppt
- **Lotus SmartSuite:**

  application/vnd.lotus-freelance: \

  description=Lotus Freelance;\

  file_extensions=.prz
- application/vnd.lotus-1-2-3: \

  description=Lotus 1-2-3;\

  file_extensions=.123
- application/vnd.lotus-wordpro: \

  description=Lotus WordPro;\

  file_extensions=.lwp

- **OpenOffice:**
  application/vnd.sun.xml.writer: \
  description=Open Office;\
  file_extensions=.sxw
- application/vnd.sun.xml.writer.template: \
  description=Open Office;\
  file_extensions=.stw
- application/vnd.sun.xml.writer.global: \
  description=Open Office;\
  file_extensions=.sxg
- application/vnd.sun.xml.calc: \
  description=Open Office;\
  file_extensions=.sxc
- application/vnd.sun.xml.calc.template: \
  description=Open Office;\
  file_extensions=.stc
- application/vnd.sun.xml.impress: \
  description=Open Office;\
  file_extensions=.sxi
- application/vnd.sun.xml.impress.template: \
  description=Open Office;\
  file_extensions=.sti
- application/vnd.sun.xml.draw: \
  description=Open Office;\
  file_extensions=.sxd
- application/vnd.sun.xml.draw.template: \
  description=Open Office;\
  file_extensions=.std
- application/vnd.sun.xml.math: \
  description=Open Office;\

file_extensions=.sxm

Maintaining Your Search Index

Successful searching within Document Manager requires an up-to-date, valid search index. These important tips and procedures will help you maintain your search index.

Backing up and Recovering the Search Index

To ensure that your Document Manager search continues to work correctly, consider performing the following steps as part of your database back up and recovery procedures.

- Each time that you back up your database(s), you should also back up the Juru search indexes that have been built and coincide with the current state of your database(s).

  To back up Juru indexes:

  You need to back up the directory tree containing the Juru indexes. After you unzip the juruIndexes.zip file, these indexes are maintained under *wp_root*/jcr/search in the Indexes directory. Use any standard zip tool or operating system command that recursively collects the contents within a directory and its subdirectories.

- To restore the Juru indexes, simply unzip the backup copy to an empty directory (this is the default).

  For z/OS, the default directory is *wp_root*/jcr/search.

Changing the Search Indexing Interval

The time between rebuilding the search indexes is set to 30 minutes by default. To change the search indexing interval, you must change a setting in the icm.properties file. To change the interval:

1. Edit the icm.properties file.
2. Edit the line
   - jcr.textsearch.indexmaintenance.interval = 30
3. Set the interval number to the desired value in minutes. For example, if the interval is set to 90 minutes, the line looks like this:
   - jcr.textsearch.indexmaintenance.interval = 90
4. Save the properties file.
5. Restart the WebSphere Portal server.

TECHNICAL PROCESSING

Major activities of this section are:

- Writing process slip for assigning call no. for the book received from the Acquisition section.
- Checking the process slip with the Catalogue and SL cards.
- Assigning call no. for the book with the help of UDC Scheme and the Authority file.
- Arranging the process slip for the preparation of NAL monthly bulletin
- Pasting the spine and date labels in the book and noting the call no. and cop. no. on the spine label and accession no on the date label along with the call no. and cop. no.
- Arranging the processed project book for informing the concerned project co-ordinator
- Arranging the library book along with other processed books to be displayed on each month.
- Merging the SL card in the cabinet alphabetically after noting the call no on it.
- Preparing the list of the processed books during a month with bibliographical details, Accession no and location using Microsoft Word.
- Announcing this list on the Library website at the beginning of the month.
- Sending the processed books for display on each month after entering the required details of the book in the OPAC.
- Removing the already displayed books to the stack after keeping the reserved books on the reservation desk .
- Reminding the Project Co-ordinator or faculty member to collect the processed books which are not collected and to be issued on Permanent Loan or Department Loan.

PHYSICAL VERIFICATION OF COLLECTION

Physical verification is a process whereby an IC layout design is checked via EDA software tools to see if it meets certain criteria. Verification involves DRC (Design rule check), LVS (Layout versus schematic), ERC (Electrical rule check), XOR (Exclusive OR), and Antenna Checks.

XOR Check

This step involves comparing two layout databases/GDS by XOR operation of the layout geometries. This check results a database which has all the mismatching geometries in both the layouts. This check is typically run after a metal spin, wherein the re-spin database/GDS is compared with the previously taped out database/GDS.

Antenna Check

Antenna checks are used to limit the damage of the thin gate oxide during the manufacturing process due to charge accumulation on the interconnect layers (metal, polysilicon) during certain fabrication steps like plasma etching, which creates highly ionized matter to etch. The antenna basically is a metal interconnect, i.e., a conductor like polysilicon or metal, that is not electrically connected to silicon or grounded, during the processing steps of the wafer. If the connection to silicon does not exist, charges may build up on the interconnect to the point at which rapid discharge does take place and permanent physical damage results to thin transistor gate oxide. This rapid and destructive phenomenon is known as the antenna effect. The Antenna ratio is defined as the ratio between the physical area of the conductors making up the antenna to the total gate oxide area to which the antenna is electrically connected.

ERC (Electrical Rule Check)

ERC (Electrical rule check) involves checking a design for all well and substrate areas for proper contacts and spacings thereby ensuring correct power and ground connections. ERC steps can also involve checks for unconnected inputs or shorted outputs. They can also check for structures suceptible to ESD damage.

Shared Responsibility for Electronic Materials Management

The CIC-EJC has provided the opportunity for the CIC libraries to define their role in electronic scholarship both independent of and in relation to publishers and computer specialists. The CIC Center for Library Initiatives has provided coordination and leadership for the CIC-EJC as it has for other CIC-wide library projects. CICNet has provided technical support, guidance, and implementation. It has conducted all development and maintenance of the technical aspects of the system, including acquisition and archiving of electronic journals, publisher relationships and permissions, organization and display of bibliographic data, development of indexing and search utilities, and hardware and software support. The CIC member librarians share responsibility for evaluation of available information resources including selection, deselection, cataloging, and quality control.

Other projects within the CIC provide an opportunity for collaboration in the development of related electronic information resources and access. The CIC libraries, with shared licences negotiated by the CIC Center for Library Initiatives, have purchased commercial databases and are sharing them across the CIC institutions' regional network. This activity has served as a model of how to work together and reach mutually beneficial collective decisions. These efforts have put CIC in the forefront in collective licensing negotiations with publishers.

The Virtual Electronic Library (VEL), funded through a US Department of Education grant, will develop the technical infrastructure required to provide seamless access to the CIC libraries' OPACs. The utility of this infrastructure will be demonstrated through user-initiated interlibrary loans and document delivery throughout the CIC. The VEL will enable the more than one-half million faculty, staff, and students to explore and take advantage of vast resources within the CIC. Inherent to the VEL project is the addition of an expanded set of electronic resources to the VEL pool of information resources. Ultimately, the CIC-EJC will be an integral part of the VEL.

The VEL has provided the impetus for the CIC libraries to sponsor numerous working groups and projects. The Task Force on the CIC Electronic Collection, which oversees the CIC-EJC, is one of these groups. Each CIC library has appointed an Electronic Resources Officer to coordinate local participation in the various projects related to building the VEL. The Task Force on Preservation and Digital Technology is exploring both digitization of materials held by the libraries and preservation of original electronic materials using digital technology. The CIC Electronic Text Group is developing a core collection of encoded humanities texts and planning for networked access among the CIC libraries. Sharing expertise among CIC library computer specialists is a central component of the e-Text project, with group members specializing in applying text encoding standards, building search engines, developing collections, and training colleagues at other CIC institutions. Groups have just been appointed to address issues around geographic information systems and government document electronic resources. All these separate and overlapping projects provide a strong environment for collaborative research and work.

SERIALS AND ELECTRONIC MATERIAL MANAGEMENT

Georgia State University is seeking an energetic, knowledgeable and visionary librarian to serve as Serials and Electronic Acquisitions Librarian. Georgia State University has an annual serials budget of approximately $3 million dollars for both print and electronic resources.

It is a full participant in GALILEO, which provides substantial online information sources, and in consortial purchases with other research libraries. Pullen Library seeks a person with serials experience for a faculty rank (non-tenure) position to manage all aspects of electronic serials acquisition, oversee the efficient operation of the Serials Unit and to serve as Assistant Department Head. The position reports to the

Head of the Acquisitions Department and will have administrative responsibility for the Acquisitions Department in the absence of the department head.

Responsibilities: The successful candidate will be responsible for, but are not limited to: coordinating the purchase and licensing of all electronic materials; overseeing all aspects of serials acquisitions including ordering, receipt, invoicing, claiming, binding, vendor assessment, and other serials-related functions; coordinating the work of the serials unit with the other appropriate areas to ensure efficient workflow and communication; serving as Assistant Department Head; and participating in university and professional activities including research and publication.

Required: ALA-accredited master's degree in library science plus two years serials experience. Computer skills. Experience supervising or organizing the work of others. PREFERRED: Experience with electronic resources including negotiating contracts and licenses for electronic resources. Some budget management experience. Experience working in an integrated automated environment, preferably Voyager. Excellent communications skills. Attention to detail. Strong analytical and problem solving skills. Demonstrated interest in professional and research activities.

Library and University Environment: Georgia State University (GSU) is a dynamic urban institution located in downtown Atlanta with an enrollment of approximately 25,000 students. The close relationship that exists between the university and its surrounding business, government and cultural communities makes GSU unique in the University System of Georgia and distinctive among universities in the South.

The William Russell Pullen Library houses over 1,300,000 volumes, subscribes to more than 8,000 serials, and is a Federal Document Depository with more than 850,000 government documents. Its growing Media Center has holdings of approximately 12,000 audio, video, and multimedia materials. The carefully selected collections are designed to serve varied research and instructional needs at the undergraduate and graduate levels of the university community. Library services are supported by GIL (GALILEO Interconnected Libraries) with integrated functions for OPAC acquisitions, cir culation systems and serials control, including a system-wide union catalog.

The University System of Georgia has a statewide system known as GALILEO providing equal access to electronic resources and other materials for libraries throughout the state. Pullen Library is a member of the Association of Southeastern Research Libraries; the Southeastern Library Network (SOLINET), and the Atlanta Regional Con! sortium for Higher Education, consisting of fourteen academic and research libraries serving nineteen institutions in the greater Atlant metropolitan area.

Materials Management

The materials management department is responsible for acquiring new library materials, preparing them for placement on the shelves, and maintaining the periodicals and serials collection. The Acquisitions Unit orders, receives, and pays for library materials. Acquisitions staff add records to the Foley Center's on-line catalog for materials which are on order. They also coordinate the selection of gifts donated to the library. Once received and paid for, new materials are routed to the Cataloging Unit. Cataloging staff search an international database to obtain cataloging records. They review records for accuracy and add holdings to the database so that other libraries will know which materials are contained in the Foley Center collection.

The cataloging records are then loaded into the Foley Center's on-line catalog. Cataloging staff physically process the materials and deliver them to the Public Services department for shelving. The Serials Unit is responsible for maintaining subscriptions and standing orders for materials such as magazines, scholarly journals, newspapers, government documents, and microforms. Serials staff also check in current issues of periodicals and prepare them for binding. They bind some volumes in-house in the Bindery located on the lower level of the Foley Center; they ship other volumes to a bindery outside of the Spokane area. Government Documents Processing: As a depository library, the Foley Center is responsible for maintaining collections of both state and federal government documents.

PRESERVATION

Preservation is a branch of library and information science concerned with maintaining or restoring access to artifacts, documents and records through the study, diagnosis, treatment and prevention of decay and damage.

It should be distinguished from conservation which refers to the treatment and repair of individual items to slow decay or restore them to a usable state. Conservation is occasionally used interchangeably with preservation, particularly outside the professional literature.

History

Antecedents: Although preservation as a formal profession in libraries and archives dates from the twentieth century, its philosophy and practice has roots in many earlier traditions. In library science, preservation is treated as an active and intentional process, as opposed to the passive sense of preservation that might be applied to paleontological or archaeological finds. The survival of these items is a matter of chance, from an information science perspective, while the preservation of them after their discovery is a matter of intentional activity.

Human record-keeping arguably dates back to the cave painting boom of the upper paleolithic, some 32,000-40,000 years ago. More direct antecedents are the writing systems that developed in the 4th millennium BC. Written record keeping and information sharing practices, along with oral tradition, sustain and transmit information from one group to another. This level of preservation has been supplemented over the last century with the professional practice of preservation and conservation in the cultural heritage community.

1. Oral tradition or oral culture, the transmission of information from one generation to the next without a writing system.
2. Antiquarian practices, including scribal practice, burial practice, the libraries at Pergamum, Alexandria and other ancient archives.
3. Medieval practices, including the scriptorium and relic collection
4. Renaissance and the changing conception of artists and works of art
5. Enlightenment and the Encyclopedists
6. Romantic movement's imperative to preserve

Significant Events

- 1933: William Barrow introduces the field of conservation to paper deacidification when he publishes a paper on the acid paper problem. In later studies, Barrow tested paper from American books made between 1900 and 1949 and learned that after forty years the books had lost on average 96 percent of their original strength; after less than ten years, they had already lost 64 percent. Barrow determined that this rapid deterioration was not the direct result of using wood-pulp fibers, since rag papers of this period were also aging rapidly, but rather due to the residual sulfuric acid produced in both rag and wood pulp papers. Manufacturing methods used after 1870 employed sulfuric acid for sizing and bleaching the paper. Earlier papermaking methods left the final product only mildly alkaline or even neutral. Such paper has maintained its strength for 300 to 800 years, despite sulfur dioxide and other air pollutants. Barrow's 1933 article on the fragile state of wood pulp paper predicted the life expectancy, or "LE," of this paper was approximately 40-50 years. At that point the paper would begin to show signs of natural decay, and he concluded that research for a new media on which to write and print was needed.

- 1966: The Flood of the River Arno in Florence, Italy damaged or destroyed millions of rare books and lead to the development of restoration laboratories and new methods in conservation. Instrumental in this process was conservationist Peter Waters, who lead a group of volunteers, called "mud angels", in restoring thousands of books and papers. This event awakened many historians, librarians, and other professionals to the importance of having a preservation plan. Many consider this flood to be one of the worst disasters since the burning of the Alexandria Library in ancient Rome. It spurred a resurgence in the profession of preservation and conservation worldwide.
- 1987: Terry Saunders releases the film Slow Fires: On the Preservation of the Human Record which examines paper embrittlement resulting from acid decay
- 1989: March 7 "Commitment Day" Major US print publishers convene at NYPL to endorse a community-wide commitment to utilizing ISO 9706 certified permanent durable paper in order to combat the acid paper epidemic.

Significant People in the History of Preservation

- William Barrow (1904 – 1967) was an American chemist and paper conservator, and a pioneer of library and archives conservation. He introduced the field of conservation to paper deacidification through alkalization.
- Paul N. Banks (1934-2000) was Conservator and Head of the Conservation Department at the Newberry Library from 1964 to 1981, and published regularly on bookbinding, book and paper conservation and problems related to conservation. He designed and

implemented a curriculum for Columbia University's School of Library Science that dealt directly with preservation training.

- Pamela Darling, author and historian, was Preservation Specialist for the Association of Research Libraries. Her works include materials to aid libraries in establishing their own comprehensive preservation programmes.
- Carolyn Harris worked as head of Columbia University Libraries' Preservation Division from 1981 until 1987, where she worked closely with Paul Banks. She published extensive research throughout her career, especially dealing with mass deacidification of wood-pulp paper.
- Peter Waters, former Conservation Officer at the Library of Congress in Washington, DC, worked in the areas of disaster recovery and preparedness, and the salvaging of water-damaged paper goods.
- Nicholson Baker is a contemporary American novelist and author of *Double Fold*, a criticism of libraries' destruction of paper-based media.
- Patricia Battin, as the first president of the Commission on Preservation and Access, worked to organize a national campaign both for the use of alkaline paper in publishing companies and for a national programme of preservation microfilming.
- John F. Dean, Preservation and Conservation Librarian at Cornell University, has made contributions towards improving preservation efforts in developing countries. Specifically, Dean has created online tutorials for library conservation and preservation in Southeast Asia and Iraq and the Middle East.

The Paul Banks and Carolyn Harris Preservation Award for outstanding preservation specialists in library and archival science, is given annually by the Association for Library Collections & Technical Services, a subdivision of the American Library Association. It is awarded in recognition of professional preservation specialists who have made significant contributions to the field. Banks/Harris award winners:

- Sally Buchanan 2001—Buchanan received the award in recognition of years of service in the preservation field while an associate professor at the University of Pittsburgh School of Information Science
- Ellen McCrady 2002—From 1975 to 2004, McCrady edited and published the "Abbey Newsletter", covering important information

for preservation professionals. She also conducted research regarding papermaking and acid testing.

- John F. Dean 2003—Since its inception in 1985, Dean has led the Department of Preservation and Conservation at Cornell University.
- Jan Merrill—Oldham 2004-As the Malloy-Rabinowitz Preservation Librarian at Harvard University, Merrill-Oldham oversees the Weissman Preservation Center and the Preservation and Imaging Department.
- Paul Conway 2005—Conway is an associate professor in the University of Michigan School of Information and has worked with Yale and Duke University after beginning his career at the Gerald R. Ford Presidential Library. His research and educational work focuses primarily on digital preservation and electronic media.
- Gary Frost 2006—Currently the University Conservator at the University of Iowa Libraries, Frost has been an educator and practitioner in the field of library preservation for almost 40 years. Frost is actively involved in library preservation and maintains an online blog at Futureofthebook.com.
- Walter Henry 2007—Henry, a conservator at the Stanford University Libraries and Academic Information Resources, is the creator of Conservation OnLine and the Conservation DistList.
- Janet Gertz 2008—Director for Preservation, Columbia University Libraries has been chair of ALCTS' Preservation and Reformatting Section (PARS). She has taught, spoken and published widely on topics ranging from traditional library preservation, disaster preparedness, commercial binding, and preservation microfilming to digital preservation, audio preservation, preservation metadata and large-scale mass digitization. She is an adjunct faculty member in the Palmer School of Library and Information Science, Long Island University, and has been a guest lecturer at Rutgers' Preservation Institute and at Queen's College.

Practices

Care and Handling:

1. Exhibitions
2. Circulating collections
3. Special collections

Environmental Controls

Environmental controls are necessary to facilitate the preservation of organic library materials and are especially important to monitor in rare and special collections. Key environmental factors to watch include temperature, relative humidity, pests, pollutants, and light exposure.

In general, the lower the temperature is, the better it is for the collection. However, since books and other materials are often housed in areas with people, a compromise must be struck to accommodate human comfort. A reasonable temperature to accomplish both goals is 65-68UF however, if possible, film and photography collections should be keep in a segregated area at 55UF.

Books and other materials take up and give off moisture making them sensitive to relative humidity. Very high humidity encourages mold growth and insect infestations. Low humidity causes materials to lose their flexibility. Fluctuations in relative humidity are more damaging than a constant humidity in the middle or low range. Generally, the relative humidity should be between 30-50% with as little variation as possible, however recommendations on specific levels to maintain vary depending on the type of material, i.e. paper-based, film, etc.

The Image Permanence Institute provides a downloadable calculator to assist in determining the ideal indoor temperature when taking into account the outdoor dew point. This calculator also provides information on the risk on condensation and how many days to mold based on the entered scenario.

Pests, such as insects and vermin, eat and destroy paper and the adhesive that secures book bindings. Food and drink in libraries, archives, and museums can increase the attraction of pests. An Integrated Pest Management system is one way to control pests in libraries.

Particulate and gaseous pollutants, such as soot, ozone, sulfur dioxide, oxides of nitrogen, can cause dust, soiling, and irreversible molecular damage to materials. Pollutants are exceedingly small and not easily detectable or removable. A special filtration system in the building's HVAC is a helpful defense. Exposure to light also has a significant effect on library materials. It is not only the light visible to humans that can cause damage, but also ultraviolet light and infrared radiation. Measured in lux or the amount of lumens/m^2, the generally accepted level of illumination with sensitive materials is limited to 50 lux per day. Materials receiving more lux than recommended can be placed in dark storage periodically to prolong the original appearance of the object.

Recent concerns about the impact of climate change on the management of cultural heritage objects as well as the historic environment has prompted research efforts to investigate alternative climate control methods and strategies that include the implementation of alternative climate control systems to replace or supplement traditional high-energy consuming HVAC systems as well as the introduction of passive preservation techniques.

Decision-Making and Criteria

Making a proper decision is an important factor before starting preservation practices. Decision making for preservation should be made considering significance and value of materials. Significance is considered to have two major components: importance and quality. "Importance" relates to the collection's role as a record, and "quality" covers comprehensiveness, depth, uniqueness, authenticity and reputation of the collection. Moreover, analysing the significance of materials can be used to uncover more about their meaning. Assessment of significance can also aid in documenting the provenance and context to argue the case for grant funding for the object and collection.

Forms of significance can be historically, culturally, socially, or spiritually significant. In the preservation context, libraries and archives make decisions in different ways. In libraries, decision-making likely targets existing holding materials, where as in archives, decisions for preservation are often made when they acquire materials. Therefore, different criteria might be needed on different occasions. In general, for archive criteria, the points include: (1) the characteristics of a record (purpose, creator, etc.); (2) the quality of the information in the record; (3) the record in context (part of a series or not); (4) potential use and possible limitations; and (5) the cost against the benefits from its existence.

For library criteria, the following are evidence of significance: (1) uniqueness, (2) irreplaceability, (3) high level of impact – over time or place, (4) high level of influence, (5) representation of a type, and (6) comparative value (rarity, completeness, integrity relative to others of its kind).

Selection

Since the 1970s, the Northeast Document Conservation Center has stated that the study of understanding the needs of the library is inherently important to the survival of archives and libraries. In order for the preservation of a collection to survive for a long time it is important that a systematic preservation plan is in place. The first step in planning a preservation programme is to assess the institution's existing preservation needs. This process entails identifying the general and specific needs of the collection, establishing priorities, and gathering the resources to execute the plan.

Because budget and time limitations require priorities to be set, standards have been established by the profession to determine what should be preserved in a collection. Considerations include existing condition, rarity, and evidentiary and market values. With non-paper formats, the availability of equipment to access the information will be a factor (for example, playback equipment for audio-visual materials, or microform readers). An institution should determine how many, if any, other repositories hold the material, and consider coordinating efforts with those that do.

Institutions should establish an environment conducive to preservation changes, involve staff, and create an understanding among administration and staff. The first steps an institution should implement, according to the NEDCC, are to establish a policy that defines and charts the course of action and create a framework for carrying out goals and priorities. There are three methods for carrying out a preservation survey: general preservation assessment, collection condition surveys, and an item-by-item survey.

Selection for treatment determines the survival of materials and should be done by a specialist, whether in relation to an established collection development policy or on an item by item basis. Once an object or collection has been chosen for preservation, the treatment must be determined that is most appropriate to the material and its repository. If the information is most important, reformatting or creation of a surrogate is a likely option. If the artifact itself is of value, it will receive conservation treatment, ideally of a reversible nature.

Research and Testing

With old media deteriorating or showing their vulnerabilities and new media becoming available, research remains active in the field of conservation and preservation. Everything from how to preserve paper media to creating and maintaining electronic resources is being explored by students and professionals in library and information science. The two main issues that most libraries tend to face are the rapid disintegration of acidic paper and water damage (due to flooding, plumbing problems, etc). Therefore, these areas of preservation, as well as new digital technologies, receive much of the research attention.

The American Library Association has many scholarly journals that publish articles on preservation topics, such as *College and Research Libraries, Information Technology and Libraries,* and *Library Resources and Technical*

Services. Scholarly periodicals in this field from other publishers include *International Preservation News, Journal of the American Institute for Conservation*, and *Collection Management* among many others.

Ethics

Conservators should refer to the AIC Code of Ethics and Guidelines for Practice, which states that the conservation professional must "strive to attain the highest possible standards in all aspects of conservation."

Ethics will play an important role in many aspects of the conservator's activities. When choosing which objects are in need of treatment, the conservator should do what is best for the object in question and not yield to pressure or opinion from outside sources.

Preservation of Cultural Objects

One instance in which these decisions may get tricky is when the conservator is dealing with cultural objects. The AIC Code of Ethics and Guidelines for Practice has addressed such concerns, stating "All actions of the conservation professional must be governed by an informed respect for cultural property, its unique character and significance and the people or person who created it." This can be applied in both the care and longterm storage of objects in archives and institutions.

The AIC Code of Ethics and Guidelines for Practice also states: "While recognizing the right of society to make appropriate and respectful use of cultural property, the conservation professional shall serve as an advocate for the preservation of cultural property." This statement speaks to the conservator's need to balance his or her duty to conserve objects and maintain a collection with society's right to have access and use of objects for their own cultural/religious purposes. While it is obvious that a member of a religion should be able to have access to an object or text that has spiritual value to them, it would be against the conservator's ethics to then allow that object to incur damage from such use. The conservator should make sure that the care of the object is kept in mind when access to an object is granted. The object should remain in the best condition possible not only so it is preserved for prosperity, but also so that it can be studied by researchers and by members of the cultural or religious group that created it.

It is important that preservation specialists to be respectful of cultural property and the societies that created it, it is also important for them to be aware of international and national laws pertaining to stolen items. The AIC Code of Ethics and Guidelines for Practice also states that:

The conservation professional should be cognizant of laws and regulations that may have a bearing on professional activity. Among these laws and regulations are those concerning the rights of artists and their estates, occupational health and safety, sacred and religious material, excavated objects, endangered species, human remains, and stolen property.

In recent years there has been a rise in nations seeking out artifacts that have been stolen and are now in museums. In many cases museums are working with the nations to find a compromise to balance the need for reliable supervision as well as access for both the public and researchers.

Conservators are not just bound by ethics to treat cultural and religious objects with respect, but also in some cases by law. For example, in the United States, conservators must comply with the Native American Graves Protection and Repatriation Act (NAGPRA). The First Archivists Circle, a group of Native American archivists, has also created Protocols for Native American Archival Materials. The non-binding guidelines are suggestions for libraries and archives with Native American archival materials.

With all these issues of respect and cultural sensitivity to consider, conservation and preservation issues are sure to arise. The care of cultural and sacred objects often affects the physical storage or the object. For example, sacred objects of the native peoples of the Western United States are supposed to be stored with sage to ensure their spiritual well being. The idea of storing an object with plant material is inherently problematic to an archival collection because of the possibility of insect infestation. When conservators have faced this problem, they have addressed it by using freeze-dried sage, thereby meeting both conservation and cultural needs.

Some individuals in the library science community have explored the possible moral responsibility to preserve all cultural phenomena, in regards to the concept of monumental preservation. Other advocates argue that such an undertaking is something that the indigenous or native communities that produce such cultural objects are better suited to perform. Currently, however, many indigenous communities are not financially able to support their own archives and museums. Still, indigenous archives are on the rise in the United States.

Preservation and the Library as a Sacred Institution

- In her book *Sacred Stacks: The Higher Purpose of Libraries and Librarianship*, Nancy Kalikow Maxwell discusses how libraries are capable of performing some of the same functions as religion. Many librarians feel that their work is done for some higher purpose. The same can be said for preservation librarians. One instance of the library's role as sacred is to provide a sense of immortality: with the ever changing world outside, the library will remain stable and dependable. Preservation is a great help in this regard. Through digitization and reformatting, preservation librarians are able to retain material while at the same time adapting to new methods. In this way, libraries can adapt to the changes in user needs without changing the quality of the material itself. Through preservation efforts, patrons can rest assured that although materials are constantly deteriorating over time, the library itself will remain a stable, reliable environment for their information needs. Another sacred ability of the library is to provide information and a connection to the past. By working to slow down the processes of deterioration and decay of library materials, preservation practices help keep this link to the past alive.

Regional Centers

- The Conservation Center for Art and Historic Artifacts in Philadelphia, PA. CCAHA is a non-profit conservation laboratory specializing in the treatment of art and historic artifacts on paper. The Center also trains museum and library professionals in disaster planning, records and archives management.
- The Northeast Document Conservation Center in Andover, MA. Since its inception in 1973, the Center has instructed institutions and organizations, as well as librarians, conservators, preservationists and museum professionals in preservation care and procedures. From 1995 to 2007, NEDCC presented its School for Scanning conference eleven times in cities across the United States. The school takes a leading role for digital preservation.
- The Southeastern Library Network is a not-for-profit membership cooperative of libraries and other information organizations in the southeastern United States. Established in 1973, as the largest regional library network in the U.S., SOLINET provides a variety of preservation education programmes and workshops.

FORMAT OF WRITING BIBLIOGRAPHY: APA STANDARD AND MLA STANDARD

Background

APA style, or APA format are the terms commonly used to describe the writing style guidelines which are developed, maintained, and periodically revised and updated by the American Psychological Association (APA). The

American Psychological Association came into being in its current form through the 1945 amalgamation of a number of different psychological societies and organizations which existed in the USA at that time, at both the national and state levels. The APA currently has almost 160,000 members and is the largest association of psychologists in the world.

Over the years, the APA has developed a standard for writing style that is now widely used by writers in the social sciences, education, business and psychology. Accordingly, the APA documentation style is now used throughout the world, in both business and academia.

The APA's writing style is documented in its manual entitled:

Publication Manual of the American Psychological Association, Fifth Edition (2001).

The APA's *Publication Manual* covers all aspects of the writing and publishing process including: organizing, writing, formatting, keying, and submitting a manuscript for publication. It provides detailed guidance on editorial style as well as on the appropriate standards for publishing research in accordance with ethical principles of scientific publishing.

There is often considerable confusion when teachers, students, editors and researchers use the terms "APA style" or APA format". To clear up that confusion I am including three paragraphs below from the APA website.

"When editors or teachers ask you to write in "APA style," they do not mean writing style. They are referring to the editorial style that many of the social and behavioral sciences have adopted to present written material in the field. Editorial style consists of rules or guidelines that a publisher observes to ensure clear and consistent presentation of written material. Editorial style concerns uniform use of such elements as:

- punctuation and abbreviations
- construction of tables
- selection of headings
- citation of references
- presentation of statistics
- as well as many other elements that are a part of every manuscript

The American Psychological Association has established a style that it uses in all of the books and journals that it publishes. Many others working in the social and behavioral sciences have adopted this style as their standard as well.

Please note that when researchers talk about APA style, they may be referring to APA's system of citations in text and reference format.

If you are unsure, you should clarify with your instructor or editor how they define "APA style." APA's style rules and guidelines are set out in a reference book called "The Publication Manual of the American Psychological Association."

APA Rules

APA documentation style (in similar fashion to MLA style) calls for "in-text" citations of sources of information to be listed within the text where they are referenced, rather than in footnotes and endnotes, as some systems require.

To assist those who would rather not wade through APA's 439 page Publication Manual, I have broken down and summarized the APA Rules for the Preparation of Manuscripts into three distinct sections as follows:

1. Overall APA Paper Format Rules
2. APA Rules For In-Text Citation of Sources
3. Compiling and Formatting the APA Reference List

Each of the above sections contains a link to an actual sample pages of of the formats being discussed. You can access this APA Rules Page at:

Basic APA Rules-Paper Format, Citations, and Samples

APA Software: StyleEase for APA Style is powerful software that automatically formats your APA paper for you. From title page to bibliography, StyleEase does it all, right from the MS-Word toolbar. Handles simple papers to major dissertations with equal ease. *If your paper is due soon, StyleEase will save the day.*

References in APA-standard

Documentation of Sources: It is important to document sources of information used in theses, reports and other papers, for several reasons. Written academic work normally builds upon previously published research and we refer to others' theories, formulations, arguments and empirical data. Readers must be able to locate your original sources of information in order to judge or confirm your work independently. In addition, it is necessary to distinguish between what is your own and what originally comes from others. If you don't document your sources you may be accused of plagiarizing. It is thus important to acknowle dge other authors' contributions, both from an ethical and an academic perspective.

References, Citations and Quotes

Three important terms used in the documentation of information sources are: references, citations and quotes.

Reference – a bibliographic description of a document which is placed after the main text. A reference includes information about the author, title, year, and publisher. References are listed alphabetically in a bibliography, also called reference list. All document types, both printed and electronic, are in the same list. References to the same author are listed chronologically, with the oldest on top.

Citation (also called in-text citation) – information in the main text which identifies the source. All citations point to references in the bibliography, and all references in the bibliography correspond to citations in the main text. The information in citations is enclosed in parentheses. The author's name can be integrated into the main text and thereby excluded from the parentheses.

Quotations

A quotation (also called quote) is a direct, word-for-word, reproduction of a source. Never quote out of context.

Short Quote: When you quote a source, the citation should include the page number, for example:

> *"The library is the heart of the school for both students and staff" writes Nierenberg et al. (2009).*
>
> or
>
> *"The library is the heart of the school for both students and staff" (Nierenberg et al., 2009).*

Long Quote (longer than 3 lines): Long quotes should be indented, with a smaller font, with white space above and below, and without quotation marks. For example:

Torras and Sætre (2008) write that:

When Parts of a Quote are Excluded: If you cut out part of a quote, fill in with 3 dots ... or 3 dots in parentheses (...), for example:

> *Nierenberg et al. maintain that "the library is the heart of the school for ... staff" (2009).*

Translated Quotation: You can translate quotes from other languages. Follow the rules for quoting sources and write "own translation" at the end of the citation, for example:

According to Dag Østerberg (1996), "many of our actions involve changing the materials which surround us: building roads, houses, equipment, signs, weapons, etc." (p. 136, own translation).

Quotations with Italics: If *italics* are found in the original text, it should also be italicized in the quotation. If you want to italicize text which isn't originally in italics, write (italics added) just after the italicized text.

APA-style: There are many different styles for handling references. The main differences are with punctuation and the order of information in the reference. Common for all styles is that they have a consistent method for handling references, and that they include the documentation necessary to identify the source. Never mix reference styles – once you've chosen one style, you must use it consistently throughout the entire paper.

Hedmark University College recommends that students and staff use the APA-style (American Psychological Association). This is a so-called author/year-system, where all references are collected at the end of the document. Footnotes should only be used to supply additional information which isn't a part of the main text. The collection below provides examples of how citations and references to different sources should be formatted in the APA-style. Many of the examples used below are fictitious.

MLA System: Parenthetical Author-Page References (humanities)

This streamlined format gives author and page in parentheses within the text of the paper, then sets out full references in a Works Cited (or Works Consulted) list. Developed by the Modern Language Association, it is now widely accepted in the humanities. The 2003 edition of the *MLA Handbook for Writers of Research Papers* gives detailed advice and examples on such matters as spacing of notes and Works Cited entries. It contains very useful sections on citing non-print sources such as films, paintings, sound recordings, and Internet sources. It's available in all campus libraries and at U of T Bookstores. See also the MLA website for recommendations on details of referring to non-print sources. The University of California at Berkeley provides a handy summary of the MLA system. Or try the University of Auckland's interactive guide for constructing references in MLA style.

NOTE: In listing a Web page as a source, include the date you read the page as well as the URL. That information lets your reader judge whether he or she is seeing the same version of the Web page you looked at. See also our note on Electronic Sources.

Example: When Hamlet protests to his mother, "Leave wringing of your hands" (III.iv.35), he is naming a universally recognizable gesture. As Smith says, similar broad physical movements are "still the most direct way of indicating inner turmoil" (960). Zygmundi confirms their continuing usefulness in contemporary productions of other sixteenth-century plays. Renaissance audiences would have recognized hand-wringing as a signal for inner distress (Brown, *Renaissance Stage* 111), specifically for a condition that the Elizabethan author Reynolds named "ague of the spirits" (qtd. in Mahieu 69). Poor sight lines in Elizabethan theatres also required highly visible body movements (Smith 964). In her new book, Brown attempts to show that such gestures are related to stylized movements from religious ceremonies, among other influences (Brown, *Ritual* 90). She argues that acting methods responded to both the physical conditions of the theatres and the audience's cultural expectations (Brown, *Ritual* 14).

ANNOTATED BIBLIOGRAPHY

An annotated bibliography is a bibliography that gives a summary of the research that has been done. It is still an alphabetical list of research sources. In addition to bibliographic data, an annotated bibliography provides a brief summary or annotation. The purpose of annotations is to provide the reader with a summary and an evaluation of the source. In order to write a successful annotation, each summary must be concise. An annotation should display the source's central idea(s) and give the reader a general idea of what the source is about. An annotation should include the complete bibliographic information for the source. It should also include some or all of the following:

- An explanation about the authority and/or qualifications of the author.
- Scope or main purpose of the work.
- Any detectable bias.
- Intended audience and level of reading
- A summary comment

An annotation should be between 100 to 200 words, ideally.

Indicative Annotations

This type of annotation defines the scope of the source, lists the significant topics and explains what the source is about. In this type of entry, there is no attempt to give actual data such as hypotheses, proofs, etc.

Informative Annotations

This type of annotation is a summary of the source. An informative annotation should include the thesis of the work, arguments or hypotheses, proofs and a conclusion.

Evaluative Annotations

This type of annotation assesses the source's strengths and weaknesses—how the source is useful and how it is not. Simply put, an evaluative annotation should evaluate the source's usefulness.

Combination Annotations

Most annotated bibliographies contain combination annotations. This type of annotation will summarize or describe the topic, and then evaluate the source's usefulness.

Writing Styles

No matter which writing style is used for annotations, all entries should be brief. Only the most significant details should be mentioned. Information that is apparent in the title can be omitted from the annotation. In addition, background materials and any references to previous work are usually excluded.

Telegraphic

A telegraphic writing style gets the information out quickly and concisely. Maintaining clarity, complete and grammatically correct sentences are not necessary.

Complete Sentences

A **complete** sentences writing style utilizes coherent sentences that are grammatically correct. Subjects and conjunctions are not eliminated even though the tone may be terse. Long and complex sentences are to generally be avoided.

Paragraph

A paragraph writing style utilizes a full, coherent paragraph. This can sometimes be similar to the form of a bibliographic essay. Complete sentences and proper grammar must be used.

Purpose

There are three main purposes behind writing an annotated bibliography. Each purpose can serve anyone in a different manner, depending on what they are trying to accomplish.

Learning about a Topic

Writing an annotated bibliography is an excellent way to begin any research project. While it may seem easier to simply copy down bibliographical information, adding annotations will force the researcher to read each source carefully. An annotation requires the source to be critically analyzed, not simply read over.

Formulating a Thesis

Any form of research paper or essay will require some form of argument. This is called a thesis. A developed thesis needs to be debatable, interesting and current. Writing an annotated bibliography will give the researcher a clear understanding about what is being said about their topic. After reading and critically analyzing sources, the researcher will be able to determine what issues there are and what people are arguing about. From there, the researcher will be able to develop their own point of view.

To Assist Other Researchers

Extensive and scholarly annotated bibliographies are sometimes published. The purpose of these annotated bibliographies is to provide a complete and comprehensive overview of any given topic. While any normal researcher may not get their own annotated bibliography published, it could be a good idea to search for previously published annotated bibliographies that are related to their topic.

Writing a Review Article

The major pulmonary and critical care journals publish more than 5,000 articles every year. To read these would requiremore than 25 hours each week. Despite the surfeit of information,the average physician is starving for wisdom. The aim of scholarshipis to increase understanding, not just accumulate discrete facts. A stack of papers no more conveys wisdom than a pile of bricksmakes a house.

If new research is to improve patient care, reports need to be fitted into the mosaic of existing knowledge. General medical journals, such as the *New England* or *Annals*, publish a much higher proportion of review articles than do sub-specialty journals.But the audience for a sub-specialty journal is different froma general medical journal. The first rule of writing is to identify your audience. Review articles that appeal to general physicians are unlikely to satisfy sub-specialists, who are expected to have a more detailed and nuanced understanding of subjects in their field.

The first step in writing a review article is selecting a suitable subject.

Authors of a review article in *AJRCCM* may pick a broadfield suited to a comprehensive overview in a State-of-the-Art(1–14), encapsulate a surge of rapid progress in a Pulmonary Perspective (15–30), turn a search light on an overlooked subject in a Critical Care Perspective (31–40), capture advances in related fields in an Update in Nonpulmonary Critical Care (41–53), convey practice pearls in a Clinical Commentary (54–63), share the secrets of scientific discovery in a How it *Really* Happened (64–78), or comment on a socialconundrum in an Occasional Essay (79–83). By definition,a review article does not include original data. Yet, the perspective should be fresh and the synthesis unique. Authors must avoid a rehash of views expressed in existing reviews.

When writing a state-of-the-art review, the author needs to a mass and synthesize a huge number of original reports. The skill is akin to that of a landscape artist. When ranging overa great sweep of scenery, the naked eye takes in millions of shapes, shades, and textures. The painter reduces this complexity to a few hundred brush strokes through ruthless selection, intensifying some contours, ignoring others, and reordering and harmonizing the relationships between elements. Great compositional skillis needed to place the elements in a coherent space, avoiding discontinuities and depth-of-field distortions, and construct a unified and expansive canvas that achieves realistic verisimilitude.

Likewise, the author of a comprehensive review article stands back to form a panoramic view of a broad field. He or she sifts through a mass of miscellaneous detail, selecting the most relevant, and omitting trifling reports and ephemeral fads. The valueof the article depends as much on the dross and minutiae omitted as on the pearls included. The author does not cover every reportin a field, because all are not of equal quality. In contrast to the deluge of references generated by a PubMed search, the good review article serves as a quality filter, directing the reader to the most influential journal and book literature. An author's selection of primary and secondary literature also conveys the legitimacy of his or her framework.

One of the most difficult tasks in writing a review articleis finding the best structure because manuscripts do not follow the fixed formula (introduction, methods, results, discussion) of research reports. The structure should facilitate sequential unfolding of ideas in a logical order. To avoid getting lost mid journey, readers need to know where an author is coming from and where he or she is going. The best structure may not become obvious until several drafts have been written; indeed, the failure to change the structure during the course of writingis a warning that it is likely wrong.

Taking the mass of raw reports, the author classifies, interprets and integrates the material, shaping it into a compact product that is more manageable for the reader. The author moves back and forth between the universal and the particular, alternating between use of a telescope and a microscope. He or she selects studies that are especially insightful, and locates them in the overall pattern. A major challenge is compression: how to take a tangled mass of facts, eliminate those that do not enhance understanding, and weave the remaining threads into a seamless fabric. The good review article is not a compendium of sequential studies in the manner of "Smith found this and Jones found that". Instead, the author integrates broad conceptual ideas into anarrative, and the primary investigators disappear into the prose.

Another challenge is how to write sentences that form a linear sequence, one connected to the next by a logical extension of thought. Sustaining reader interest over the course of a long review requires the skill of a storyteller. A good narrative pulls readers along without them noticing the tug.

Some journals classify narrative review articles as less reliableand of lower intellectual caliber than "systematic reviews"(84). The compulsive tracking down of every trial on a topicis imperative when writing a review article on the basis of a metaanalys is of randomized clinical trials; it is also important to tabulate numbers, inclusion and exclusion criteria, and other such detail of the trials. A scrupulous search system might be expected to limit bias, although vigilant peer review willafford greater reassurance against this flaw (85–88).The uniformity of the approach to writing such review articles enables a formulaic presentation. But the compulsive retrieval of every original paper is only one essential when writing are view article (and the least challenging). A punctilious listing of every detail produces prose that is prolix. It may also detract rather than enhance understanding, which is based on being able to see a forest among the trees. A catalog approach is ill suited to communicating a deeper understanding of biological principles garnered from the commingling of molecular research in animals with bedside studies of pathophysiologic mechanisms in patients. A catalogue approach is in appropriate for subjects reviewed in *Nature Medicine, PNAS, JCI*—and most subjects reviewed in *AJRCCM*.

That a review article does not carry the epithet "systematic" is not to say it was written in a desultory manner and the presentation chaotic. The skills in writing a narrative review are more intellectual than mechanical. Teams of "systematic reviewers" of questionable provenance are no substitute for wisdom derived from years of marinating in a subject and reflecting on its complexities. The worth of the final product depends on the author's conceptual sophistication, power of apprehension, cogency of analysis, sense of proportion, skill in condensation ,explanatory force, and felicity of exposition—qualities not emphasized in "quantitative systematic reviews" (89–91).

A reader's best guide that a review article will be worth reading is a foreknowledge of the journal's peer-review standards (92). At *AJRCCM*, peer review starts when the author submits a letter of intent and an outline of a planned article. (Details of information to include in a proposal are provided in our *Instructions for Contributors.*) Proposals are reviewed anonymously by six or more experts. Many proposals are declined, and authors getting a green light are also given concrete recommendations for improving the planned manuscript. Completed manuscripts undergo rigorous peer review and only the fraction satisfying the highest standards is published. The criteria differ from those used for original research reports. Referees of research reports focus on novelty of a hypothesis, rigor of experimental design, soundness of the methodology, approach to data analysis, and plausibility of the findings. With a review article, referees evaluate the importance and relevancy of the subject, comprehensiveness ofthe author's coverage, emphasis given to individual studies, legitimacy of the analyses, new insights and ideas being offered, ability to synthesize and integrate disparate observations, and the cogency and lucidity of the prose.

Scientific journals rightly set great store on original research. But much research consists of mopping up operations (93), and the amount of truly new information is less than we think. George Stigler (94), the 1982 Nobel Laureate in Economics, pointed out that "originality is a more complicated virtue than most discussion seems to recognize, and that its role in progressis not easy to state or assess." He continues that, "originality may also impair progress. Originality means difference, not improvement, and one may invent new errors as well as new truths."Moreover, new truths do not emerge fully formed. Accordingly, review articles help advance science. Progress in science dependson a certain aging process, whereby earlier findings are reanalyzed, previously undetected ambiguities are identified, residues of truth are extracted before a disproved theory is discarded, concepts are refined, and the range of applicability of new ideas is identified. *AJRCCM* contributes to a bountiful harvest of research reports. We hope that our review series also speed up scientific fermentation.

REVIEW PAPER

The purpose of a review paper is to succinctly review recent progress in a particular topic. Overall, the paper summarizes the current state of knowledge of the topic. It creates an understanding of the topic for the reader by discussing the findings presented in recent research papers.

A review paper is not a "term paper" or book report. It is not merely a report on some references you found. Instead, a review paper synthesizes the results from several primary literature papers to produce a coherent argument about a topic or focused description of a field.

Examples of scientific reviews can be found in:

- Scientific American
- Science in the "Perspectives" and "Reviews" sections
- Nature in the "News and Views" section
- Compilations of reviews such as:

    Current Opinion in Cell Biology

    Current Opinion in Genetics & Development

    Annual Review of Plant Physiology and Plant Molecular Biology

    Annual Review of Physiology

    Trends in Ecology & Evolution

- Almost every scientific journal has special review articles.

You should read articles from one or more of these sources to get examples of how your paper should be organized.

Scientists commonly use reviews to communicate with each other and the general public. There are a wide variety of review styles from ones aimed at a general audience (e.g., *Scientific American*) to those directed at biologists within a particular subdiscipline (e.g., *Annual Review of Physiology*).

A key aspect of a review paper is that it provides the evidence for a particular point of view in a field. Thus, a large focus of your paper should be a description of the data that support or refute that point of view. In addition, you should inform the reader of the experimental techniques that were used to generate the data.

The emphasis of a review paper is interpreting the primary literature on the subject. You need to read several original research articles on the same topic and make your own conclusions about the meanings of those papers.

How to Write the Paper?

Overview of the Paper: Your paper should consist of four general sections:

- Introduction
- The body of the paper
- Conclusion and future directions
- Literature cited

Review articles contain neither a materials and methods section nor an abstract.

Organizing the Paper: Use topic headings. Do not use a topic heading that reads, “Body of the paper.” Instead the topic headings should refer to the actual concepts or ideas covered in that section.

BOOK REVIEW

A book review (or book report) is a form of literary criticism in which a book is analysed based on content, style, and merit. It is often carried out in periodicals, as school work, or online. Its length may vary from a single paragraph to a substantial essay. Such a review often contains evaluations of the book on the basis of personal taste. Reviewers, in literary periodicals, often use the occasion of a book review for a display of learning or to promulgate their own ideas on the topic of a fiction or non-fiction work. At the other end of the spectrum, some book reviews resemble simple plot summaries.

General

The book review is assigned to develop analytical skills. First, the reviewer has to depict the content, regardless of the type of novel, a historical or critical book. In the subsequent narration the goal of the book reviewer is to discuss the content of the book and provide analysis of what he/she had read, and deduce if the author managed to reveal the core, whether he/she kept to the thesis or properly achieved the purpose of the book. The last thing the reviewer has to do is to speculate on the topic him/herself. The book reviewer should also undertake through their own research to discuss the theme, assess the authors ability to express and explore this theme, and provide an opinion of the novel.

The determination of the book review is to communicate to the readers mind the ideas and sensations book reviewer experienced while researching the content, in this way explaining the reader what exact meaning the author presumed to transmit, or what did the reviewer experienced while during the reading. The book reviewer, then, stands as reporter, who informs the third party of the events, as an analyst, who makes judgments basing them on own experience, and as the observer from the side, who pretends to act as the reader him/herself should do by expressing own opinion, desires and expectations.

Making book review implies some special skills, as well as obliges with some precise responsibilities. Professional reviewer has not just to read and scrutinize the text, but to realize concealed, implied meaning the author obviously had dropped hints about. Skilled book reviewers' explanations make the reader feel this "that is just what I thought" sensation. The reviewer must also state the main points of the reviewed book. While some aspects are less meaningful, others are have to be marked out as prerogative issues. The task is even more complicated as the writer could unintentionally imply the idea the reviewer of the book can notice.

Then, the book reviewer has to decide upon authors points validity. The reviewer has to be the judge and say "did the writer persuade the audience, or were his/her evidences not sufficient and weak". The reviewer here makes judgment on the adequacy of the book topic to the content.

The book review is also the expertise of the contents authenticity. By comparing the reviewed book to other materials in the given category the reviewer work implies potential danger for those writers, who admit plagiarism. If the reviewer finds the book authentic and, perhaps, unique, the points and attitudes of the reviewer are discussed.

Textbooks

In reviewing a textbook, the reviewer has a different set of considerations. Unlike the language in a monograph, that in a textbook must be no technical and jargon must be avoided. The reader will be a student, not a peer of the scientist who wrote the book. Technical terms will be used, of course, but each should be carefully defined at first use. The function of the book reviewer is to determine whether the subject of the text is treated clearly, in a way that is likely to enable students to grasp and to appreciate the knowledge presented. The textbook reviewer has one additional responsibility. If other texts on the same subject exist, which is usually the case; the reviewer should provide appropriate comparisons.

Imprint Information

At the top of a book review, the reviewer should list complete imprint information. The usual order is as follows: title of the book, edition (if other than the first), name of author(s) or editor(s), publisher, place (city in which the publisher is located), year of publication, number of pages, and list price of the book. Conventionally, well-known cities are not followed by state or country names. A publisher located in New York is listed "New York" not "New York, NY" and London is listed as "London" not "London, U.K."

Professional Book Review

Books, as well as professional book reviews are important in all professions, but they are especially important in the sciences, which defines the specialization of the book reviewer. That is because the basic unit of scientific communication, the primary research paper, is short (typically five to eight printed pages in most fields) and narrowly specific. Therefore, to provide a general overview of a significant slice of science, professional writers of scientific books organize and synthesize the reported knowledge in a field into a much larger, more meaningful package. In other words, new scientific knowledge is made meaningful by sorting and sifting the bits and pieces into book reviews to provide a larger picture. Thus, the individual plants and flowers, and even the weeds, become a landscape.

Scientific, technical, and medical books are of many types, let alone reviews and overviews. In broad categories, they can be considered as monographs, reference books, textbooks, and trade books. Because there are significant differences among these four types, a professional book reviewer should understand the distinctions.

How to Find Reviews of a Given Book?

Some book reviews are available on the Internet, but not most and perhaps not the most important. There are many special journals devoted to book reviews and they are indexed in special databases such as *Book review Index*, but many more book reviews can be found in newspaper databases and in scholarly databases such as *Arts and Humanities Citation Index*, *Social Sciences Citation Index* and discipline specific databases. Ask the librarian about how to identify reviews of the books which reception you would like to study. Among the reviews of a given book there may be one that changes your view of that book.

Problems with Book Reviews

Principally book reviews are good sources for evaluating the quality of books. Sometimes, however, book reviews have been considered problematic. Katz (1985-1986) found that there are too few critical book reviews. This is also documentated by Novick (1988) in the field of history. Typically are book reviews in scholarly journals of a much higher quality than book reviews in newspapers.

PREPARING ABSTRACT AND INDEXES

While abstracts are not required in grades K-4 they are encouraged. They are strongly recommended for 5th Grade to 8th grade students, as abstracts are required for those nominated for the Discovery Channel Young Scientist Challenge (DCYSC). Selections for this nomination are based upon a well written abstract in addition to the science they have done.

An abstract is a brief (250 words or less), written discussion/summary of your Science Project. It includes:

- The Project Title,
- The purpose of your project/ experiment: An introductory statement explaining the reason for the research, or a statement of the problem, hypothesis or question
- A summary/description of the procedures, emphasizing the key points or steps
- The results and observations made
- Conclusions of your investigation, and it may also include any possible research applications or goals.
- If there is space, you may also include where this will take you next.

Abstracts are helpful to the judges to understand more about the student's ability to write succinctly and show the degree of understanding of the project. Abstracts should never exceed 250 words. For the students in grades 5, 6, 7 and 8, the abstract will play considerably more importance than in the K-4 grades. It is a good learning tool and should be encouraged at all grade levels, even Kindergarten, but in the lower grades its absence will not downgrade a project. Its presence, however, could be the tie breaker. Abstracts are a good learning device at even the Kindergarten level. A Kindergarten abstract may only have 20 words, but he/she is learning how to tell their science story. As the student progresses in grade level, that ability to communicate with the written word becomes more and more important. Abstracts should be edited for correct spelling and grammar. Even the best writers and scientists have their work edited. A mentor, parent or teacher should review and help by editing your abstract AFTER you have written it.

DO NOT send abstracts to SARSEF. Bring your abstracts with you to set up for SARSEF at the Tucson Convention Center. They may be placed either on the table in front of the project or affixed to the display board (recommended).

The Sample High School Abstract below is Copied from the Science Service Link

The colour coding below in the Sample abstract indicates Purpose of the Experiment, Procedures Used, Observation/Data/Results, and Conclusions as explained below:

Purpose of the Experiment

- An introductory statement of the reason for investigating the topic of the project.
- A statement of the problem or hypothesis being studied

Procedures Used

- A summarization of the key points and an overview of how the investigation was conducted.
- An abstract does not give details about the materials used unless it greatly influenced the procedure or had to be developed to do the investigation.
- An abstract should only include procedures done by the student. Work done by a mentor (such as surgical procedures) or work done prior to student involvement must not be included.

Observation/Data/Results

- This section should provide key results that lead directly to the conclusions you have drawn.
- It should not give too many details about the results nor include tables or graphs.

Conclusions

- Conclusions from the investigation should be described briefly.
- The summary paragraph should reflect on the process and possibly state some applications and extensions of the investigation.

Sample Abstract

Effects of Marine Engine Exhaust Water on Algae: This project in its present form is the result of bioassay experimentation on the effects of two-cycle marine engine exhaust water on certain green algae. The initial idea was to determine the toxicity of outboard engine lubricant. Some success with lubricants eventually led to the formulation of "synthetic" exhaust water which, in turn, led to the use of actual two-cycle engine exhaust water as the test substance.

Toxicity was determined by means of the standard bottle or "batch" bioassay technique. Scenedesmus quadricauda and Ankistrodesmus sp. were used as the test organisms. Toxicity was measured in terms of a decrease in the maximum standing crop. The effective concentration-50% (EC 50) for Scenedesmus quadricauda was found to be 3.75% exhaust water; for Ankistrodesmus sp. 3.1% exhaust water using the bottle technique.

Anomalies in growth curves raised the suspicion that evaporation was affecting the results; therefore, a flow-through system was improvised utilizing the characteristics of a device called a Biomonitor. Use of the Biomonitor lessened the influence of evaporation, and the EC 50 was found to be 1.4% exhaust water using Ankistrodesmus sp. as the test organism. Mixed populations of various algae gave an EC 50 of 1.28% exhaust water. The contributions of this project are twofold. First, the toxicity of two-cycle marine engine exhaust was found to be considerably greater than reported in the literature (1.4% vs. 4.2%). Secondly, the benefits of a flow-through bioassay technique utilizing the Biomonitor was demonstrated.

Index (Database)

A database index is a data structure that improves the speed of operations on a database table. Indexes can be created using one or more columns of a database table, providing the basis for both rapid random look ups and efficient access of ordered records. The disk space required to store the index is typically less than that required by the table (since indexes usually contain only the key-fields according to which the table is to be arranged, and excludes all the other details in the table), yielding the possibility to store indexes in memory for a table whose data is too large to store in memory.

In a relational database an index is a copy of part of a table. Some databases extend the power of indexing by allowing indexes to be created on functions or expressions. For example, an index could be created on upper(last_name), which would only store the upper case versions of the last name field in the index. Another option sometimes supported is the use of "filtered" indexes, where index entries are created only for those records that satisfy some conditional expression. A further aspect of flexibility is to permit indexing on user-defined functions, as well as expressions formed from an assortment of built-in functions.

Indexes may be defined as unique or non-unique. A unique index acts as a constraint on the table by preventing duplicate entries in the index and thus, the backing table.

Index Architecture

Index architectures can be classified as clustered or non-clustered.

Unclustered

An Unclustered index is structured in a way that does not correspond to the order of the actual data records. It resembles the words index at the back of a book. For this reason, it will perform worse than clustered indexes on ranged searches where the result set is large, since each result could cost an additional I/O-operation to get the actual data record. One can have any number of these kinds of indexes, since all that is required is the space to store the index itself—one does not copy the actual data to create a new index.

Clustered

Clustering re-orders the data block in the same order as the index, hence it is also an operation on the data storage blocks as well as on the index. A phone book ordered by last name resembles a clustered index in its structure and purpose. Exact operation of database systems vary, but because storing the row data more than once is never done in practice (since it is usually too expensive), the row data can only be stored in one order physically. Therefore, only one clustered index can be created on a given database table. Clustered indexes can greatly increase access speed, but usually only where the data is accessed sequentially in the same or reverse order of the clustered index, or when a range of items are selected.

Since the physical records are in this sort order on disk the next row item in the sequence is immediately before or after the last one, and so fewer data block reads are required. The primary feature of a clustered index is therefore the ordering of the physical data rows in accordance with the index blocks that point to them. Some databases separate the data and index blocks into separate files, while others intermix the two different types of data blocks within the same physical file(s). Databases that use the latter scheme may be said to store the actual data in the leaf node of the index, whereas, in fact there is still a distinction between the index and the data block, and the data blocks can be traversed without using the index by way of a link list that links the data blocks in order.

Index Implementations

Indexes can be implemented using a variety of data structures. Popular indexes include balanced trees, B+ trees and hashes.

In Microsoft SQL Server, the leaf node of the clustered index corresponds to the actual data, not simply a pointer to data that resides elsewhere, as is the case with a non-clustered index. Each relation can have a single clustered index and many unclustered indexes.

Column Order

The order in which columns are listed in the index definition is important. It is possible to retrieve a set of row identifiers using only the first indexed column. However, it is not possible or efficient (on most databases) to retrieve the set of row identifiers using only the second or greater indexed column.

For example, imagine a phone book that is organized by city first, then by last name, and then by first name. If you are given the city, you can easily extract the list of all phone numbers for that city. However, in this phone book it would be very tedious to find all the phone numbers for a given last name. You would have to look within each city's section for the entries with that last name. Some databases can do this, others just won't use the index.

Applications and Limitations

Indexes are useful for many applications but come with some limitations. Consider the following SQL statement: SELECT first_name FROM people WHERE last_name = 'Smith';. To process this statement without an index the database software must look at the last_name column on every row in the table (this is known as a full table scan). With an index the database simply follows the b-tree data structure until the Smith entry has been found; this is much less computationally expensive than a full table scan.

Consider this SQL statement: SELECT email_address FROM customers WHERE email_address LIKE '%@yahoo.com';. This query would yield an email address for every customer whose email address ends with "@yahoo.com", but even if the email_address column has been indexed the database still must perform a full table scan. This is because the index is built with the assumption that words go from left to right. With a wildcard at the beginning of the search-term the database software is unable to use the underlying b-tree data structure. This problem can be solved through the addition of another index created on reverse (email_address) and a SQL query like this: SELECT email_address FROM customers WHERE reverse (email_address) LIKE reverse('%@yahoo.com');. This puts the wild-card at the right-most part of the query (now moc.oohay@%) which the index on reverse(email_address) can satisfy.

Types

Bitmap Index: A bitmap index is a special kind of index that stores the bulk of its data as bit arrays (bitmaps) and answers most queries by performing bitwise logical operations on these bitmaps. The most commonly used index, such as B+trees, are most efficient if the values it indexes do not repeat or repeat a relatively smaller number of times. In contrast, the bitmap index is designed for cases where the values of a variable repeat very frequently. For example, the gender field in a customer database usually contains two distinct values: male or female. For such variables, the bitmap index can have a significant performance advantage over the commonly used trees.

Dense Index: A dense index in databases is a file with pairs of keys and pointers for every record in the data file. Every key in this file is associated with a particular pointer to *a record* in the sorted data file. In clustered indices with duplicate keys the dense index points *to the first record* with that key.

Sparse Index: A sparse index in databases is a file with pairs of keys and pointers for every block in the data file. Every key in this file is associated with a particular pointer *to the block* in the sorted data file. In clustered indexes with duplicate keys the sparse index points *to the lowest search key* in each block.

Covering Index: In most cases an index is used to quickly locate the data record(s) from which the required data is read. In other words, the index is only used to locate data records in the table and not to return data.

A covering index is a special case where the index itself contains the required data field(s) and can return the data.

Consider the following table (other fields omitted):

ID	Name	Other Fields
12	Plug	...
13	Lamp	...
14	Fuse	...

To find the Name for ID 13 an index on (ID) will be useful, but the record must still be read to get the Name. However, an index on (ID, Name) contains the required data field and eliminates the need to look up the record.

A covering index can dramatically speed up data retrieval but may itself be relatively large due to the additional keys, which slows down data insertion & update. To reduce such index size some systems allow non key fields to be included in the index. Non key fields are not themselves part of the index ordering but only included at the leaf level, allowing for a covering index with less overall index size.

COLON CLASSIFICATION

GENESIS

Method of Choice in a Danish University in 1967: This communication describes the trend of the proceedings of a meeting held at Odense on 18 April 1967, and attended by twenty representatives of the Danish University and Specialist Libraries and of the Classification Committee of the Danish Public Library System. The discussion at the meeting was based on the report made to Torkil Olsen, Chief Librarian of the newly formed University Library at Odense, by the two librarians M Weitemeyer and A Tiedje.

These two librarians had never used either DC or LC or UDC. They were asked to examine the result of classifying an assortment of 225 books picked out from the field of humanities and history according to DC, LC, and UDC; and to compare the respective sequences and report their findings on their relative merits. The Meeting considered also a report by K Birket-Smith on the possible adoption of LC by the Odense University Library.

Method of Choice in Delhi University in 1943: The method of choosing a scheme for classification, described in the preceding section, was not available in India about a generation ago. In 1943, S. Das Gupta took charge of the University Library at Delhi. He had to choose a scheme for classification. At that time, the library profession had not been well established. The number of professional librarians was very small. Therefore, he used the preference of scholars as the test. He made an assorted collection of books in a subject. He also made a duplicate collection. There were only two schemes to be considered - Colon Classification and Decimal Classification. He classified one of the collections by CC and labelled its book case 'Classification A'; and the second collection by DC and labelled its book case 'Classification B'. Then some of the professors in the subject spent a fairly long time in comparing the relative helpfulness of the two arrangements. Their verdict was unanimously in favour of 'Classification A' - that is, Colon Classification.

Das Gupta used the names A and B to denote the two schemes for classification for a definite reason. In these early years, which belonged to the British Period, there was inherent preference to anything of foreign origin and an equally inherent prejudice to anything of Indian origin.

Further, the few librarians in the country had cultivated an emotional aversion to Colon Classification, without gaining any experience with it and even without haying read the scheme and the literature which had grown around it. Das Gupta knew this. He knew also that two librarians had been doing some propaganda in the matter. He explained this as the reason for his not disclosing the names of the two schemes to the professors until they made the choice.

General

Preliminaries: In any comparison of Schemes for Classification, clarity and consistency will be gained and fault in communication will be minimised, if start is made with

1. Definition of the term 'Classification';
2. Concept of Class Number as a translation of the name of a subject from a natural language to a preferred ordinal language;
3. Making unique the name of a subject in the preferred ordinal language - i.e., making its Class Number unique;
4. Providing for the approach of the minority of readers not by changing Class Numbers but by other means; and
5. Purpose to be served by classification.

Definition of the Term 'Classification'

The term 'Classification' should not be taken in the sense of:

1. Either merely as a division of the Universe of Subjects into near-homogeneous groups of subjects;
2. Or merely as division into groups plus arrangement of the groups in a preferred helpful sequence.

The term 'Classification' should be taken to include also the representation of each group of subjects - that is, each subject or each subject-complex of any possible degree of intension - by a unique ordinal number of its own. This is necessary to re-insert, in its correct place, any book taken out of the shelves or any entry taken out of the classified part of the catalogue. It is believed that there is no difference of opinion on this today.

Concept of Class Number

The definition of the term 'Classification', given in the preceding section, is equivalent to the concept that Class Number is a unique translation of the name of a subject in a natural language into the preferred Classificatory Language of ordinal numbers. In this view, the system of all the Class Numbers of a Scheme for Classification, taken together, may be deemed to be a Classificatory Language. This concept was not perhaps easily acceptable about 30 years ago. But, Sayers endorsed it and it is believed that it is now widely accepted.

Uniqueness of Class Number

The term 'Uniqueness of Class Number' emphasizes that the preferred Classificatory Language should be homonym-free and synonym-free. In other words, no Class Number can represent more than one subject and no subject can be represented by more than one Class Number. To use mathematical terminology there should be a strict one. One correspondence between subjects on the one side and the Class Numbers on the other. Unless there is such a uniqueness, pestering cross classification will arise.

Books on one and the same subject will get scattered and mixed up in the sequence. A system of unique Class Numbers and such a system alone can provide a unique sequence of subjects. Of course, care must be taken to see that such a sequence should be the one satisfying the approach of a majority of readers. No doubt, it is not easy to determine such a sequence by direct experience gained by observing the approach of readers' books in all kinds of libraries. Leaving it altogether to conjecture at the level of actual Class Numbers, will lead to great divergence of opinion.

The chief contribution of CC is the taking of this problem to the near-seminal level. Its Postulate of the Five Fundamental Categories and of Rounds and Levels of manifestation of each of them in a subject; and the Postulates and Principles for the helpful sequence of the isolates in a facet and of the facets among themselves belong to this near-seminal level. The sequence of facets thus determined is nearly the one determined by Absolute Syntax. This System of Postulates and Principles has given at the phenomenal level a unique sequence of subjects helpful to the majority of readers. UDC has not yet realized the importance of maintaining uniqueness of Class Numbers. It is time for UDC to examine this problem afresh. The question will be again taken up in Sec 4 of this paper.

Minority Approach

The Laws of Library Science are democratic to the finish. They will not be satisfied unless they are respected in the service to even a minority of one reader.

Purpose of Classification: Finding of the Odense Meeting

The difference in the old and the new purposes of classification is brought out categorically by the following finding of the Odense Meeting: " DC and LC belong to the type of systems which were designed for shelving purposes, while UDC from the beginning was developed as a bibliographic system, designed for retrieval purposes and consequently belong to the same - more advanced - type of systems as the BC system (Bliss Bibliographic Classification) and the CC system (Colon Classification by Ranganathan)" (Para 6). In respect of DC, this observation is confirmed by the following statement by the Editor of DC: "The latest ... full edition of DC was prepared as a shelf classification which could meet the needs of general libraries of any size, though not necessarily those of special libraries ...it is not intended to be used for deep bibliographicanalysis". In respect of LC, the observation of the Odense Meeting is confirmed by the following statement of Putnam: "The system of classification... is one devised from ... a consideration of the particular conditions in this Library (Library of Congress), the character of its present and probable collection and of its probable use ... '. LC is thus a scheme tailored to meet the arrangement of the books of a particular library on its shelves.

Fallacy of Resisters

The antithesis between a Scheme for Classification for shelf arrangement of books and one for bibliographical classification- that is, a Scheme for Classification for the arrangement of the main entries in the classified part of a documentation list of micro subjects - arises from a fallacy. Without actual experience, the resisters to the adoption of a so-called "Bibliographical Classification" to 'Shelf Arrangement' assume that the Class Numbers of books also will have many facets and will be as long as those for micro documents. If the resisters actually apply a so-called "Bibliographical Classification", such as CC, to an assortment of a few hundreds of books, then they will see that a Classificatory Language which gives co-extensive Class Numbers with many facets, though long to subjects of minute extension and deep intension, can give for books Class Numbers with very few facets and as short as and perhaps even shorter than, the so-called "Library Classification '. The versatility of CC is comparable to that of the trunk of an elephant which has at once the amazing strength to uproot a tree with ease and also the nimble simplicity to pick out a grain with equal ease.

Facts of the Case

The correct way of deciding the issue is the statistical one. A sample of 1,300 books consisting of those lent out during one month from the Madras University Library was used as the basis for statistical study. They were classified by CC and DC. It was found that the average number of digits for a Class Number was 4-8 in CC - a so-called "Bibliographical Classification" - and 5.8 in DC -a so-called "Library Classification". Thus, the view of the resisters to the use of one and the same scheme for classification both for shelf arrangement and for documentation lists is without basis.

SEQUENCE OF MAIN SUBJECTS

Finding of the Odense Meeting: A finding of the Odense Meeting concerns the sequence of the Main Subjects in the different schemes. It is as follows: "The main structure (that is, the sequence of the Main Subjects) of all the three systems (BC, LC, and UDC) is antiquated and not consistent with the consensus of the scientists of today. This is of course very regrettable from the point of view of a modern library" (Para 5).

Recent Changes in UDC: Being based on DC, the sequence of the Main Subjects in UDC is substantially the same as in DC. These Main Subjects are to be found among the 1,000 subjects enumerated in the Third Summary in DC. The Odense Meeting noted that attempts were being recently made to modify the sequence of the Main Subjects in UDC at certain points. One such change is bringing the Main Subjects Literature and Language in juxtaposition. Here is the direction in the Schedule of UDC: "To bring together Linguistics and Literature in libraries or private collections, Sec 4 may be abandoned and Linguistics grouped here [in Sec 8] by means of the special subdivision ".07" which is also attachable to any specific language number under 82/89. Thus,

8 Languages, Literature, and Linguistics.

8.07 Philology, Linguistics generally. As in 41.

839.3.07 Dutch philology, Linguistics".

This change has been rightly appreciated by the Odense Meeting (Para 5). But there are other spots in the sequence of the Main Subjects in UDC, needing rearrangement to bring UDC into conformity to the "consensus of the scientists of today". An important need is to bring social sciences and history into juxtaposition, and philosophy, religion, fine arts, literature, and linguistics - which are collectively known as humanities - into juxtaposition.

Historical Setting: To go the whole hog in the matter of the sequence of the Main Subjects, we should take a historical view of the matter. During recent years, we have begun to distinguish between the "Classification of the Universe of Knowledge" and the "Classification of the Universe of Subjects". Here, the term 'Subject' means, "An organized or systematised body of ideas, whose extension and intension are likely to fall coherently within the field of interest and comfortably within the intellectual competence and the field of inevitable specialisation of a normal person".

Main Subject: In the early years, ideas of large extension were organized and systematised into subjects and were embodied in books. During the last few centuries the extension of the ideas organized and systematised into subjects is becoming progressively narrow. Moreover, even subjects of extension, too narrow for embodiment in books, are being embodied in articles in periodicals. These too have to be provided for in the Schedule for Classification. Therefore, it is no longer sufficient for a Scheme for Classification to have the capacity to arrange macro subjects alone in a helpful sequence; it should also be able to arrange micro subjects similarly. The need for this came to be realised forcibly after World War II, as a social necessity for the prevention of the dissipation of research potential. A Micro Subject is found to be a subdivision of a Macro Subject. In fact, we get a hierarchy or a chain of subjects of varying degrees of extension, beginning at one end with a small "bit" of Micro Subject and ending at the other end with a large Macro Subject. We have for example the chain:

History

|

History of India

|

President of India

|

Functions of the President of India

|

Veto power of the President of India

|

Veto power of the President of India in 1968

Here, "History" is the ultimate Macro Subject; and "Veto power of the President of India in 1968" is the ultimate "bit" of Micro Subject. The top two links of the chain are certainly Macro Subjects; and equally certainly, the last two links have only the status of Micro Subject at the present time. Of the links 3 and 4, it is difficult to assert about their status. The trend in the world of books is to upgrade Micro Subjects as Macro Subjects.

The different topmost or ultimate Macro Subjects are called `Main Subjects'. Obviously,the number of Main Subjects will be small, while the number of "bits" of Micro Subjects will be very large and tend towards infinity as time goes on. Therefore, it is usual to divide the Universe of Subjects into Main Subjects, at the first step. Traditionally a few Main Subjects have been recognized; and these are being added to in small doses. Due to the exigencies of notation, DC and therefore UDC have moved one step backwards and introduced in the schedule certain Comprehensions of Main Subjects and treated them as if each Comprehension of Main Subjects were itself a Main Subject. These are, "3 Social Sciences", "5 Pure Sciences", "6 Technology", and "9 General Geography, History, etc".

Consensus of Philosophers

Vedic System: From the Vedic times downwards, the philosophers have been interested in the division of knowledge qua knowledge and not of subjects qua subjects. Moreover, they had only attempted to break down the Universe of Knowledge into a few broad divisions and arrange them in a helpful sequence. The Vedic sequence consisted of the following four Divisions of knowledge:

1. 'Dharma', comprehending the ensemble of the modern Main Subjects collectively of law, religion, ethics, and sociology;
2. 'Artha', comprehending the ensemble of the modern Main Subjects denoted by the term `applied sciences' - natural as well as social;
3. 'Kama', comprehending the ensemble of the modern Main Subjects collectively of linguistics, fine arts, Literature, and those denoted by the term 'pure sciences'; and
4. 'Moksha', comprehending the ensemble of the modern Main Subjects collectively of philosophy and mystical experience.

Greek System: In the Greek period several systems were introduced by different philosophers and the influential system was that of Aristotle. The outline of his system consisted of economics politics, law, creative art, mathematics, physics, and theology (metaphysics).

Scholastic System: The universities have been influenced by the Greek System; so also the libraries. It was modified by them into what is known as the Scholastic System.

Baconian System: In the early seventeenth century Francis Bacon gave the following system:

1. History, comprehending the ensemble of natural history, arts including literature, and civil history;
2. Poetry, comprehending the ensemble of lyrics, fables, and allegories; and
3. Philosophy, comprehending the ensemble of natural theology, physical sciences, philosophy proper, sociology, and economics.

Inverted Baconian System: The above-mentioned philosophical systems exercised a great influence on the design of library classification in the nineteenth century; in particular, Bacon held sway for a long time. The sequence of the Main Subjects in DC is said to be a kind of an inverted Baconian sequence. If this be true, the sequence of Main Subjects in UDC also should be described as inverted Baconian. Perhaps, in a way the sequence of the Main Subjects in DC and in UDC may be taken to be consistent with the consensus of the philosophers as it had reached at the beginning of the nineteenth century.

Consensus of Scientists: Serial System

The pressure of natural sciences led the philosophers of the early nineteenth century to abandon the socio-centred sequence of the Vedic system, the universitycentred sequence of the scholastic system, and the psychology-centred sequence of the Baconian system. This pressure led to the concept of the Serial Dependence of subjects. In the first half of the nineteenth century, Auguste Comte started off a Serial System of knowledge : His sequence of Main Subjects was: mathematics, astronomy, physics, chemistry, biology, social physics. Each of these main divisions of knowledge was dependent for its development on the use of the preceding one. On the same principle, Herbert Spencer arrived at the sequence: logic, mathematics, mechanics, physics, chemistry, astronomy, geology, psychology, and sociology. These Serial Systems concerned themselves with pure disciplines only. However, they show the new trend in the consensus of scientists. About the same time, Ampere recommended the interpolation of each applied science next to the pure discipline on the use of which it was believed to be essentially dependent.

Sequence of Main Subjects in CC: CC divides the Universe of Subjects into three major groups arranged as follows:

1. Natural sciences and their applications;
2. Humanities; and
3. Social sciences and their applications.

In the first group, the progression of the pure discipline consists of mathematics, physics, chemistry, geology, botany, and zoology. This is a progression from the abstract to the concrete. These are described as forming successive "Levels of Integration". After each pure discipline, is inserted an applied subject mainly depending on it. Thus, engineering after physics; technology after chemistry; mining after geology; agriculture after botany; animal husbandry and medicine after zoology; and the residual applications of sciences after medicine. In the subjects in the two groups humanities and social sciences taken together, the progression is from the natural to the artificial. Fine arts and literature are the most natural. Law is the most artificial.

There is also some attempt to bring the pure disciplines of these groups and their applications in juxtaposition. Social service after sociology is an example. Political science and history are in the same relation though they come in the inverted sequence. The reason for this inversion is that political science was evolved as a discipline comparatively later than the other pure disciplines. The interval was much greater than that in the natural sciences. The juxtaposition of psychology and education may be taken as an example. Thus the sequence of the Main Subjects in CC conforms to the current consensus among the scholars and the scientists.

Not Wholly Important

In any Scheme for Classification the sequence of the Main Subjects is not however very important. In the first place each Main Subject will have thousands of books on it forming a single block. Whatever be the sequence of the Main Subjects in the scheme, these blocks will usually be arranged in a different sequence, in order to satisfy Law 4 of Library Science - Save the Time of the Reader. For example, in a Generalist Library, literature is the most popular. Therefore, it saves the time of the majority of readers if this block of books is inserted first. Linguistics has only very low priority in the attraction of readers. On the other hand, a subject like history or economics or philosophy will attract more readers. Therefore, to satisfy Law 4 of Library Science, these blocks may have to be inserted between the literature block and the linguistics block. In other words, a library will have to adopt only a "Broken Sequence" of the Main Subjects. But this need not be done in the catalogue. Secondly, the number of possible sequences of Main Subjects runs to millions. It is impossible to pick one of them as the most helpful sequence. What is wanted is only a reasonably helpful sequence.

Preference of a Scheme With Helpful Sequence of Main Subjects

This statement should not be taken to imply

1. Either that an outmoded scheme may be chosen for a new library;
2. Or that it should be continued in an old library. A new library will do well to choose, as its Scheme for Classification, a scheme that gives a reasonably helpful sequence according to the current consensus amongst scholars and scientists. Even a library on a system with a very unhelpful sequence of Main

Subjects may change over to a better scheme, before the number of volumes becomes too large. Perhaps even in huge library collections, it may be desirable to introduce a new system conforming to the current consensus among scholars and scientists. This can be done, without undue cost of revision, by adopting the "Method of Osmosis".

New Main Subjects

Attribute of Main Subjects: One of the attributes of a Main Subject scheduled by a Scheme for Classification is that it cannot be a subdivision of any other Main Subject. We should also exclude from Main Subjects any subject comprehending two of more Main Subjects. Each Main Subject has its own distinctive field in the Universe of Subjects and also its own distinctive technique of study. Even this criterion may not prove sufficient to be taken as a rigid definition of the term 'Main Subject'. It is for this reason that, while observing these attributes of a Main Subject, a Scheme for Classification safeguards its position by way of abundant caution with the statement that it "Postulates the Main Subjects".

New Main Subjects emerge often, though slowly. A few Main Subjects, that have emerged in recent years are, Pure Theory of Standardization, Pure Theory of Management, Pure Theory of Communication, Pure Theory of Conduct of Meetings, and Social Work. Presently, we are finding that a new Main Subject can be formed by the "Fusion" of two Main Subjects; Bio-physics and Bio-chemistry are examples. In the choice of a Scheme for Classification, the capacity of the notational system to accommodate newly emerging Main Subjects in a fairly helpful place among the already existing Main Subjects is important. In a sense it is even more important than the existing sequence of the Main Subjects in the Scheme.

Main Subjects in DC: As stated in Sec 22, the Main Subjects in DC are to be picked out from the "Third Summary, the 1000 Sections". Here is a schedule of them:

02	Library Science	574	Biology
1	Philosophy	58	Botany
15	Psychology	59	Zoology

2	Religion	61	Medicine
32	Political Science	62	Engineering
33	Economics	63	Agriculture
34	Law	634.9	Forestry
36	Social Welfare	636	Animal Husbandry
37	Education	64	Home Science
4	Linguistics	65	Management
51	Mathematics	66	Technology
519.2	Statistical Methods	7	Fine Arts
52	Astronomy	8	Literature
53	Physics	91	Geography
54	Chemistry	93/99	History
55	Geology		

The number of Main Subjects recognizable as such are thus 31. It will be noticed that 5 Main Subjects are represented each by a single digit; 22 by two digits; 2 by three digits; and 2 by four digits. Of the 1000 Class Numbers in the Third Summary, many have been given over to subdivisions of Main Subjects rather extravagantly; with the result that two Main Class Numbers have to have three digits each and two four digits each. The table of three digited numbers is thus choked up. The accommodation in DC of any newly emerging Main Subject is going to be a problem. Moreover, Main Subjects with three or four digits come in as a wedge between the subdivisions of one and the same Main Subject. This is not helpful. This is the penalty to be paid by DC for its using the pure base of Indo-Arabic numerals for its notational system.

Main Subjects in UDC: UDC has adopted the Main Subjects of DC with the following changes in the Class Numbers:

159.9	Psychology
634.0	Forestry

Al the remarks on DC apply also to UDC.

2.8.4 Main Subjects in CC

We shall next examine the capacity of the notational system of CC to accommodate the Main Subjects. Its notational system uses the Indo-Arabic numerals, the Roman capitals, and the Roman smalls as its base making allowance for certain omissions and other considerations. There are eight digits in the Sector of Indo-Arabic numerals; twenty-four in the Sector of Roman capitals; and twenty-three in the Sector of Roman smalls. Further, the digits z,Z, and 9 are made semantically empty digits though retaining the ordinal value. The three digits T, V, and X are postulated to be Emptying Digits - that is, they empty the preceding digit of its semantic value though the ordinal value is allowed to be retained. Further, the three digits U, W, and Y are both Empty and Emptying Digits. By this arrangement CC has accommodation for about 5000 Main Subjects. There are 32 single digited numbers to represent Main Subjects. All these have already been used up; there are 184 two digited numbers to represent Main Subjects; of these 44 have already been used up; there are still 140 numbers free. Of the three digited numbers, only a few have been brought into use till now. GYC for biophysics and GYE for bio-chemistry are examples. The others are free.

New Criterion: The number of available Class Numbers with not more than three digits, which can be used for representing Main Subjects, should be an important criterion in the choice of a Scheme for Classification for a new library or for an old library desiring to modernise its Scheme for Classification for all new accessions and for the active books in the old stock using the "Method of Osmosis" (28). Also, the capacity to accommodate new Main Subjects should be given due weight in the design of new Schemes for Classification.

CLASSIFICATION MANUAL FOR LIBRARIES

CLASS STEM

The class stem is the classification number up to the colon. It consists of letter author symbols for the parent issuing body, numbers indicating subordinate offices, followed by a period, and numbers designating category classes, series, or serial title, followed by a colon.

Section 1

Author Symbols

The first letter or letters in the classification number represent the department or independent agency issuing the publication. Each department or independent agency has a unique letter or combination of letters assigned to it.

Originally, when the classification system was first established, the executive departments were assigned a single letter (Example: A for

Agriculture Department), and other agencies were assigned two letters (Example: GP for Government Printing Office). This practice was changed, however, as more departments were established, sometimes resulting in conflicts.

For example T was assigned to Treasury Department; therefore, T could not be used alone for the Transportation Department when it was established later. The TD designation was assigned to the Transportation Department.

A. Choice of Letter Designations

Generally, the letter or letters chosen as the author symbols correspond to the letter beginning a significant subject word or words in the name of the agency.

For example:

A Agriculture

C Commerce

D Defence

E Energy

Exceptions to this principle are the X and Y designations used for publications of the United States Congress. The boards, commissions, and committees established by Act of Congress or under authority of an Act of Congress, not specifically designated in the Executive Branch of the Government, are grouped under Y 3., one of the symbols assigned to Congressional publications. Series designations are handled differently in the X and Y classes and are covered in Chapter 5 of this manual.

1. *New Agency Classes:* It is important to determine the enabling authority when a new agency or department is established, so that the agency can be assigned to its correct place in the classification system. The enabling authority may be a public law, an executive order of the President, or a departmental directive. It may be necessary to phone the new agency to locate this information.
2. *Determining the Identity of the Issuing Office:* Occasionally a publication will appear without an issuing office name printed on the cover, resulting in classification difficulties. Usually, somewhere inside the publication is a letter of transmittal, preface, or foreword which gives information or at least an agency contact, where more information may be obtained to help identify the publication. At the

Government Printing Office, jacket number identification is another source for determining the issuing agency.

B. Joint Publications

A publication may be issued jointly by two or more agencies. If this is the case, all of the agency names will be listed on the publication with more or less equal treatment. Classify the publication under the first agency listed.

1. *Revised Editions:* A revised edition of a joint publication should be classified with the original if both agencies are issuing the revision, regardless of the order in which the agencies are listed on the publication.

   However, if only one of the agencies issued the revision, it should be classified under the revising agency regardless of where it was classified originally.

2. *Publications Prepared by One Agency for Another:* Publications prepared by one agency for another pose a somewhat different problem. First, determine which agency is the actual publisher of the publication in question, and classify under that agency.

   In most cases, the agency for which the publication was prepared is the issuing agency; however, on occasion the preparing agency will publish it. Usually this can be determined by the title page or cover format.

   For example, a publication may be prepared by the Department of Interior's US Geological Survey for the Commerce Department. If the Commerce Department issued the publication, that is where it should be classified, even though a US Geological Survey open-file report number may appear on the publication. If the US Geological Survey is determined to be the issuing office, use the series printed on the publication to determine the class.

3. Serial and Series Treatment

   a) *Serial:* If the publication is a serial and the printed order of the agencies changes with later issues, retain the original class if the first agency is still listed as a publisher.

   b) *Series:* The publication may carry one or more series. The presence of a series does not necessarily determine the class number of a joint publication. Do not conclude immediately that the series class is where the publication belongs.

First, decide the issuing agency to be used in the class. After the proper issuing agency has been determined, classify in the series appropriate to that agency. It may be the first or second series listed, but it must agree with the issuing office.

For example, the National Institute of Standards and Technology (NIST), Commerce Department, and the National Institute for Occupational Safety and Health, Health and Human Services Department, issues a booklet in the NISTIR/NIOSH Publication series. The publication carries a NIOSH number as well as the series NISTIR 90-3945. The National Institute of Standards and Technology is the first agency listed, so the class number is: C 13.58:90-3945.

If a double series is issued routinely by two agencies, and the publications are not consistent in presenting the agency and series in uniform order, classify the publications in one class consistently.

A joint publication may carry only one series. If the agency listed first is not the agency associated with the series, then the series is not used in the class. The publication should be classified in a general class under the agency selected as the issuing agency.

C. Sources of Information

A publication should be classified under the subordinate office printed on the title page, the verso of the title page, pages 1, 2, 3 and 4 of the cover, or the spine. Under ordinary circumstances, use the source that provides the most complete information. However, in cases of conflict, prefer the information found on the title page.

Pages 1-4 of cover are both sides of the front and back cover. In general, a subordinate office from a letter of transmittal, preface, or foreword should not be used as the issuing office. Also, the bureau or office listed with a personal author, in most cases, should not be used as a determining factor.

Section 2: Subordinate Offices

A. First and Second Levels

A number designating a subordinate office follows the letter designation of the parent issuing body. The numbers, followed by a period, are used to identify subordinate offices one level below the parent agency.

The parent agency, always designated by the number 1, is the first-level office. The number 1 is always used for the office of the secretary of a department or the administrator of an independent agency. The 1 class also should be used for any publication carrying only the department or agency name with no subordinate bureau listed.

The numbers 2 through 99 are used for subordinate bureaus, administrations, offices, etc., immediately below the level of the head of the agency. The classification number does not generally include designations for offices below the second level.

For example:

A 1. Agriculture Department (including Secretary's Office)

A 13. Forest Service

A 68. Rural Electrification Administration

A 88. Agricultural Marketing Service

In some classes, notably Defence, 3 digits are used before the period to designate second-level subordinate bodies. The use of 3 digits is exceptional, however, and was necessary with Defence because of the vast number of subordinate issuing agencies.

For example:

D 1. Defence Department

D 101. Army Department

D 201. Navy Department

D 301. Air Force Department

1. *Arrangement of Classes:* When the classification system was established, the subordinate offices were arranged alphabetically with numbers assigned sequentially. It is rarely possible to obtain enough information on new departments and their plans for organization to continue following this practice. Also, new departments and agencies frequently reorganize and change the names of the subordinate offices.

   New classes are therefore arranged in chronological order, determined by the order in which publications are received.

2. *New Classes for Subordinate (Level 2) Offices:* New level 2 classes should be assigned as offices are established and issue publications. The next higher number should be assigned beginning with number 2 after the author symbol.

B. Third and Fourth Levels

On occasion, classes are created for third and fourth level offices, to provide a finer organization of the agency's publications. An office immediately subordinate to a second-level office is a third-level office. Fourth-level offices are immediately subordinate to third-level offices.

Classes are broken down to the third and fourth levels by using 100 and 1000 numbers after the parent agency's assigned number, after the period. The decision on how far to go in the breakdown depends upon how small a breakdown is necessary for clarity.

For example:

C 1. Commerce Department (level 1)

C 55. National Ocean and Atmospheric

Administration (level 2)

C 55 .100's National Weather Service (level 3)

.200's Environmental Data & Information

Service (level 3)

.300's National Marine Fisheries Service (level 3)

.400's National Ocean Service (level 3)

HE 1. Health and Human Services

Department (level 1)

HE 20. Public Health Service (level 2)

HE 20 .3000's National Institutes of Health (level 3)

.3150's National Cancer Institute (level 4)

.3200 to.3249 National Heart, Lung, and Blood

Institute (level 4)

.3250's National Institute of Allergy &

Infectious Diseases (level 4)

.3600's National Library of Medicine (level 3)

In the case of the Public Health Service, National Institutes of Health, there are so many separate institutes that the 3000 numbers are broken by 50's to have a number for each of the institutes. Currently, the Health and Human Services Department classes are the only ones using 1000 numbers.

1. *Slash Numbers Added:* Third and fourth level offices not expected to issue many publications may be treated the same as series or category classes. In these cases, a slash and a number are added after the number for the subordinate office.

   A 13.40 has been reserved for publications of the Southern Forest Experiment Station. Each of the forest service experiment stations has a number reserved for it. As new classes are established, new slash numbers are used as necessary.

2. *New Classes for Third and Fourth Level—Organizations:* When a new subordinate office is established, determine the name of its parent organization and how the office fits into the agency organization.

Determine how many levels there are between the new organization and the departmental secretary or independent agency administrator. Use the letter of the agency, the number for the first level breakdown followed by a period, then a 100, 200, or 300 class as appropriate, followed by a colon.

If not many publications are expected, consider assigning a series class rather than a subordinate agency class.

If the agency is expected to issue many publications and has many smaller offices, all of which will produce many publications, you may use 1000 numbers to differentiate between offices. There are very few cases where this will be necessary. If it does become necessary, the Public Health Service classes under HE 20. will serve as a guide. Each of the subordinate offices in the Public Health Service issues many publications, and the finer breakdown is necessary to keep the publications of each institute together.

C. Joint Publications

When a joint publication, not in a numbered series, carries two equally subordinate bureaus under the same department, classify the publication under the bureau which is listed first on the document. If three or more equally subordinate offices are named, ignore them and classify the publication under the parent agency. To determine which is the parent agency, and whether subordinate offices are equally subordinate, consult: (1) the issuing agency; (2) a cataloger; or (3) an on-line database.

D. Name Changes, Reorganizations, etc.

1. *Name Changes:* Certain agencies in their infancy have been very

inconsistent and changeable in naming their subordinate offices. Frequent name changes present many problems.

Sometimes, because organizational information was unclear, certain classes which should have been treated as level 3 or 4 offices have been established under the parent agency. An example of this problem is found in the publications of the Environmental Protection Agency. The subordinate office names changed frequently during the first years of its existence.

A name change does not necessarily demand a class number change. If the agency's function and position within the parent organization remain the same, the class number will remain the same. When it appears that a name has changed, the agency should be contacted to verify the nature of the change.

2. *Reorganizations:* Reorganizations within an agency present other problems. Sometimes offices and functions are moved from one subordinate office to another. It is important to note the issuing office on each publication in order to determine whether a reorganization has taken place that will affect the class. The class number must be changed when an agency is moved from one parent agency with one author symbol to a second parent agency with a separate author symbol.

Reorganization is a particular problem in serials when the name of the serial remains the same, the publication looks the same, and the numbering follows along logically; but the issuing office has been transferred to another bureau or office.

For example:

ED 1.116/2:

Institutions of higher education index, by state and congressional district.

Previously classed: HE 19.322:

The publisher, the National Centre for Education Statistics, at one time was a subordinate office of the Department of Health, Education, and Welfare.

The class number must be changed when the issuing body is moved to another agency.

It is important to change the class with the first issue carrying the name of the new department or bureau. Always glance at the parent agency of any publication being classified to be sure that the subordinate office class is still correct. By checking constantly, the necessity for changing class numbers retroactively can be avoided.

Changes within Classes

The use of adequate references will eliminate many errors. Notes should be placed in appropriate places when classes are changed, or when the method of classifying within the class is changed. This may involve changing from Cutters to numbers, from the 2-figure to the 3-figure Cutter table, changing the Cutter word of a particular title for one reason or another, etc.

BOOK NUMBERS RULE FOR LIBRARIES

WHAT IS A BOOK NUMBER?

Book numbers are parts of call numbers, together with collection numbers and class numbers. Book numbers come at the end, and arrange books about the same subject so that they can be given useful order on the shelf and a unique location in the collection. The collection number, if used, indicates a major grouping within a library or library system, *e.g.* REF for reference or J for the juvenile collection. The class number of a book tells what it is about, but many books can be about the same thing and share the same class number. Book numbers are different for each book having the same class number and will make the full call number completely individual.1 Just as different classification schemes lead to different class numbers, so do the different book number systems lead to incompatible book numbers. The library of the Faculty of Information Studies at the University of Toronto uses the Dewey Decimal Classification (DDC).2. Their policy for making book numbers is to make an author number from the main entry,3 then add a title mark equal to the first letter of the title.

For example, Satija and Comaromi (1992) has the call number 025.428 S2523B MC. MC is the collection number, indicating in which of the many campus libraries it can be found. (The name has since changed, which is confusing.) 025.428 is the class number, indicating the subject is shelflisting. There are many books in the library about shelflisting. How to tell them apart? With a book number: for this book, S2523B. S2523 is from Satija, and B is from Book Numbers. A Library of Congress (LC) example is a copy of David Copperfield by Charles Dickens, found in the main University of Toronto library at PR 4558.A1 1947 ROBA 1. PR 4558 is class number, and stands for for David Copperfield, while A1 indicates that copies are arranged in chronological order and 1947 is the year of this particular edition. The library has appended its own collection mark (ROBA) and a copy number. S.R. Ranganathan devised his own, very detailed, faceted book number system, and in Colon Classification (1964), he helpfully includes a complete call number on the copyright page: 2:51N3 qN60. 2:51N3 is the class number (2 for Library Science, 51 for Generalia Bibliography/Technical Treatment/ Classification, N3 for Colon Classification), and qN60 is the book number (q to show the form is "Code," N for 1900-1999, 60 to make the year 1960).

"Book number" means slightly different things to different people. Comaromi (1981) says a book number is a "combination of author numbers, Cutter numbers, author letters, and any other shelflisting device." Chan (1994) defines item number as "[t]hat part of a call number which designates a specific individual item within its class." Sartap and Comaromi (1992) say, "Class numbers alone produce groupings whose size depends upon the depth of the library classification and the closeness with which the classification used is applied. To organize or provide order within a class grouping, documents are given a further notation called a book number." Ranganathan (1964) said the book number "of a book is a symbol used to fix position relatively to the other books having the same Ultimate Class.... The Book Number of a book individualises it among the books sharing the same class number."

Book numbers do not usually reflect the subject of a book, but instead are based on external attributes such as author name or year of publication. Satija and Comaromi (1992) say that book numbers "may be based on one or a combination of some of the attributes of the document, such as author, title, language, year or place of publication, physical size, and physical make-up." (Book numbers may sometimes reflect a subject-related aspect of a book, such as when it is a volume of criticism. Ranganathan used a g at the end of the call number for that, and that the Library of Congress system uses its own indicators in some cases. This brings together on the shelf books and their criticism, a very helpful collocation.) Ranganathan (1964) said the book number "may consist of one or more of the following successive Facets: Language Number; Form Number; Year Number; Accession Part of Book Number; Volume Number; Supplement Number; Copy Number; Criticism Number; and Accession Part of Criticism Number."

In general, book number = author number + title (or work) mark + edition mark + date of publication + volume number + copy number + anything else library policy dictates. Call number = class number + book number, with the collection number at the start or end.

WHY ARE THEY NEEDED?

Book numbers give a unique shelf location to each book in a collection. They bring a defined and consistent order to all books on a given topic, an order that may apply more generally to all subject groupings in the library. Depending on the size of the collection and the depth of classification, it may happen that very rarely do two books collide and share a class number, so book numbers are not thought necessary. Satija and Agriwal (1990) forcefully object to such imprecision:

> For a rigorously fine arrangement of books, book numbers are simply indispensable. Yet their value is debated if not totally doubted. A sizeable number of librarians do not value them highly in shelf arrangement, no wonder then if these are meted out a step-motherly treatment in some libraries. Literature on them is thin and rare. Even those who use book numbers think of them as merely and adjunct--a tool of the perfectionist only. Yet their value in impeccable shelf classification cannot be underestimated. In close access libraries these have comparatively more value in pinpointing the location of books.
>
> And for collocation of host and associated books, and to bring together a book and its sequels, the book numbers are quite indispensable. Their utility and importance becomes more pronounced in libraries using broad classification such as Rider's International Classification or even the DDC. It is not to suggest that in use with depth classification systems these are less desired. Whatever be the size of the library and the kind of classification used, book numbers add [the] last touch to the ultimate shelf arrangement.

In 1937 Bertha Barden listed six important reasons for using book numbers (though bar codes have made numbers four and six less relevant now):

> Book numbers in addition to class numbers are needed:
>
> 1. To arrange books in order on the shelves.
> 2. To provide a brief and accurate call number for each book.
> 3. To locate a particular book on the shelf.
> 4. To provide a symbol for charging books to borrowers.
> 5. To facilitate the return of books to the shelves.
> 6. To assist in quick identification of a book when inventories are taken.

Broad classifications will make many books share the same class number. Deep classifications will mean fewer do. Some libraries, such as in elementary schools, may use very broad classifications, perhaps Dewey to the tens. What happens when books collide? Ordering the books alphabetically by author's last name (the most basic of book numbers, though perhaps an invisible one if the name is only on the book cover and not on the spine label) seems obvious. For some collections this is enough. It will not be enough in large or specialized libraries or any library where precision and detail are valued, in order that the needs of both the librarian who organizes material, and the user who searches for it, are best served.

EARLY HISTORY

Before the DDC, books had fixed locations on the shelf. Call numbers identified where on which particular shelf a book could be found. Books might be grouped by subject, but new books were added at the end of a shelf, not mixed in. Melvil Dewey introduced relative location: his call numbers tell what a book is about, and organize the books "in terms of their relationship to one another without regard to the shelves or rooms where they are placed" (Chan, 1994). When a new book comes in, it can be placed between two existing books. One small effect of Dewey's work was the need for book numbers, because two books could now share the same class number. Dewey first tried using the author's full name, but then switched to accession numbers, ordering books by their arrival in the library: "3428.3 and 3428.28 were respectively the third and twenty-eighth books in the child care class" (Comaromi, 1981). This might bring a rough chronological ordering, but it was not good enough.

CUTTER AND SANBORN

Making rules for book numbers was a busy field in the late nineteenth century (Lehnus, 1980; Comaromi, 1981). Several schemes were devised, some using author names and some publication date. One man's work has survived: Charles Cutter's. The two- and three-figure Cutter tables and the Cutter-Sanborn table are the basis for modern author numbers, and "to cutter" is a common expression when cataloguing.

Cutter began turning author names into letter-number combinations in 1879, first published about it in 1880, and by the mid-1880s, after several editions and with Dewey's imprimatur, his system had become common (Satija and Comaromi, 1992). A copy of the two-figure author table is attached (it is long out of copyright, but updated versions are still in print). The rules are neatly specified: "Use one letter for words beginning with consonants (except S), two for words beginning with vowels or with S, three for words beginning with Sc" (Cutter, n.d.). For example, to turn Denton into an author number, go to the fragment on the table that precedes it alphabetically: "Deno 43." If there are no other names in the Deno-Dent range already, then Denton would become D43. If Denovich had already claimed D43, Denton could become D435, leaving room for 431-434 to be used for other nearby names. The numbers are to be treated as decimal fractions, as in the DDC. Bruce Sterling would become St4, Albert Einstein Ei6, and Joseph Schumpeter Sch8. The three-figure table, which Cutter published in 1901 after Kate Sanborn's work, is an extension of and compatible with the two-figure table, and is suitable for larger libraries (Comaromi, 1981).

Kate Sanborn (later Jones) was asked by Cutter to revise the two-figure table but ended up making a new table that was incompatible. Author numbers would be one letter plus one to three letters. The distribution of numbers through the letters of the alphabet was different from Cutter's original work. Her table of name fragments and numbers was large, with more than 12,000 numbers, but Cutter's later three-figure table was larger still, with more than 20,000 (Lehnus, 1980).

Cutter also included instructions for complete book numbers: one could add title marks based on the first one or two letters of the title to distinguish different books by the same writer; copy numbers could be indicated with a 2 or 3; translations could be marked with the initial letter of the language of origin; biographies would be filed by subject but with an additional letter to show the writer; commentaries would add a -Y; dictionaries and concordances would add a -Z (Cutter and Jones, n.d.)

The Cutter and Cutter-Sanborn tables are still popular, but though the detail may help with the distribution as names are turned into numbers, constantly referring to lookup tables is tiresome. Various other marks are still used with DDC much as Cutter set out: title marks being the first letter of the title; biographies indicated by inserting a "z" between the Cutter number and work mark; commentaries done the same way but with a capital "Z;"edition marks shown with edition numbers or year of publication; copy and volume numbers shown with a "c" or "v" (Chan, 1994).

LIBRARY OF CONGRESS

The LC classification removes the worry about how to specify book numbers. The rules are laid out in the system because it specifies almost complete call numbers. For book numbers, they use simplified Cutter numbers and a variety of indicators that show when books are collected works, commentaries, being ordered chronologically, etc. Their numberings are chosen to fit their shelving needs. "The Library of Congress classification is a very close classification and if numbers from either the Cutter-Sanborn table or the Cutter three-figure table were used many call numbers would be unnecessarily long. Therefore the Library of Congress developed its own author number table to be used with is classification schedules" (Lehnus, 1980). The table has five short rules and can be found in any book that covers LC cataloguing (*e.g.* Chan, 1994).

(1) After initial vowels

for the second letter: bdl-mnprs-tu-y

use number:23 4 567 89

(2) After initial letter S

for the second letter: acheh-im-ptuw-z

use number:2 34 56 78 9

(3) After initial letters Qu

for the second letter: aeiorty

use number:3456789

For initial letters Qa-Qt, use:2-29

(4) After other initial consonants

for the second letter: aeioruy

use number:3456789

(5) For expansion

for the letter:a-de-hi-lm-op-st-v w-z

use number: 345678 9

D 644.M32 2002 is the LC call number for Paris 1919: *Six Months That Changed the World*, by Margaret MacMillan. D 644 indicates History (General)/World War I/Peace/General works, M32 is MacMillan (a short Cutter number), and 2002 is the year of publication. This is a fairly simple call number. Some classes include "A" and "Z" Cutter numbers, where "a span of Cutter numbers at the beginning or end of the alphabetical sequence is assigned special meanings" (Chan, 1994). Works about a person have this: A2 is appended for collected works by date, A4 for letters by date, A5 for speeches and lectures by date, etc. This will collocate such collections in chronological order after books written by the person in question. That a book is a translation, or other such details, is shown by a second Cutter number.

Work marks can be added to the year of publication ("a" for the second edition that year, "b" for the third), but that is the limit of detail in LC call numbers. QA 76.76.T49 G64 1997, for Writing GNU Emacs Extensions by Bob Glickstein, is about as complicated as they get. It has a decimal in the class number and two Cutter numbers (albeit no work letter for the year of publication). Libraries can add collection numbers, and copy and volume numbers, as needed.

CHRONOLOGICAL ORDERING

All of the book number systems seen so far (except for Dewey's first attempt, using accession numbers) arrange books within a topic by author's last name. This is an obvious and sensible method of ordering. It will bring together all the books by one writer on the same topic, a helpful arrangement. However, the chronological ordering will be completely disrupted. Books on evolution by Charles Darwin will be followed by those by Richard Dawkins (metaphorically apt, since he is an important Darwinist). What of the 150 years between them? There is little room for names between Darwin and Dawkins, but they span the entire history of thought on evolution. A chronological ordering would put Darwin first (or near it), and moving across the shelf would show how the science progressed up to the latest work in the field.

Satija and Comaromi outline the arguments for and against chronological book numbers. In their favour, they are simple; there is no confusion when the same writer gets different Cutter numbers in different classes; when a book has multiple authors, one is not favoured over the others; the development of a subject can be traced; they are an aid to weeding out of date books; there are no problems making Cutter numbers for non-European names. Against them, they note there is no well-developed system for using chronological numbers; that the arrangement is more helpful for organization than retrieval; that it separates different editions of the same book; and most importantly, that people remember names, not years.

Chronological book numbers are as old as author numbers. W.S. Biscoe, a disciple of Dewey, devised a system that the great man admired. James Duff Brown and Fremont A. Rider created their own systems (Satija and Comaromi, 1992). All have rules for how to turn year numbers into shorter combinations of letters and numbers, which is their great fault. Biscoe's rules included (Satija and Comaromi, 1992):

A (B.C.)

B up to 999 (B33 = A.D. 33, B 685 = 685)

C 1000-1499 (C236 = 1236, C423 = 1432)

D 1500-1599 (D20 = 1520, D 85 = 1585)

...

V 1950-1959

W 1960-1060

X 1970-1979

Y 1980-1989 (Y5 = 1985, Y6 = 1986)

Z 1990-1999

"Biscoe was not concerned that his table would reach its limit with the letter Z in the year 1999, and commented that before this limit was reached someone would have devised a better scheme" (Lehnus 1980). Brown's Extended Date Table covered 1450-2125 using pairs of lower case letters (Satija and Comaromi 1992):

1450-1475 aa-az

1476-1501 ba-bz

...

1970-1995 ua-uz (up = 1985, uq = 1986, ur = 1987)

1996-2021 va-vz

2022-2047 wa-wz

All these systems have an enormous failing: they are needlessly and overwhelmingly complicated. The Indo-Arabic numerals are the best system for counting anything in western civilization, and they are recognized all around the world by speakers of many other languages.

To save one or two characters at the cost of making library users memorize an obscure conversion mechanism is no bargain. Proper names are made up of letters, and trimming them down to author numbers may not be as informative as using the full name, but they are still easy to read and ordered alphabetically. There are no such advantages to turning 1985 into Y5 or up.

One particular advantage that chronological orderings have is that they do away with problems about making author numbers for non-European names. Cutter's tables try to spread numbers around so that the distribution over the range of names is proportional, but when Chinese, Indian, Arabic, and other names are in the collection, the tables do not work as well.

Librarians in those cultures have made their own tables. Indeed, "[i]n view of the multiplicity of languages almost every Indian script and language has its own author number table for book numbers" (Satija and Agriwal, 1990). There are different calendars used around the world, but far fewer than the number of languages, and the Gregorian calendar is widely known. Arranging chronologically leads to fewer problems when managing a varied and multicultural, multilingual collection.

COLON CLASSIFICATION BOOK NUMBERS

S.R. Ranganathan's faceted Colon Classification (CC) is extremely detailed, precise, and informative, as is the book number system he made to go with it. In his Colon Classification (6th ed.) (Ranganathan, 1964) he defined these terms:

03 The Book Number of a book is a symbol used to fix position relatively to the other books having the same Ultimate Class.

030 The Book Number of a book individualises it among the books sharing the same class number.

031 The Book Number of a book is the translation of the names of certain of its specified features into the artificial language of ordinal numbers, specified and elaborated in the rest of this chapter.

03012 The Book Number consists of an intelligible concatenation of one or more of the following symbols: the twenty-four Roman capitals got by omitting I and O; the twenty-three Roman smalls got by omitting i, l, and o; the punctuation marks dot, hyphen, semicolon and colon; and the ten Indo-Arabic numerals.

0302 The Book Number may consist of one or more of the following successive facets: Language Number; Form Number; Year Number; Accession Part of Book Number; Volume Number; Supplement Number; Copy Number; Criticism Number; and Accession Part of Criticism Number.

He also defined this formula for book numbers:

[L][F][Y][A].[V]-[S];[C]:Cr[Cr#]

[L]= language number (can be left out)

[F]= form number (can be left out)

[Y]= year (the most important; comes from a table: *e.g.* N=1900-1999, P=2000-2099)

[A]= accession part of year number (if more than one book from the same year)

[V]= volume number

[S]= supplement number

[C]= copy number

Cr = g indicates a volume of criticism

[Cr #] = accession part of criticism indicator

This is the most orderly book number system discussed. The language and form facets can be left out if they are the default (*e.g.*, English books), leaving the year of publication, which Ranganathan felt was the most important facet, first. He believed strongly in chronological ordering.

In many of the schemes of Book Numbers the name of the author is used to individualise a book. In the Colon Classification the year of publication and some other characteristics also in some cases, are used for the purpose. For except in literature and in the case of the classics in any subject, where the author is made into a class in the Colon Classification, it is felt that the year of publication will be a more relevant and helpful characteristic than the name of the author for individualising a book.

If we remember that the library is a growing organism, it is more often the year of publication that determines the value of a book in all cases except the ones excluded above. The majority of readers are interested in the latest books in an ultimate class, while antiquarians may be interested in the oldest books. Most pedestrian works cease to have value to an ordinary reader at the expiry of ten to twenty years after publication. Any work with long-persisting value is likely to come out again in a new edition (Ranganathan, 1964).

For example, a 1987 book written in Urdu about Indian history would have call number V,44 168 M7 where V,44 is the class number and 168 M7 is the book number (168 showing it is written in Urdu and M7 standing for 1987) (Satija and Agriwal, 1990). A more complicated book number is 15w1K8.1g which indicates a book of criticism of volume 1 of a 1968 book of Sanskrit verse: 15 for Sanskrit (language), w1 for form (verse), K8 for year (1968), .1 for volume 1, and g for criticism.

As with all chronological systems, one writer's books on a topic will not be collocated. Further, different editions of the same book will be separated. A book published in 1968 with a second edition in 1975 would have copies filed at K8 and L5, with many books in between. Ranganathan said that if editions were to be kept together, it could be done by treating later editions as copies of the first. In this example, the first edition would be K8 and the second K8;L5.

This brings together different editions of the same book, but at the same time destroys the chronological ordering that shows the progression of knowledge.

Ranganathan knew that not everyone would like complete chronological ordering, but he felt its advantages outweighed its faults. He liked the ordering, and ways of turning numbers into shorter coded forms, so much so that in Colon Classification (1964) he includes two tables for doing this. One is especially for book numbers and turns four-number calendar years into three-character letter and number combinations.

Conclusion

Book numbers are not as interesting as class numbers. The methods for making them are straightforward and can be defined in a couple of pages, while classification systems can take many volume to define class numbers.

Nevertheless, book numbers are important. They are the final step in classification, the one that gives a book a unique place in a collection. Books about the same subject need to be ordered in a useful and helpful manner so that users can find the books arranged in an informative way that will save their time in choosing a title.

The most important part of choosing a book number system is whether to arrange books alphabetically by author or chronologically by year of publication. Most people are familiar with alphabetical arrangements, and this is what the Cutter and Cutter-Sanborn tables and LC do. Chronological ordering has its partisans, but its unfamiliarity would make it uncomfortable to most users.

Both systems attempt to save space (especially on the spine label) by turning names and years into coded short forms. That is useful for alphabetical arrangements, but confusing and unhelpful for chronological orderings, where using the full year is much clearer. Chronological book numbers may be useful when dealing with a collection that includes many non-European names.

Little has been written about book numbers. A search in the Library and Information Science Abstracts database on "book number*" with a filter to exclude International Standard Book Numbers showed only seven articles between 1990-2003. "Item number*" showed four articles. Though mostly ignored, book numbers should be appreciated by all librarians who value precision.

It will be interesting to see how book numbers fare in the future, when more and more documents are available electronically, not on a shelf. Even shelved books can be virtually reordered by doing different sorts on fields from the catalogue database. Metadata systems like the Dublin Core will mean that everything is catalogued and classified with so much detail that there is no more need for book numbers.

Book numbers, which bring so much detail and accuracy to DDC, LC, or CC, become blunt and unrefined instruments of arrangement when compared to very thorough description and classification systems.

LIBRARY CLASSIFICATION SYSTEMS

As a result of differences in notation, history, use of enumeration, hierarchy, facets, classification systems can differ in the following ways

- *Type of Notation :* Notation can be pure (consisting of only numerals for example) or mixed (consisting of letters, numerals, and other symbols).
- *Expressiveness:* This is the degree in which the notation can express relationship between concepts or structure.
- *Whether they Support Mnemonics:* For example the number 44 in DDC notation usually means it concerns some aspect of France. For example 598.0944 concerns “Birds in France”. the 09 signifies country code, and 44 represents France.
- *Hospitality:* The degree in which the system is able to accommodates new subjects
- *Brevity:* Length of the notation to express the same concept
- *Speed of Updates and Degree of Support:* The best classification systems are constantly being reviewed and improved.
- Consistency
- Simplicity

BLISS BIBLIOGRAPHIC CLASSIFICATION

The Bliss bibliographic classification (BC) is a library classification system that was created by Henry E. Bliss (1870–1955), published in four volumes between 1940 and 1953. Although originally devised in the United

States, it was more commonly adopted by British libraries than by American ones. A second edition of the system (BC2) has been developed in Britain since 1977.

ORIGINS OF THE SYSTEM

Bliss was born in New York in 1870 and in 1891 began work in the library of the College of the City of New York (now City College of the City University of New York).

Bliss had a lifelong interest in the organization, structure and philosophy of knowledge and was very critical of the library classification systems that were available to him. He believed that because the popular Library of Congress system had been designed for a specific library (the Library of Congress) it had no use as a standard system outside that library. He also greatly disliked the Dewey Decimal system.

Bliss wanted a classification system that would provide distinct rules yet still be adaptable to whatever kind of collection a library might have, as different libraries have different needs. His solution was the concept of "alternative location," in which a particular subject could be put in more than one place, as long as the library made a specific choice and used it consistently. In 1908 Bliss reclassified 60,000 of his library's books, and in 1910 he published an article with a rough scheme of his general ideas. But as he continued to develop his system he realized that it was going to be a much larger project than he had anticipated. The first of his four volumes appeared in 1940 (the year he retired) and the last in 1953, two years before his death.

Some of the underlying policies of the BC system were:

- alternative location
- brief, concise notation
- organizing knowledge according to academic expertise
- subjects moving gradually from topic to topic as they naturally related to one another.

Examples

Bliss deliberately avoided the use of the decimal point because of his hatred of Dewey's system. Instead he used capital and lower-case letters, numerals, and every typographical symbol available on his extensive and somewhat eccentric typewriter.

In the revised edition (BC2), only capital letters are used, with numerals occasionally used for special purposes. Here is an extract:

- HJ Preventive medicine
- HL Curative medicine
- HLK Primary care; general practice
- HLY Secondary care, aftercare

ADOPTION AND CHANGE

BC was not used by many North American Libraries. The system was not without its flaws (the result of being largely a one-person project), and the layout of Bliss's text was difficult to read. A few library schools sometimes taught the BC system to their students, but only in a minor way.

The failure of the system to catch on in North America was partly because of its internal deficiencies but also because the Dewey Decimal and Library of Congress systems were already well established.

The City College library continued to use Bliss's system until 1967, when it reluctantly switched to the Library of Congress system. It had become too expensive to train new staff members to use BC, and too expensive to maintain in general. Much of the Bliss stacks remain, however, as noone has recatalogued the books.

The case was different, however, in Britain. BC proved more popular there and also spread to other English-speaking countries. Part of the reason for its success was that libraries in teachers' colleges liked the way Bliss had organized the subject areas on teaching and education. By the mid-1950s the system was being used in at least sixty British libraries and in a hundred by the 1970s. In 1967 the Bliss Classification Association was formed. Its first publication was the *Abridged Bliss Classification* (ABC), intended for school libraries. In 1977 it began to publish and maintain a much-improved, revised version of Bliss's system, the Bliss Bibliographic Classification (Second Edition) or BC2.

DEWEY DECIMAL CLASSIFICATION

The Dewey Decimal Classification (DDC, also called the Dewey Decimal System) is a proprietary system of library classification developed by Melvil Dewey in 1876, and has since then been greatly modified and expanded through twenty-two major revisions, the most recent in 2004.

HOW IT WORKS?

The DDC attempts to organize all knowledge into ten main classes. The ten main classes are then further subdivided. Each main class has ten divisions, and each division has ten sections. Hence the system can be summarized in 10 main classes, 100 divisions and 1000 sections. DDC's advantage in choosing decimals for its categories allows it to be both purely numerical and infinitely hierarchical.

It also uses some aspects of a faceted classification scheme, combining elements from different parts of the structure to construct a number representing the subject content (often combining two subject elements with linking numbers and geographical and temporal elements) and form of an item rather than drawing upon a list containing each class and its meaning.

Except for general works and fiction, works are classified principally by subject, with extensions for subject relationships, place, time or type of material, producing classification numbers of no less than three digits but otherwise of indeterminate length with a decimal point before the fourth digit, where present (*e.g.* 330 for economics + 9 for geographic treatment + 4 for Europe = 330.94 European economy; 973 for United States + 05 form division for periodicals = 973.05, periodicals concerning the United States generally).

Books are placed on the shelf in increasing numerical order; the whole number to the left of the decimal is in counting order, while the digits to the right of the decimal are compared one digit at a time, with a blank coming before zero. (Example: 050, 220, 330.973, 331 etc.) When two books have the same subject, and therefore the same classification number, the second line of the call number, which usually has the first letter or first several letters of the author's last name (or the title if there is no identifiable author), is placed in alphabetical order.

It is a common misconception that all books in the DDC are non-fiction. The DDC has a number for all books, including those that generally become their own section of fiction. If DDC rules are strictly followed, American fiction is classified in 813. Most libraries create a separate fiction section to allow shelving fiction in a more generalised fashion than Dewey provides for, or to avoid the space that would be taken up in the 800s.

DDC COMPARED TO OTHER CLASSIFICATION SYSTEMS

DDC's numbers formed the basis of the more expressive but complex Universal Decimal Classification, which combines the basic Dewey numbers with selected punctuation marks (comma, colon, parentheses etc.). Besides its frequent revision, DDC's main advantage over its chief American rival—the Library of Congress Classification system developed shortly afterward—is its simplicity. Thanks to the use of pure notation, a mnemonics system and a hierarchical decimal place system, it is generally easier to use for most users.

DDC and UDC are also more flexible than Library of Congress Classification because of greater use of facets (via auxiliary tables) while Library of Congress Classification is almost totally enumerative.

On the flip side, DDC's decimal system means that it is less hospitable to the addition of new subjects, as opposed to Library of Congress Classification which has 21 classes at the top level. Another side effect of this is that DDC notations can be much longer compared to the equivalent class in other classification systems.

Another disadvantage of DDC is that it was developed in the 19th century, by essentially one man, and was built on a top down approach to classify all human knowledge which made it difficult to adapt to changing fields of knowledge. In contrast, the Library of Congress Classification system was developed based mainly on the idea of literary warrant; classes were added (by individual experts in each area) only when needed for works owned by the Library of Congress.

As a result, while the Library of Congress Classification system was able to incorporate changes and additions of new branches of knowledge, particularly in the fields of engineering and computer science (the greater hospitability of the Library of Congress Classification was also a factor), DDC has been criticized for being inadequate for covering those areas. As a result, most major academic libraries in the US do not use the DDC because the classification of works in those areas is not specific enough.

The Library of Congress Classification system is not without problems; because each area is developed by an expert according to demands of cataloguing, there is little consistency. It is also highly US-centric (more so than DDC) because of the nature of the system, and compared to DDC and UDC it has been translated into far fewer languages.

OWNERSHIP AND ADMINISTRATION

The Online Computer Library Centre of Dublin, Ohio, acquired the trademark and any copyrights associated with the Dewey Decimal System when it bought Forest Press in 1988. OCLC maintains the classification system and publishes new editions of the system. The work of assigning a DDC number to each newly published book is performed by a division of the Library of Congress, whose recommended assignments are either accepted or rejected by the OCLC after review by an advisory board; to date all have been accepted.

In September 2003, the OCLC sued the Library Hotel for trademark infringement. The settlement was that the OCLC would allow the Library Hotel to use the system in its hotel and marketing. In exchange, the Hotel would acknowledge the Center's ownership of the trademark and make a donation to a nonprofit organization promoting reading and literacy among children.

LIBRARY OF CONGRESS CLASSIFICATION

The **Library of Congress Classification** (LCC) is a system of library classification developed by the Library of Congress. It is used by most research and academic libraries in the US and several other countries — most public libraries and small academic libraries continue to use the Dewey Decimal Classification (DDC). It is not to be confused with the Library of Congress Subject Headings or Library of Congress Control Number.

The classification was originally developed by Herbert Putnam with the advice of Charles Ammi Cutter in 1897 before he assumed the librarianship of Congress. It was influenced by Cutter Expansive Classification, DDC, and was designed for the use by the Library of Congress. The new system replaced a fixed location system developed by Thomas Jefferson. By the time of Putnam's departure from his post in 1939 all the classes except K (Law) and parts of B (Philosophy and Religion) were well developed. It has been criticized as lacking a sound theoretical basis; many of the classification decisions were driven by the particular practical needs of that library, rather than considerations of epistemological elegance.

Although it divides subjects into broad categories, it is essentially enumerative in nature. It provides a guide to the books actually in the library, not a classification of the world.

The National Library of Medicine classification system (NLM) uses unused letters *W* and *QS-QZ*. Some libraries use NLM in conjunction with LCC, eschewing LCC's R (Medicine). Of documents within corporate archives and repositories has resulted from the widespread adoption of the Internet; the consequent rise of enterprise software systems such as e-mail, portals and content management; and customer relationship management (CRM). This condition is commonly referred to as "infoglut" or "information overload." Most of the information causing infoglut is in the form of documents that contain text, images or other unstructured data that cannot be readily stored in relational databases. We refer to these documents as "semistructured."

A number of "content intelligence" techniques are available to work with semistructured documents. The last two techniques in the list, basic search and advanced search (both discussed in earlier chapter), have been broadly integrated into enterprise applications. Frontier because just as a schema structure represents the contents of a database and enables queries, an information hierarchy or taxonomy organizes a repository of semistructured documents. This lets the user navigate a hierarchical structure of categories analogous to the folder systems of Microsoft Windows and the Macintosh OS, which research has shown to be highly effective for locating information.

Classification has long been used in libraries as a way to organize books, periodicals and other texts, as well as for organizing technical collections. However, in 1995 classification leapt into public view. That year, Yahoo! introduced a Website, later known as a Web portal, which organized a broad variety of information into categories. Soon, portals covering every conceivable subject area appeared. Yahoo!'s directory of Websites, unlike many of the other portals, spans thousands of categories and employs teams of human editors who manually classify news and information. For most organizations, this manual approach is economically unfeasible. This, in turn, has stimulated a flurry of research into automatic classification methods. This research has resulted in a new generation of technologies and products, and some of the leading vendors offering these products are identified.

Yet the question remains: Will this new generation of products be able to carry automatic classification into the mainstream enterprise market? Before we attempt to answer this question, let us first look at the latest technology. We will then examine several representative applications as well as the tools used to construct them.

From Words to Concepts

The goal of all text classification is to assign documents into one or more content categories. While categories are generally predefined, they may be automatically generated based on the content. Any type of document containing text can be classified, including traditional documents such as reports and memos as well as e-mails, Web pages, call-centre notes and other less traditional types.

Classification is either performed on a document repository, such as a library, or operated on a stream of incoming documents, such as that which might arrive from a news agency or field sales staff.

On the technology front in the past few years, vendors have brought the ability to extract and classify concepts, rather than words. This has required considerable language processing. Words are first *stemmed*; that is, they are reduced to their root form. Next, *stop words* are eliminated. These include words such as *a, an, in,* and *the* – words that add little semantic information. Then, words with similar meanings are equated using a thesaurus. In the example, the words *IBM, Big Blue,* and *International Business Machines* are treated as equivalent.

Finally, the classifying tool will use statistical or language-processing techniques to identify noun phrases, or *concepts,* such as "Polaris missile" or "red bicycle." In the example, six noun phrases are identified. Further, using a thesaurus or lexicon, these noun phrases are reduced to three distinct concepts that will be associated with the document. In the example, there are three instances of IBM, two instances of acquisition and one instance of Widget, Inc.

Approaches to Classification

Manual: Often used in library and technical collections as well as in call centres and forms-processing environments, manual classification requires individuals to assign each document to one or more categories. These individuals are usually domain experts who are thoroughly versed in the category structure or taxonomy being used. Manual classification can achieve a high degree of accuracy – although even domain experts will occasionally disagree on how to categorize a document. However, manual classification is more labour-intensive and therefore more costly than automated techniques.

Rule-Based: In this form of classification, keywords or Boolean expressions are used to categorize a document. This is typically used when a few words can adequately describe a category. For example, if a collection of medical papers is to be classified according to a disease, then a medical thesaurus that lists each disease together with its scientific, common and alternative names can be used to define the keywords for each category.

Another example involves e-mail systems which typically provide rule-based methods for routing messages to specific mailboxes. The e-mails are routed based either on the sender's name or the occurrence of specific words in the subject line. For example, the occurrence of the word "remove" would cause the sender's name to be dropped from an e-mail list.

While rule-based approaches are effective for carefully tuning a limited number of categories, the expense of defining and maintaining categories is generally prohibitive for large-scale classification systems.

Supervised Learning: Most approaches to automated text classification require a human subject-expert to initiate the learning process by manually classifying or assigning a number of "training documents" to each category.

This classification system first analyzes the statistical occurrences of each concept in the example documents and then constructs a model or "classifier" for each category that is used to classify subsequent documents automatically. The system refines its model, in a sense "learning" the categories as new documents are processed.

Each vendor has a favoured algorithm. For example, Autonomy and Stratify favour Bayesian algorithms, while Inxight and Verity use a form of the k-nearest neighbour (kNN) approach. Microsoft uses support vector machines (SVM) in its SharePoint portal and other products.

Both vendors and researchers have recently undertaken a number of studies to evaluate the performance of various algorithms in different situations. While the studies point out some of the strengths and weaknesses inherent in the various approaches, they also highlight the importance of testing a corpus of documents that is representative of the actual documents an organization wants to handle. Criteria that need to be tested include performance, efficiency (the percentage of documents correctly classified), errors and left-outs (the percentage of documents that are not assigned to any category).

Unsupervised Learning: These systems identify both groups, or clusters, of related documents as well as the relationships between these clusters. Commonly referred to as *clustering,* this approach eliminates the need for training sets because it does not require a preexisting taxonomy or category structure. The Autonomy Corporation cluster map tool groups all articles concerning the Venezuelan oil strike in a collection of news articles. However, clustering algorithms are not always good at selecting categories that are intuitive to human users. For this reason, clustering generally works hand-in-hand with the previously described supervised learning techniques.

Which Approach is Best?

Each of the four approaches is optimal for a different situation. As a result, classification vendors are quickly moving to support multiple methods. As Stratify chief technology officer Ramana Venkata explains, "No single technique outperforms the others in all situations since categories vary in how 'precisely' or 'diffusely' they can be described. Therefore, we need to provide different approaches that can be used simultaneously and an appropriate way to combine the results so that users can achieve optimum results."

Classification in Practice

Thus far, we have discussed state-of-the-art technology; but what about the state of the market? Most real-world implementations combine search, classification and other techniques such as identifying similar documents to provide a complete information retrieval solution. Following are several examples.

A Research Portal

Cancer.gov (www.cancer.gov), the National Cancer Institute's portal for government cancer research, aims to be the definitive source for research on cancer. The portal provides access to more than 200,000 documents located on roughly 150 Web servers throughout the National Cancer Institute (NCI). According to its project manager, Josh Stella, Cancer.gov has two main goals: making the site easily searchable and navigable for patients, and providing the tools for health professionals to find specialized research. "It's important to include the patients," Stella says, "since they use this as a way of augmenting information provided by their doctors."

When NCI's content specialists process new documents, they review meta data provided by the author, such as author name, title, abstract and keywords. Then they classify the article using UMLS (Unified Medical Lexigraphic System), a comprehensive medical thesaurus containing more than 2 million terms. However, the Cancer.gov site exposes a much smaller category structure through its Website—in the order of 100 nodes – so that it can be easily navigated by specialists and non-specialists alike.

In building this system, Cancer.gov looked for a product that could combine sophisticated search capabilities such as *spidering* across many repositories (that is, locating documents, extracting meta data and indexing them), load balancing and distribution. Ultimately, Cancer.gov selected Verity's K2 Enterprise search product. It has since developed a highly customized application using K2's comprehensive application programming interface. Project manager Stella notes that Verity K2 was one of the few products that would let him implement "best bets," in which the results of queries that contain common search terms such as "breast cancer" or "colon cancer" would return a preselected list of documents, followed by the actual search results.

Automating Customer Support

Cadence Design Systems, a leading provider of electronic design technology and services, has moved aggressively to provide Web-based customer support. The company has done so by integrating its existing Siebel CRM system with its Web-based customer support portal, SourceLink. On the back end, support engineers answer questions and resolve issues using the Siebel system, regardless of which contact channel the problem enters from – call, Web, e-mail, etc. On the Web side, SourceLink (sourcelink.cadence.com) provides application notes, FAQs and other information, and enables customers to enter service requests, receive case numbers and track the case.

Because Cadence uses Interwoven's TeamSite content management system to manage its Web site, it was a natural step to implement Interwoven's MetaTagger product to create a unified meta data repository that would integrate the SourceLink and Siebel systems. MetaTagger extracts meta data, including product name, release, type of document and modification date, from the Siebel documents and then automatically classifies the documents. The user can then browse documents according to a simple three-level taxonomy: product, release, type of document.

The meta data repository created and managed by MetaTagger is also used for document searches by the Verity K2 search engine used by SourceLink. It further enables Cadence to respond quickly to product changes. For example, changing key product information, such as name or release number, can be accomplished within MetaTagger without touching the documents themselves. "Our goal has been to streamline the cycle of publishing a change or introducing a new product onto the Web site," says Vianne Sha, the SourceLink knowledge architect. "With Sourcelink, we've shortened the cycle from months to days."

CHAPTER 4

Library Network

LIBRARY AUTOMATION

This Library has the distinction of being the first University Library in India to have fully automated all its house keeping operations.

- The Library has started its automation activity in the year 1989, by procuring a PC-AT Intel 80286 with 4mb RAM, 80mb Hard disk, MS-DOS operating system.
- Initially some programmes were developed in dbase III+. In this process, the data for the new books became available in machine readable form. The database was created for searching by author, title, subject and call number. Simultaneously catalogue cards were printed on the continuous card stationery and monthly list of additions to the library was also generated using dot matrix printer.

Integrated Library Operations with Libsys

- During the year 1990, an integrated library application software (LIBSYS) was procured using XENIX as operating system. All the new book records available in machine readable form under dbase III+ were converted into the LIBSYS software package. XENIX is a multi-user operating system on which LIBSYS: an integrated library application software provided facilities for acquisition, cataloguing, circulation and serial control and OPAC (online public access catalogue) to provide quick search of books to the users.
- During the year 1991, the hard-disk was upgraded from 80MB to 200MB and again upgraded in 1993 its systems by acquiring a new

PC 80486 system with 3 VT-220 terminals and UNIX operating system.

- During the year 1994, with the special grant from the UGC under modernization of library facilities, the library acquired a mini computer system DEC Alpha 2000 model with 6 GB hard disk, 16 numbers of 80386 PCs, 4 multimedia printers, 7 drive CD-ROM network server. Library has started using Bar-code technology at the circulation desk for issue and return transactions.
- By February 1995, the library could convert all the book records i.e. 2, 35,000 volumes of data base by entering the data from the shelf list catalogue cards and was made available for campus wide access across the Local Area Network (LAN) for the benefit of users in various Schools/Departments.

Automation and Digital Library with Vtls Software and Sun Microsystems

- During 2001, the Library switched over to VTLS software package for Library Automation and Digital Library. A Cyber Storage System (DF-1000) with facility for 400 GB hard disk storage to capture digital data from the CD/DVDs was made available for network access.

Online Public Access Catalog (OPAC)

- Library has replaced its card catalogue with Online Public Access Catalogue (OPAC) terminals for users in the central lobby of the Library and 4 + 3 terminals near the stack/ reading areas. The Library database consists of all the books, back volumes of periodicals, current journals and theses & dissertations.
- Users can search the database by author, title, classification number, subject, Journal title, Accession Number to know whether a book/ document is there in the Library or not, its status with reservation facility if the book is issued out. Users can also access the new books list from OPAC. Multimedia links are provided to enable users access digitized text of Thesis and few books and web pages of Journals to access Table of Contents, Abstracts and also the Full text. Library initiated linking the scanned pages of Table of Contents to Language Journals and few Indian Journals, where publishers are not providing such links.

DIGITAL LIBRARY

A digital library is a library in which collections are stored in digital formats (as opposed to print, microform, or other media) and accessible by computers. The digital content may be stored locally, or accessed remotely via computer networks. A digital library is a type of information retrieval system.

The *DELOS Digital Library Reference Model* defines a digital library as:

An organization, which might be virtual, that comprehensively collects, manages and preserves for the long term rich digital content, and offers to its user communities specialized functionality on that content, of measurable quality and according to codified policies.

The first use of the term *digital library* in print may have been in a 1988 report to the Corporation for National Research Initiatives The term *digital libraries* was first popularized by the NSF/DARPA/NASA Digital Libraries Initiative in 1994. The older names electronic library or virtual library are also occasionally used, though *electronic library* nowadays more often refers to portals, often provided by government agencies.

Types of Digital Libraries

The term *digital library* is diffuse enough to be applied to a wide range of collections and organizations, but, to be considered a digital library, an online collection of information must be managed by and made accessible to a community of users. Thus, some web sites can be considered digital libraries, but far from all. Many of the best known digital libraries are older than the web including Project Perseus, Project Gutenberg, and ibiblio. Nevertheless, as a result of the development of the internet and its search potential, digital libraries such as the European Library and the Library of Congress are now developing in a Web-based environment. Public, school and college libraries are also able to develop digital download websites, featuring eBooks, audiobooks, music and video.

A distinction is often made between content that was created in a digital format, known as born-digital, and information that has been converted from a physical medium, e.g., paper, by digitizing. The term hybrid library is sometimes used for libraries that have both physical collections and digital collections. For example, American Memory is a digital library within the Library of Congress. Some important digital libraries also serve as long term archives, for example, the ePrint arXiv, and the Internet Archive.

Academic Repositories

Many academic libraries are actively involved in building institutional repositories of the institution's books, papers, theses, and other works which can be digitized or were 'born digital'. Many of these repositories are made available to the general public with few restrictions, in accordance with the goals of open access, in contrast to the publication of research in commercial journals, where the publishers often limit access rights. Institutional, truly free, and corporate repositories are sometimes referred to as digital libraries.

Digital Archives

Archives differ from libraries in several ways. Traditionally, archives were defined as:

1. Containing primary sources of information (typically letters and papers directly produced by an individual or organization) rather than the secondary sources found in a library (books, etc.);
2. Having their contents organized in groups rather than individual items;
3. Having unique contents.

The technology used to create digital libraries has been even more revolutionary for archives since it breaks down the second and third of these general rules. The Oxford Text Archive is generally considered to be the oldest digital archive of academic physical primary source materials.

Digital Preservation

Project Gutenberg, Google Book Search, Windows Live Search Books(shutdown), Internet Archive, Cornell University, The Library of Congress World Digital Library, The Digital Library at the University of Michigan, and Carnegie Mellon University's Million Book Project are considered leaders in the field of digital library creation and management.

The Future

Large scale digitization projects are underway at Google, the Million Book Project, MSN, and Yahoo!. With continued improvements in book handling and presentation technologies such as optical character recognition and ebooks, and development of alternative depositories and business models, digital libraries are rapidly growing in popularity as demonstrated by Google, Yahoo!, and MSN's efforts. Just as libraries have ventured into audio and video collections, so have digital libraries such as the Internet Archive.

Searching

Most digital libraries provide a search interface which allows resources to be found. These resources are typically deep web (or invisible web) resources since they frequently cannot be located by search engine crawlers. Some digital libraries create special pages or sitemaps to allow search engines to find all their resources. Digital libraries frequently use the Open Archives Initiative Protocol for Metadata Harvesting (OAI-PMH) to expose their metadata to other digital libraries, and search engines like Google Scholar, Google, Yahoo! and Scirus can also use OAI-PMH to find these deep web resources.

There are two general strategies for searching a federation of digital libraries:

1. distributed searching, and
2. searching previously harvested metadata.

Distributed searching typically involves a client sending multiple search requests in parallel to a number of servers in the federation. The results are gathered, duplicates are eliminated or clustered, and the remaining items are sorted and presented back to the client. Protocols like Z39.50 are frequently used in distributed searching. A benefit to this approach is that the resource-intensive tasks of indexing and storage are left to the respective servers in the federation. A drawback to this approach is that the search mechanism is limited by the different indexing and ranking capabilities of each database, making it difficult to assemble a combined result consisting of the most relevant found items.

Searching over previously harvested metadata involves searching a locally stored index of information that has previously been collected from the libraries in the federation. When a search is performed, the search mechanism does not need to make connections with the digital libraries it is searching-it already has a local representation of the information.

This approach requires the creation of an indexing and harvesting mechanism which operates regularly, connecting to all the digital libraries and querying the whole collection in order to discover new and updated resources. OAI-PMH is frequently used by digital libraries for allowing metadata to be harvested. A benefit to this approach is that the search mechanism has full control over indexing and ranking algorithms, possibly allowing more consistent results. A drawback is that harvesting and indexing systems are more resource-intensive and therefore expensive.

Construction and Organization

Frameworks: A digital library can be built around specific repository software. The best known examples of this are DSpace, Eprints, Fedora, dLibra(Poland), and Greenstone Digital Library Software.

The Reference Model for an Open Archival Information System (OAIS) provides a framework to address Digital preservation.

Other formal frameworks include the DELOS Reference Model(Agosti, et al., 2006) and the Streams, Structures, Spaces, Scenarios, Societies (5S) formal framework (Gonçalves, Fox, Watson, & Kipp, 2004)

Digitization: In the past few years, procedures for digitizing books at high speed and comparatively low cost have improved considerably with the result that it is now possible to plan the digitization of millions of books per year for creating digital libraries.

Advantages: The advantages of digital libraries as a means of easily and rapidly accessing books, archives and images of various types are now widely recognized by commercial interests and public bodies alike. Traditional libraries are limited by storage space; digital libraries have the potential to store much more information, simply because digital information requires very little physical space to contain it. As such, the cost of maintaining a digital library is much lower than that of a traditional library. A traditional library must spend large sums of money paying for staff, book maintenance, rent, and additional books. Digital libraries do away with these fees. Both types of library require cataloguing input to allow users to locate and retrieve material. Digital libraries may be more willing to adopt innovations in technology providing users with improvements in electronic and audio book technology as well as presenting new forms of communication such as wikis and blogs; conventional libraries may consider that providing online access to their OPAC catalogue is sufficient. An important advantage to digital conversion is increased accessibility to users. There in also availability to individuals who may not be traditional patrons of a library, due to geographic location or organizational affiliation.

- *No Physical Boundary:* The user of a digital library need not to go to the library physically; people from all over the world can gain access to the same information, as long as an Internet connection is available.
- *Round the Clock Availability:* A major advantage of digital libraries is that people can gain access to the information at any time, night or day.
- *Multiple Access:* The same resources can be used simultaneously by a number of institutions and patrons. This may not be the case for copyrighted material: a library may have a license for "lending out" only one copy at a time; this is achieved with a system of digital rights management where a resource can become inaccessible after

expiration of the lending period or after the lender chooses to make it inaccessible (equivalent to returning the resource).

- *Information Retrieval:* The user is able to use any search term (word, phrase, title, name, subject) to search the entire collection. Digital libraries can provide very user-friendly interfaces, giving clickable access to its resources.
- *Preservation and Conservation:* Digitization is not a long-term preservation solution for physical collections, but does succeed in providing access copies for materials that would otherwise fall to degradation from repeated use. Digitized collections and born-digital objects pose many preservation and conservation concerns that analog materials do not. Please see the following "Problems" section of this page for examples.
- *Space:* Whereas traditional libraries are limited by storage space, digital libraries have the potential to store much more information, simply because digital information requires very little physical space to contain them and media storage technologies are more affordable than ever before.
- *Added Value:* Certain characteristics of objects, primarily the quality of images, may be improved. Digitization can enhance legibility and remove visible flaws such as stains and discoloration.

Problems

Digital Preservation: The work needed to ensure that digital content is maintained and accessible into the future is beginning to be addressed: see digital preservation. Technological standards change over time and forward migration must be a constant consideration of every library. Migration is a means of transferring an unstable digital object to another more stable format, operating system, or programming language. Migration allows the ability to retrieve and display digital objects that are in danger of becoming extinct.

This is a rather successful short-term solution for the problem of ageing and obsolete digital formats, but with the ever-changing nature of computer technologies, migration becomes this never-ending race to transfer digital objects to new and more stable formats. Migration is also flawed in the sense that when the digital files are being transferred, the new platform may not be able to capture the full integrity of the original object. There are countless artifacts sitting in libraries all over the world that are essentially useless because the technology required to access the source is obsolete. In addition to obsolescence, there are rising costs that result from continually replacing the older technologies. This issue can dominate preservation policy and may put more focus on instant user access in place of physical preservation.

Copyright and Licensing

Some people have criticized that digital libraries are hampered by copyright law, because works cannot be shared over different periods of time in the manner of a traditional library. The republication of material on the Web by libraries may require permission from rights holders, and there is a conflict of interest between them and publishers who may wish to create Web versions of their content for commercial purposes.

There is a dilution of responsibility that occurs as a result of the spread-out nature of digital resources. Complex intellectual property matters may become involved since digital material isn't always owned by a library. The content is, in many cases, public domain or self-generated content only. Some digital libraries, such as Project Gutenberg, work to digitize out-of-copyright works and make them freely available to the public. An estimate of the number of distinct books still existent in library catalogues from 2000BC to 1960, has been made.

The Fair Use Provisions (17 USC § 107) under copyright law provide specific guidelines under which circumstances libraries are allowed to copy digital resources. Four factors that constitute fair use are purpose of use, nature of the work, market impact, and amount or substantiality used.

Some digital libraries acquire a license to "lend out" its resources. This may involve the restriction of lending out only one copy at a time for each license, and applying a system of digital rights management for this purpose.

Metadata Creation

The ability to find works of interest in large libraries is directly related to how well they are catalogued. While cataloguing electronic works digitised from a libraries' existing holding may be as simple as copying moving a record for the print to the electronic item, with complex and born-digital works require substantially more effort. While full text search can be used for some searches, there are many common catalog searches which can't be performed using full text, including:

- finding texts which are the translation of other texts
- linking texts published under pseudonyms to the real author (Samuel Clemens and Mark Twain, for example)

- differentiating non-fiction from parody (The Onion from The New York Times, for example)

ELECTRONIC LIBRARY

Unique Attributes

The Electronic Library is devoted to the applications and implications of new technology, automation, digitisation, the Internet, user interfaces, and networks in all types of libraries, information centres and museums throughout the world as well as the development of software and hardware for such applications. It provides a vehicle for the latest research and ongoing developments in today's digital library and information environments in different countries, and offers practical advice, useful information and descriptions of specific applications around the globe.

Key Benefits

Subscribers enjoy access to:

- International contributions
- Comment on existing and developing systems and technologies
- First hand user experience of techniques and applications
- Practical information on the application of digital technology
- Analysis of underlying trends and their likely effects

Coverage

The Electronic Library covers a broad range of topics including:

- Libraries and the web
- The digital library
- Software and hardware developments
- Library networking and automation – integrated library systems, OPACs
- User interfaces – web usability
- Internet access and use
- E-books and e-journals
- E-governance and e-readiness
- Online and distance learning

Key Journal Audiences

- Senior Library Managers
- Collection Development Officers
- Acquisitions Librarians
- Reference Librarians

The Electronic Library is indexed and abstracted in:

- CINAHL
- Computer Science Index
- Current Awareness Abstracts
- Current Contents/Social and Behavioral Sciences
- Emerald Management Reviews
- The Informed Librarian
- Information Management & Technology Abstracts
- Information Science & Technology Abstracts
- INSPEC (Electrical & Electronics Abstracts)
- Internet and Personal Computing Abstracts
- ISI Alerting Services
- Journal Citation Reports/Social Sciences Edition
- Library and Information Science Abstracts
- Library, Information Science and Technology Abstracts
- Scopus
- Social Sciences Citation Index
- Social SciSearch
- Referativnyi Zhurnal
- Compendex
- Paperchen (CPX)
- Library Literature and Information Science
- zetoc

VIRTUAL LIBRARY

"*Virtual reality* (VR) is an environment that is simulated by a computer.

Most virtual reality environments are primarily visual experiences, displayed either on a computer screen or through special stereoscopic displays, but some simulations include additional sensory information, such as sound through speakers or headphones. Some advanced and experimental systems have included limited tactile feedback." Given this definition of VR a virtual library could be a library environment simulated by a computer. An example is the Book House System developed by Annelise Mark Pejtersen.

Another definition of a virtual library is synonymous with a digital library:

Virtual Library *means library without walls. The resources are available in digital format, there is no paper, microforms etc. The resources are locally held or accessed through computer networks.*

The World Wide Web Virtual Library *was the first index of content on the World Wide Web. It was started by Tim Berners-Lee, the creator of HTML and the Web itself, in 1991 at CERN in Geneva.*

ERNET (EDUCATION AND RESEARCH NETWORK)

ERNET (Education and Research Network) has made a significant contribution to the emergence of networking in the country. It practically brought the Internet to India and has built up national capabilities in the area of net-working, especially in protocol software engineering. It has not only succeeded in building a large network that provides various facilities to the intellectual segment of Indian society—the research and education community, it has over the years become a trendsetter in the field of networking. UNDP has lauded ERNET as one of the most successful programmes it has funded. The Government of India has committed itself to further strengthen the project by including it in the 9th Plan with the allocation of funds and by creation of a new organizational set-up in the form of a society. The science community of the country has also recognized ERNET's contribution—both for infrastructure services as well as for R&D. The Scientific Advisory Committee to the Cabinet has adopted ERNET as the platform for launching an S&T network in the country.

How it Began?

ERNET was initiated in 1986 by the Department of Electronics (DoE), with funding support from the Government of India and United Nations Development Programme (UNDP), involving eight premier institutions as participating agencies—NCST (National Centre for Software Technology) Bombay, IISc (Indian Institute of Science) Bangalore, five IITs (Indian Institutes of Technology) at Delhi, Bombay, Kanpur, Kharagpur and Madras, and the DoE, New Delhi. ERNET began as a multi protocol network with both the TCP/IP and the OSI-IP protocol stacks running over the leased-line portion of the backbone. Since 1995,however, almost all traffic is carried over TCP/IP.

The Objectives of ERNET Indfia

ERNET operations, i.e. providing state-of-the-art communication infrastructure and services to Academic and research institutions, government organisations, NGOs, private sector R&D organizations, and various other non-commercial organisations;

Research and development;

Training and Consultancy;

Content development.

Achievements

Foundation of national capability building in the area of computer networking laid through:

Setting up of a chain of core groups at the participating agencies with a minimal set of lab facilities and creation of skilled manpower to carry out R&D.

Generating man power at different levels.

Making the world of standards (TCP/IP, OSI etc.) well understood.

Providing an insight into emerging issues such as ATM networks, networked multi-media, and information infrastructure.

Network infrastructure and services set up, including:

Installation, maintenance and operation of large Campus LANs.

Design, commissioning and testing of SATWAN hub and the installation of VSATs.

Seamless interconnection of LAN-WAN segments, and multi-protocol capability provided.

Provision of the whole range of Internet services.

Deployment of TDM/TDMA based VSAT network for Internet access.

DELNET

DELNET was started at the India International Centre Library in January 1988 and was registered as a society in 1992. It was initially supported by the National Information System for Science and Technology (NISSAT), Department of Scientific and Industrial Reseach, Government of India. It was subsequently supported by the National Informatics Centre, Department of Information Technology, Ministry of Communications and Information Technology, Government of India and The Ministry of Culture, Government of India.

DELNET has been established with the prime objective of promoting resource sharing among the libraries through the development of a network of libraries. It aims to collect, store, and disseminate information besides offering computerised services to users, to coordinate efforts for suitable collection development and also to reduce unnecessary duplication wherever possible.

INFLIBNET

Information and Library Network (INFLIBNET) Centre is an Autonomous Inter-University Centre (IUC) of University Grants Commission, Government of India, involved in creating infrastructure for sharing of library and information resources and services among academic and research institutions. INFLIBNET works collaboratively with Indian university libraries to shape the future of the academic libraries in the evolving information environment.

Introduction

Information and Library Network (INFLIBNET) Centre is an autonomous Inter-University Centre of the University Grants Commission (UGC) of India. It is a major National Programme initiated by the UGC in 1991 with its Head Quarters at Gujarat University Campus, Ahmedabad. Initially started as a project under the IUCAA, it became an independent Inter-University Centre in 1996.

INFLIBNET is involved in modernizing university libraries in India and connecting them as well as information centres in the country through a nation-wide high speed data network using the state-of-art technologies for the optimum utilization of information. INFLIBNET is set out to be a major player in promoting scholarly communication among academicians and researchers in India

Objectives

The primary objectives of INFLIBNET are:

To promote and establish communication facilities to improve capability in information transfer and access, that provide support to scholarship, learning, research and academic pursuit through cooperation and involvement of agencies concerned.

To establish INFLIBNET: Information and Library Network a computer communication network for linking libraries and information centres in universities, deemed to be universities, colleges, UGC information centres, institutions of national importance and R & D institutions, etc. avoiding duplication of efforts.

Functions

In order to fulfil the broad objectives, INFLIBNET will do the following:

Promote and implement computerisation of operations and services in the libraries and information centres of the country, following a uniform standard.

Evolve standards and uniform guidelines in techniques, methods, procedures, computer hardware and software, services and promote their adoption in actual practice by all libraries, in order to facilitate pooling, sharing and exchange of information towards optimal use of resources and facilities.

Evolve a national network interconnecting various libraries and information centres in the country and to improve capability in information handling and service. Provide reliable access to document collection of libraries by creating on-line union catalogue of serials, theses/dissertations, books, monographs and non-book materials (manuscripts, audio-visuals, computer data, multimedia, etc.) in various libraries in India.

Provide access to bibliographic information sources with citations, abstracts etc. through indigenously created databases of the Sectoral Information Centres of NISSAT, UGC Information Centres, City Networks and such others and by establishing gateways for on-line accessing of national and international databases held by national and international information networks and centres respectively.

Develop new methods and techniques for archival of valuable information available as manuscripts and information documents in different Indian languages, in the form of digital images using high density storage media. Optimise information resource utilization through shared cataloguing, inter-library loan service, catalogue production, collection development and thus avoiding duplication in acquisition to the extent possible.

Enable the users dispersed all over the country, irrespective of location and distance, to have access to information regarding serials, theses/ dissertations, books, monographs and non-book materials by locating the sources wherefrom available and to obtain it through the facilities of INFLIBNET and union catalogue of documents. Create databases of projects, institutions, specialists, etc. for providing on-line information service. Encourage co-operation among libraries, documentation centres and information centres in the country, so that the resources can be pooled for the benefit of helping the weaker resource centres by stronger ones.

Train and develop human resources in the field of computerized library operations and networking to establish, manage and sustain INFLIBNET. Facilitate academic communication amongst scientists, engineers, social scientists, academics, faculties, researchers and students through electronic mail, file transfer, computer/audio/video conferencing, etc.

Undertake system design and studies in the field of communications, computer networking, information handling and data management. Establish appropriate control and monitoring system for the communication network and organize maintenance. Collaborate with institutions, libraries, information centres and other organisations in India and abroad in the field relevant to the objectives of the centre. Create and promote R&D and other facilities and technical positions for realizing the objectives of the centre. Generate revenue by providing consultancies and information services. Do all other such things as may be necessary, incidental or conducive to the attainment of all or any of the above objectives.

DOCUMENTATION CENTRE

A big library like NUEPA Library and Documentation Centre are situated in a building of the University covering 750 sq. meter of carpet area of three floors. It has a wide collection of more than 53,500 volumes on educational planning and management including books, documents, government publications, annual reports, project reports, UNESCO, International Institute of Educational Planning (IIEP), World Bank and International Monetary Fund (IMF) publications. It has about 4,141 bound volumes of journals. In addition, the library has audio-visual facilities containing about 380 items of non-book material such as audio cassettes, video cassettes, films, micro films, microfiches and CD-ROMs on education and its allied disciplines. Users can view video films from the library collection in audio-visual room. The library subscribes to more than 250 journals and magazines both national and international in the core area of education, planning and management.

NUEPA's Documentation Centre comprises of a unique collection of the central and state governments' publications such as Census of India, State Census Reports, State Gazetteers, Statistical Handbooks of States, All India Educational Surveys, Economic Survey, State Economic Surveys, State Educational Plans, Five-Year Plans, NUEPA Research Studies, NUEPA Occasional Paper Series, NUEPA Training Programme Reports, Annual

Reports of various ministries, International Institute of Educational Planning (IIEP), Paris. Moreover, it holds a rich collection of theses and dissertations on International Diploma in Educational Planning and Administration (IDEPA) and Diploma in Educational Planning and Administration (DEPA). Documentation Centre subscribes to 25 national and regional newspapers and maintains the press clippings for the use of faculty and other users.

It has computerized all its operations by using an integrated software LibSys 4.0. Moreover, the Library and Documentation Centre are equipped with electronic databases like Educational Resources and Information Centre (ERIC), Census of India and Internet facilities. The Library and Documentation Centre have a membership of DELNET (Developing Library Network) to promote the sharing of resources at national and international level.

Moreover, the Library and Documentation Centre have developed an online library that provides access to more than 200 full-text Indian and foreign journals, national and international indexing databases, current contents of periodicals, newspapers and full-text reports both national and international.

It has air-conditioned facility, which provides conducive environment for the readers of the library and documentation centre. The Library and Documentation Centre have the reading-cum reference room that having the capacity of more than 75 readers on three floors. It meets the information needs of faculty, researchers and participants of workshops, seminars and training programmes conducted by NUEPA time to time.

NASSDOC

National Social Science Documentation Centre (NASSDOC), was established in 1969 as a Division of the ICSSR with the objective to provide library and information support services to researchers in social sciences; those working in academic institutions, autonomous research organizations, policy making, planning and research units of government departments, business and industry etc. NASSDOC also provides guidance to libraies of ICSSR Regional Centres and ICSSR supported Research Institutes.

Facilities Available at NASSDOC

- Documentation Library and Reference Service;
- Collection of unpublished doctoral dissertations, research project reports, current and old volumes of social science journals of Indian and foreign origin;

- Literature Search Service from printed and digital databases, i.e CD-ROMS, floppies, online database etc.,
- Compilation of short bibliographies on request;
- Study grant to doctoral students for collection of research material from various libraries located in different parts of India;
- Financial assistance is provided for taking up bibliographical and documentation projects;
- Document Delivery Service is provided by procuring books and journals on inter-library loan or by photocopying the documents;
- Short-term training courses are organized for the research scholars, social scientists, librarians and IT professionals to acquaint them with the latest information and communication technology;and
- Cyber Cafe, to facilitate access to internet resources on social sciences.

INSDOC

Indian National Scientific Documentation Centre (INSDOC) is a premier organization dealing with library, documentation and information science, technology, services and systems. It is a national laboratory under the Council of Scientific and Industrial Research (CSIR) providing information and documentation services both at the national and the international level. INSDOC's activities fall under five broad categories:

1. Services, Products and Publications
2. Projects in Competency Areas
3. National Information Resource
4. Education and Training
5. International Collaboration

Since its inception in 1952, INSDOC has been providing information services that aim at fulfilling the information needs of researchers and scientists in the country. Over the years, INSDOC has designed several information products and services for the corporate and business sector as well. Keeping pace with technological developments, new information products are being brought out on CD-ROMs and floppies and many services are being offered on networks like the Internet.

INSDOC's competency areas include: library automation, library networks, computer networking, electronic libraries, CD-ROM networking, design and development of databases, access to international information sources, on-line system, feasibility studies, and design, establishment and operational management of library-cum-information centres.

INSDOC houses the National Science Library that acts as a major information resource centre in the country in the area of science and technology and a strong reference collection in general S&T aspects. It receives over 3,320 periodicals both Indian and foreign. A significant number of these periodicals are received in electronic form in CD-ROMs. An Electronic Library Division is set up with facilities to access information from CD-ROMs.

INSDOC has a strong academic and training programme. As part of the academic programme INSDOC offers a Master's level programme in Information Science called Associateship in Information Science. INSDOC also conducts regular short-term courses and attachment training programmes on various topics, including the application of computers and information technology in the field of library, documentation and information. To support its academic and training programme, INSDOC has set up an information technology laboratory which is equipped with the state of the art computer and networking facilities to ensure high quality education and training to the students.

INSDOC works closely with counterpart institutions in other countries to bring about global information exchange. INSDOC is associated with the activities of International Federation for Information and Documentation (FID), International Federation of Library Associations(IFLA) and the Documentation Centre of the South Asian Association for Regional Co-operation(SAARC).

Wide dissemination of S&T information is an important aim of INSDOC. For this purpose, it has a network of regional centres located at Bangalore, Kolkata and Chennai to provide information services in these regions. In addition, INSDOC's services are available through Communications Research Consultants, Kolkata for the eastern and north-eastern regions of the country.

A team of about 300 personnel comprising scientific, technical and administrative staff handling the programmes of INSDOC. Over 120 persons of the staff are graduates or post-graduates in science, engineering or computers. Many of them have specialized in Library, Documentation of Information Science.

Objectives

- To meet the information needs of scientific research organisations, universities, government establishment, industries and individuals.

- To harness information technology applications in information management with particular reference to modernising libraries and information centres.
- To act as a single point access for science and technology information generated in India.
- To develop human resources in the areas of library, documentation and information science, technology, management, systems, services, products and marketing.
- To act as a facilitator in furthering economic, social, industrial, scientific and commercial development by providing timely access to relevant and accurate information.
- To collaborate with international information agencies to evolve as an integral part of the globalisation process in the field of information and documentation.

INTERNET

The Internet is a global network of interconnected computers, enabling users to share information along multiple channels. Typically, a computer that connects to the Internet can access information from a vast array of available servers and other computers by moving information from them to the computer's local memory. The same connection allows that computer to send information to servers on the network; that information is in turn accessed and potentially modified by a variety of other interconnected computers. A majority of widely accessible information on the Internet consists of inter-linked hypertext documents and other resources of the World Wide Web (www). Computer users typically manage sent and received information with web browsers; other software for users' interface with computer networks includes specialized programmes for electronic mail, online chat, file transfer and file sharing.

The movement of information in the Internet is achieved via a system of interconnected computer networks that share data by packet switching using the standardized Internet Protocol Suite (TCP/IP). It is a "network of networks" that consists of millions of private and public, academic, business, and government networks of local to global scope that are linked by copper wires, fiber-optic cables, wireless connections, and other technologies.

WWW

The World Wide Web (commonly abbreviated as "the Web") is a system of interlinked hypertext documents accessed via the Internet. With a Web browser, one can view Web pages that may contain text, images, videos, and other multimedia and navigate between them using hyperlinks. Using concepts from earlier hypertext systems, the World Wide Web was started in 1989 by the English physicist Sir Tim Berners-Lee, now the Director of the World Wide Web Consortium, and later by Robert Cailliau, a Belgian computer scientist, while both were working at CERN in Geneva, Switzerland. In 1990, they proposed building a "web of nodes" storing "hypertext pages" viewed by "browsers" on a network, and released that web in December.

Connected by the existing Internet, other websites were created, around the world, adding international standards for domain names and the HTML language. Since then, Berners-Lee has played an active role in guiding the development of Web standards (such as the markup languages in which Web pages are composed), and in recent years has advocated his vision of a Semantic Web.

The World Wide Web enabled the spread of information over the Internet through an easy-to-use and flexible format. It thus played an important role in popularizing use of the Internet. Although the two terms are sometimes conflated in popular use, *World Wide Web* is not synonymous with *Internet*. The Web is an application built on top of the Internet.

History

The underlying ideas of the Web can be traced as far back as 1980, when, at CERN in Switzerland, Sir Tim Berners-Lee built ENQUIRE (a reference to *Enquire Within Upon Everything*, a book he recalled from his youth). While it was rather different from the system in use today, it contained many of the same core ideas (and even some of the ideas of Berners-Lee's next project after the World Wide Web, the Semantic Web).

In March 1989, Berners-Lee wrote a proposal which referenced ENQUIRE and described a more elaborate information management system. With help from Robert Cailliau, he published a more formal proposal (on November 12, 1990) to build a "Hypertext project" called "WorldWideWeb" (one word, also "W3") as a "web of nodes" with "hypertext documents" to store data. That data would be viewed in "hypertext pages" (webpages) by various "browsers" (line-mode or full-screen) on the computer network, using an "access protocol" connecting the "Internet and DECnet protocol worlds".

The proposal had been modeled after EBT's (Electronic Book Technology, a spin-off from the Institute for Research in Information and Scholarship at Brown University) Dynatext SGML reader that CERN had licensed. The Dynatext system, although technically advanced (a key player in the extension of SGML ISO 8879:1986 to Hypermedia within HyTime), was considered too expensive and with an inappropriate licensing policy for general HEP (High Energy Physics) community use: a fee for each document and each time a document was changed.

A NeXT Computer was used by Berners-Lee as the world's first Web server and also to write the first Web browser, WorldWideWeb, in 1990. By Christmas 1990, Berners-Lee had built all the tools necessary for a working Web: the first Web browser (which was a Web editor as well), the first Web server, and the first Web pages which described the project itself.

On August 6, 1991, he posted a short summary of the World Wide Web project on the alt.hypertext newsgroup. This date also marked the debut of the Web as a publicly available service on the Internet.

The first server outside Europe was set up at SLAC in December 1991.

The crucial underlying concept of hypertext originated with older projects from the 1960s, such as the Hypertext Editing System (HES) at Brown University—among others Ted Nelson and Andries van Dam—Ted Nelson's Project Xanadu and Douglas Engelbart's oN-Line System (NLS). Both Nelson and Engelbart were in turn inspired by Vannevar Bush's microfilm-based "memex," which was described in the 1945 essay "As We May Think".

Berners-Lee's breakthrough was to marry hypertext to the Internet. In his book *Weaving The Web*, he explains that he had repeatedly suggested that a marriage between the two technologies was possible to members of *both* technical communities, but when no one took up his invitation, he finally tackled the project himself. In the process, he developed a system of globally unique identifiers for resources on the Web and elsewhere: the Uniform Resource Identifier.

The World Wide Web had a number of differences from other hypertext systems that were then available. The Web required only unidirectional links rather than bidirectional ones. This made it possible for someone to link to another resource without action by the owner of that resource. It also significantly reduced the difficulty of implementing Web servers and browsers (in comparison to earlier systems), but in turn presented the chronic problem of link rot. Unlike predecessors such as HyperCard, the World Wide Web was non-proprietary, making it possible to develop servers and clients independently and to add extensions without licensing restrictions.

On April 30, 1993, CERN announced that the World Wide Web would be free to anyone, with no fees due. Coming two months after the announcement that the Gopher (protocol) protocol was no longer free to use, this produced a rapid shift away from Gopher and towards the Web. An early popular Web browser was ViolaWWW, which was based upon HyperCard.

Scholars generally agree that a turning point for the World Wide Web began with the introduction of the Mosaic Web browser in 1993, a graphical browser developed by a team at the National Center for Supercomputing Applications at the University of Illinois at Urbana-Champaign (NCSA-UIUC), led by Marc Andreessen. Funding for Mosaic came from the US. *High-Performance Computing and Communications Initiative*, a funding programme initiated by the *High Performance Computing and Communication Act of 1991*, one of several computing developments initiated by US Senator Al Gore. Prior to the release of Mosaic, graphics were not commonly mixed with text in Web pages, and its popularity was less than older protocols in use over the Internet, such as Gopher and Wide Area Information Servers (WAIS). Mosaic's graphical user interface allowed the Web to become, by far, the most popular Internet protocol.

The World Wide Web Consortium (W3C) was founded by Tim Berners-Lee after he left the European Organization for Nuclear Research (CERN) in October, 1994. It was founded at the Massachusetts Institute of Technology Laboratory for Computer Science (MIT/LCS) with support from the Defense Advanced Research Projects Agency (DARPA)—which had pioneered the Internet—and the European Commission.

INTERNET FOR TEACHER EDUCATORS

More than eight out of ten teachers (84 percent) believe that computers and access to the Internet improve the quality of education, according to a survey by education technology nonprofit NetDay, and 75 percent of teachers said the Internet is an important tool for finding new resources to meet new standards.

Two-thirds of teachers, however, agree the Internet is not well integrated into their classrooms and only 26 percent of them feel pressure to use it in learning activities.

Net Day also found that nearly every teacher has access to the Internet at his or her school and 80 percent of classrooms have computers that are online. Seventy-seven percent of teachers agree that teachers without Internet access in the classroom are at a disadvantage.

Teachers cite multiple uses for the Internet, but most primarily see its potential as a research tool, and say it has not changed the way they teach.

Forty-eight percent of teachers say the Internet has become an important tool for teaching over the last two years, yet across every demographic group of teachers, half or more use the Internet at school for less than 30 minutes a day.

Other findings from NetDay's survey include:

- 78 percent of teachers cited lack of time as the number one reason for not logging on to the Internet
- 46 to 50 percent list lack of equipment, speed of access or lack of technical support as hindering their use of online resources
- 44 percent of teachers cite lack of knowledge about how to use the Internet, and 32 percent list lack of leadership from the principal or administrators as reasons for not logging on.

Net Day's research suggests the critical challenge ahead is to find ways to help teachers go beyond the research functions of the Internet. Most teachers do not use the Internet in daily activities such as communication with students, parents and other teachers, or for organizational activities. Sixty-seven percent of teachers believe the Internet is not well integrated into their classroom. Those teachers most likely to use the Internet and say it is well integrated into their classrooms are sixth through eighth grade teachers.

Less than half of teachers use the Internet when building new lessons or engaging in classroom projects (42 percent), and an even greater number (62 percent) do not update lesson plans with material found online. Teachers in private and parochial schools engage in technology integration more often than teachers in public schools. Fifty-two percent of private and parochial teachers use the Internet for class projects and for updating lesson plans; compared to 40 percent of public school teachers who use the Internet for these activities.

Nearly three-quarters (73 percent) of teachers say they do not feel pressure to use the Internet in classroom instruction or the curriculum.n Of those teachers who reported feeling pressure, 54 percent say district administrators, colleagues and peers are the source of that pressure. Only 10 percent say the pressure comes from principals. The lack of pressure that teachers feel from principals suggests the need for more guidance to help principals learn how to best utilize technology to support education. In addition, learning how to provide leadership on educational technology is a new development area for many principals.

Internet Training and Support for Teachers

How do teachers prepare to guide their students wisely and effectively in using the Internet, a medium to which they are just gaining access? Teachers have received little preparatory support for using computers as they exist today. Of 219 teachers consulted in a recent Canadian needs assessment (McLeod, 1995), 118 teachers believed they required more computer instruction. Training has often focused primarily on technical matters and needs to deal as well with pedagogical concerns (Bennett, 1993; Siegel, 1995). An integrated support programme using carefully trained peer mentors is described by MacArthur, Pilato *et al.* (1995). A well-rounded programme of preparation is matched to school resources and curriculum and includes technical and pedagogical training, examining what other teachers have done, ready access to guide materials, opportunities for peer collaboration, and ongoing support from experienced classroom teachers, librarians, support staff, and principals.

Training, support, and professional development activities only have value when the technical infrastructure is in place. Ministries of education and school boards are trying to install the resources needed for Internet use at the same time that education budgets in many provinces are being reduced. Fournier and MacKinnon (1994) suggest that one new, fully networked computer be provided for each four students every three years—a goal far beyond the current reach of most school boards—but the authors acknowledge that simply having networked computers in place and working well will not ensure proper use. Once teachers are aware of the potential of the Internet, they are keen to include its use in their repertoire of teaching techniques, but they do not have time to mess about unproductively without guidance. They need enough equipment to provide convenient access, and they need support that is well adapted to their teaching situation.

Often the most effective training and support comes from teachers themselves. About one-third of the teachers consulted in McLeod's study (1995) indicated that they were teaching computer skills to their colleagues. The new medium can be of considerable service to teachers in seeking and offering peer support (Bascia, 1994, 1995). Using e-mail and computer conference systems, teachers request information and guidance from distant and often unknown colleagues and publish resources and notes on their experience. In this way, they take initiative and responsibility for their own professional development. In Ontario, approximately 40,000 of the province's 130,000 teachers have accounts on the Education Network of Ontario (1995), part of an initiative of the Ontario Teachers Federation called "Creating a Culture of Change" (Bascia, 1994, 1995). In Newfoundland nearly all teachers have access to STEM~Net, "a high-quality computer network for educators in Newfoundland and Labrador... to support teaching, curriculum and professional development activities related to their work" (TILE, 1994). Canada's SchoolNet is encouraging peer support through a moderated list, inclass@schoolnet.carleton.ca, and through the School Net Grass Roots Project, which offers modest funding in exchange for reports of successful telecommunications-based learning projects. All of these programmes and systems help teachers help themselves in exchanging information, in questioning underlying assumptions, and in realigning values and practice.

In addition to knowing how to use Internet resources and knowing what is available, teachers need to figure out how to organize the classroom depending on the resources available, how to plan, develop, undertake, and assess telecommunications-based activities and projects, how to justify their work to parents and the public, and how to collaborate on all of this with colleagues. Much of this they can figure out on their own once they have initial support and guidance, based on well-developed ministry and board policy. Excellent guides have been written by experienced teachers on planning, organizing, and conducting telecommunications-based projects in schools (Walker, 1994; Andres & Rogers, 1995). Warren (1995) advises paying attention to the aim, rationale, context, objectives, participant requirements, time line, student assessment and project evaluation, contact information, logistics, and follow-up. Little work has been done in the area of assessment and evaluation of telecommunications-based learning; the author is supervising an M.Ed. thesis that is a case study on such work.

In faculties of education, where access to Internet resources is provided to all teacher candidates, it is possible, with considerable effort, to establish habits of using the new media. At York University, all teacher candidates are given access to a computer conference system which they use extensively for peer-moderated discussion of the practicum. That discussion spills over into course work and helps to keep the whole B.Ed. programme moving ahead (Crossland & Egnatoff, 1996). In some teacher education programmes, teacher candidates are able to provide leadership in the use of computers during their practicum simply because they have had more opportunity to work with computers. Faculties are also working diligently to use telecommunications to support close collaboration with schools in the preparation of new teachers. These efforts are the beginning of a continuum of professional development for both new and experienced teachers, including faculty instructors themselves.

A recent survey report (Crossland & Egnatoff, 1996), provides information on the availability, organization, content, and scope of various Canadian teacher professional development programmes emphasizing telecommunications and information technology. In some cases, programmes of support are related to work on distance education, for which instructors need special preparation. The British Columbia Open Learning Agency has programmes that include a three-day residential training programme coupled with on-site or telecommunications-based support. The Open Learning Agency views professional development as the teacher's responsibility and staff development and training the responsibility of the organization. Some provinces have major networks designed to increase communication and peer-mediated professional development and support. The survey of such programmes was conducted to set in context a particular pilot programme, the SchoolNet Support Teachers Pilot Project.

The SchoolNet Support Teachers Pilot Project

The SchoolNet Support Teachers Pilot Project was a collaborative experiment in supporting teachers wishing to enrich their students' learning through the use of new tele-communications tools and resources (Egnatoff, 1996). The project began in September 1995 as a four-month pilot to provide training and professional development for interested teachers. The sponsors—SchoolNet and six school boards—extended the project for the entire 1995-96 school year.

The project employed a "SchoolNet Support Teacher" in each of six urban-region school boards of which two were francophone and four anglophone, and three were public and three Roman Catholic separate. These boards varied greatly in size, computer resources, and support, but were all highly committed to making the project work well. The project had four distinguishing characteristics:

- Most of the teacher training—technical and pedagogical—in the project was done by certified teachers;
- The SchoolNet Support Teachers were newly certified teachers, having just graduated from a faculty of education;
- Most of the training was done on site, in the schools, during the school day, and was related directly to the work of the teachers;
- The support teachers worked in close cooperation with board administrative personnel to expand or establish sustainable on-site professional development programmes in keeping with board plans for the educational use of telecommunications.

For the work to be sustained, it was felt that the project needed to address four areas of concern:

- development of teacher knowledge, skills, and attitudes;
- curriculum integration;

- school-level site-based planning; and
- board-level planning.

The SchoolNet Support Teachers were expected to deal primarily with the first three areas of concern. Board-wide matters were to be a concern for the project team to address as a whole, with the guidance of PARTNERS, an organization contracted as project facilitator.

The entire project had three objectives:

- to establish a pilot project in an urban region having several school boards;
- to evaluate the effectiveness of the project; and
- to promote similar projects nationally.

The work of the support teachers included many tasks of the sort normally done by coordinators, special assignment teachers, and resource teachers. One of the SchoolNet Support Teachers conducted a detailed survey of computer resources, use, knowledge, and needs which the board used to assess and reconsider its resource allocation. With varying emphasis, all support teachers introduced teachers—in hands-on workshops, presentations, and small-group or individual tutorials—to the Internet and to various ways of working on it; developed guides to Internet use; developed acceptable use policies; taught in the classroom along with the regular classroom teachers; trained teachers who would later train their peers; started teachers and classes on Internet projects; collaborated across boards to share resources; made presentations to parents, board officials, and trustees to bring the work into focus and to assure continuing support; and provided reports for the author's evaluation study.

Findings from the evaluation study of the first half of the project attest to its success. The success was due in part to the work of PARTNERS, a coordinating agency that drew together all the stakeholders to plan and coordinate the work and that ensured that the results were well known to the public and to those who set and implement board policy. The success was due in equal measure to the high degree of collaboration of teachers, principals, coordinators, SchoolNet staff, and, most important, the SchoolNet Support Teachers themselves.

The promotion phase of the project began just prior to the writing of this paper. Organizers of a related project in Alberta that began in the spring of 1996 studied the SchoolNet Support Teachers Pilot Project and adapted its approach. Several other variations are under development elsewhere in Canada.

Findings of the Evaluation Study

Partnership was a key to the success of the project. The project grew out of the agenda of the Training, Research, and Evaluation committee of Canada's SchoolNet National Advisory Board, which represents government, business, and educational stakeholders. PARTNERS invited the boards to collaborate and worked behind the scenes to ensure that the project ran smoothly at all stages.

The SchoolNet Support Teachers began with little specialized training, but quickly learned on the job, took initiative, and were very soon providing strong leadership. Collaboration emerged naturally within a few weeks of startup, taking the form of sharing resource documents, discussing solutions to common problems, and sharing accomplishments and approaches in bimonthly meetings.

The coordinators and support teachers worked very well together, often learning from and with each other, and working side by side. Having indefinite plans turned out to be an advantage because it required the support teachers to take ownership of their work. Even though the support teachers quickly became quite independent, they nevertheless kept the coordinators well-informed of the work. Several coordinators were in attendance at any given project meeting. The support teachers worked very much for the board, with only minimal direction or guidance from SchoolNet staff.

The support teachers conducted their own research and kept their own records of teacher progress according to the needs of the boards. Report writing helped them see what they had accomplished and sharing those reports gave them a sense of being part of an enterprise whose significance went beyond the boundaries of the individual boards. In the words of one superintendent, the support teachers helped get the board vision "over the mountain" from board office to classroom.

Initially, it was expected that after a few weeks of training and support, some teachers would be ready to use telecommunications as part of curriculum projects, a strong wish of the SchoolNet staff. For most participants, a focus on projects had to be postponed until the infrastructure was more secure and until basic skills and knowledge were more highly developed. Project work was more evident in the second term.

The support teachers found that the teachers they encountered were keen to use telecommunications when infrastructure development, training, and support were well coordinated. In one board especially, knowing that new equipment was coming and that the network would be connected was a strong motivator. Participating teachers all agreed that it was very important to have support from a qualified teacher when it came to working with classes and planning learning activities. Teachers also agreed on the value of sustained support rather than isolated workshops.

Many telecommunications activities worked well because the support teachers, like all dedicated teachers, did a lot of work behind the scenes. This included preparing guide materials for teachers, editing HTML documents produced by students, arranging for Internet access services, assisting with software installation and LAN setup, and keeping up an email dialogue with teachers and students.

Evidence of sustainability began to appear towards the end of the second month, even though it seemed clear that the boards would not be able to support a SchoolNet Support Teacher on their own, especially given impending layoffs due to government cutbacks. The project very quickly took on a life of its own. Once the basic design was established in consultation with the partners, all the players pulled their weight and did their own work. Because board leaders were involved, and because the support teachers were self-starters, the researchers were able very quickly to focus on the research without worrying about project management or animation. Many expectations were realized without deliberate planning. That happened in large measure because there was a commonly understood purpose.

ONLINE SEARCH OF TEACHER EDUCATION DATABASE

Training Provided by Online Training Directory Online Research Techniques is a seven day online course.

This course will help you develop online research skills and gain knowledge on Grolier Online and GaleNet resources.

This course is offered by a State Accredited University and offers State Board Continuing Education credits for Michigan teachers.? If you are located in a state other than Michigan, please check to see if your State Board will honour the Continuing Education Credit.? The course provider will be happy to provide you with appropriate documentation.

This course is designed for K12 teachers but the concepts and examples will translate for any online course developer.

SEARCH ENGINES

A Web search engine is a tool designed to search for information on the World Wide Web. The search results are usually presented in a list and are commonly called *hits*. The information may consist of web pages, images, information and other types of files. Some search engines also mine data available in newsbooks, databases, or open directories. Unlike Web directories, which are maintained by human editors, search engines operate algorithmically or are a mixture of algorithmic and human input.

History

Before there were web search engines there was a complete list of all webservers. The list was edited by Tim Berners-Lee and hosted on the CERN webserver. One historical snapshot from 1992 remains. As more and more webservers went online the central list could not keep up. On the NCSA Site new servers were announced under the title "What's New!" but no complete listing existed any more.

The very first tool used for searching on the (pre-web) Internet was Archie. The name stands for "archive" without the "v." It was created in 1990 by Alan Emtage, a student at McGill University in Montreal. The programme downloaded the directory listings of all the files located on public anonymous FTP (File Transfer Protocol) sites, creating a searchable database of file names; however, Archie did not index the contents of these sites.

The rise of Gopher (created in 1991 by Mark McCahill at the University of Minnesota) led to two new search programmes, Veronica and Jughead. Like Archie, they searched the file names and titles stored in Gopher index systems. Veronica (Very Easy Rodent-Oriented Net-wide Index to Computerized Archives) provided a keyword search of most Gopher menu titles in the entire Gopher listings. Jughead (Jonzy's Universal Gopher Hierarchy Excavation and Display) was a tool for obtaining menu information from specific Gopher servers. While the name of the search engine "Archie" was not a reference to the Archie comic book series, "Veronica" and "Jughead" are characters in the series, thus referencing their predecessor.

In June 1993, Matthew Gray, then at MIT, produced what was probably the first web robot, the Perl-based World Wide Web Wanderer, and used it to generate an index called 'Wandex'. The purpose of the Wanderer was to measure the size of the World Wide Web, which it did until late 1995. The search engine Aliweb appeared in November 1993. Aliweb did not use a web robot, but instead depended on being notified by website administrators of the existence at each site of an index file in a particular format.

JumpStation (released in December 1993) used a web robot to find web pages and to build its index, and used a web form as the interface to its query programme. It was thus the first WWW resource-discovery tool to combine the three essential features of a web search engine (crawling, indexing, and searching) as described below. Because of the limited resources available on the platform on which it ran, its indexing and hence searching were limited to the titles and headings found in the web pages the crawler encountered.

One of the first "full text" crawler-based search engines was WebCrawler, which came out in 1994. Unlike its predecessors, it let users search for any word in any webpage, which has become the standard for all major search engines since. It was also the first one to be widely known by the public. Also in 1994 Lycos (which started at Carnegie Mellon University) was launched, and became a major commercial endeavor.

Soon after, many search engines appeared and vied for popularity. These included Magellan, Excite, Infoseek, Inktomi, Northern Light, and AltaVista. Yahoo! was among the most popular ways for people to find web pages of interest, but its search function operated on its web directory, rather than full-text copies of web pages. Information seekers could also browse the directory instead of doing a keyword-based search.

In 1996, Netscape was looking to give a single search engine an exclusive deal to be their featured search engine. There was so much interest that instead a deal was struck with Netscape by 5 of the major search engines, where for $5Million per year each search engine would be in a rotation on the Netscape search engine page. These five engines were: Yahoo!, Magellan, Lycos, Infoseek and Excite.

Search engines were also known as some of the brightest stars in the Internet investing frenzy that occurred in the late 1990s. Several companies entered the market spectacularly, receiving record gains during their initial public offerings. Some have taken down their public search engine, and are marketing enterprise-only editions, such as Northern Light. Many search engine companies were caught up in the dot-com bubble, a speculation-driven market boom that peaked in 1999 and ended in 2001.

Around 2000, the Google search engine rose to prominence. The company achieved better results for many searches with an innovation called PageRank. This iterative algorithm ranks web pages based on the number and PageRank of other web sites and pages that link there, on the premise that good or desirable pages are linked to more than others. Google also maintained a minimalist interface to its search engine. In contrast, many of its competitors embedded a search engine in a web portal.

By 2000, Yahoo was providing search services based on Inktomi's search engine. Yahoo! acquired Inktomi in 2002, and Overture (which owned AlltheWeb and AltaVista) in 2003. Yahoo! switched to Google's search engine until 2004, when it launched its own search engine based on the combined technologies of its acquisitions.

Microsoft first launched MSN Search (since re-branded Live Search) in the fall of 1998 using search results from Inktomi. In early 1999 the site began to display listings from Looksmart blended with results from Inktomi except for a short time in 1999 when results from AltaVista were used instead. In 2004, Microsoft began a transition to its own search technology, powered by its own web crawler (called msnbot).

As of late 2007, Google was by far the most popular Web search engine worldwide. A number of country-specific search engine companies have become prominent; for example Baidu is the most popular search engine in the People's Republic of China.

How Web Search Engines Work?

A search engine operates, in the following order:

1. Web crawling
2. Indexing
3. Searching

Web search engines work by storing information about many web pages, which they retrieve from the WWW itself. These pages are retrieved by a Web crawler (sometimes also known as a spider) — an automated Web browser which follows every link it sees. Exclusions can be made by the use of robots.txt. The contents of each page are then analysed to determine how it should be indexed (for example, words are extracted from the titles, headings, or special fields called meta tags). Data about web pages are stored in an index database for use in later queries. Some search engines, such as Google, store all or part of the source page (referred to as a cache) as well as information about the web pages, whereas others, such as AltaVista, store every word of every page they find.

This cached page always holds the actual search text since it is the one that was actually indexed, so it can be very useful when the content of the current page has been updated and the search terms are no longer in it. This problem might be considered to be a mild form of linkrot, and Google's handling of it increases usability by satisfying user expectations that the search terms will be on the returned webpage. This satisfies the principle of least astonishment since the user normally expects the search terms to be on the returned pages. Increased search relevance makes these cached pages very useful, even beyond the fact that they may contain data that may no longer be available elsewhere.

When a user enters a query into a search engine (typically by using key words), the engine examines its index and provides a listing of best-matching web pages according to its criteria, usually with a short summary containing the document's title and sometimes parts of the text. Most search engines support the use of the boolean operators AND, OR and NOT to further specify the search query. Some search engines provide an advanced feature called proximity search which allows users to define the distance between keywords.

The usefulness of a search engine depends on the relevance of the **result set** it gives back. While there may be millions of web pages that include a particular word or phrase, some pages may be more relevant, popular, or authoritative than others. Most search engines employ methods to rank the results to provide the "best" results first. How a search engine decides which pages are the best matches, and what order the results should be shown in, varies widely from one engine to another. The methods also change over time as Internet usage changes and new techniques evolve.

Most Web search engines are commercial ventures supported by advertising revenue and, as a result, some employ the practice of allowing advertisers to pay money to have their listings ranked higher in search results. Those search engines which do not accept money for their search engine results make money by running search related ads alongside the regular search engine results. The search engines make money every time someone clicks on one of these ads. Revenue in the web search portals industry is projected to grow in 2008 by 13.4 percent, with broadband connections expected to rise by 15.1 percent. Between 2008 and 2012, industry revenue is projected to rise by 56 percent as Internet penetration still has some way to go to reach full saturation in American households. Furthermore, broadband services are projected to account for an ever increasing share of domestic Internet users, rising to 118.7 million by 2012, with an increasing share accounted for by fiber-optic and high speed cable lines.

SEARCH TECHNIQUES

Guidance for getting good results with online searching, whether you are using the library catalogue, research databases, or the web.

- *Keyword searching*
  - How it works
  - Advantages of keyword searching
  - Choosing keywords
  - Combining keywords with connectors
  - Searching for phrases
  - Truncation
  - Common words
- *Subject heading searching*
  - How it works
  - Advantages of subject heading searching
  - Choosing subject headings
- *Natural language searching*
  - How it works
  - Advantages of natural language searching
- *Refining your search strategy*
  - Limit your search results
  - Select different search terms
  - Try a different type of search
  - Try a different resource
  - Ask a librarian for suggestions

Security Search Techniques: Baggage

DVD Format: Searching baggage is far more complex than simply opening it up to see what is inside. Proper practices and procedures need to be followed to comply with the law and to avoid an oversight that might create a security breach or worse, lead to a catastrophe.

The ISPS Code explicitly states that "In liaison with the port facility, the ship should ensure that designated secure areas are established in which inspections and searching of persons, baggage (including carry-on items), personal effects, vehicles and their contents can take place." Security Search Techniques: Baggage examines the most important features of conducting successful searches. The video presents how to prepare for the search, how to conduct a thorough search and how to respond if contraband or prohibited items are discovered.

The first step in a thorough search begins with the establishment of identity and an examination of credentials. The importance of posting a search policy is explored. Coordinating with the port facility and establishing a secure area for searches are shown to be critical elements in the process. Reference is made to the Ship Security Plan as the primary document for appropriate levels of search at various ship security levels. Dealing with unaccompanied baggage is described.

The methods demonstrated in Security Search Techniques: Baggage are based on what is required in the ISPS Code and the expertise of Ravi Shankar, security consultant to some of the largest shipping companies in the world. Security Search Techniques: Baggage allows your crew to see a thorough and careful baggage search, to hear from an industry expert why such care must be taken, and to understand what needs to be done to prevent unauthorized or illegal items from gaining access to your ship.

What you will learn:

- Establishing a secure search area
- The importance of the Ship Security Plan
- What to do with unaccompanied baggage
- Proper response to finding contraband

Search Techniques

Free Text Search: The most simple search involves a free text search. This is based on a word or phrase of your choice appearing anywhere in the source material. Most bibliographic databases have their own individual controlled language which is composed of keywords. These are organized in a structured hierarchy (Thesaurus). This demonstrates the relationship between them, and enables the user to include all the terms that are relevant to their search. The Thesaurus permits a more controlled and detailed search to be undertaken because keywords are used in the indexing of the database.

Boolean Logic

If the only thing you learn about effective searching is how to use Boolean logic, you will not go far wrong. Boolean logic breaks a subject down into concepts and uses "operators" such as:

AND – narrows down a search using a combination of terms

OR – broadens a search by searching for a number of different terms

NOT – narrows down a search by eliminating terms that are not associated with something you are trying to find

For example:

- Salmonella AND eggs will retrieve records that contain both terms
- Salmonella OR eggs will retrieve all records containing a reference to either salmonella or eggs
- Salmonella NOT eggs will retrieve records that contain Salmonella but have no reference to eggs

Boolean logic can be improved by "nesting" which involves the use of parentheses to combine several search requests, for example:

- (Salmonella OR Listeria) AND (chocolate OR eggs) will retrieve records on Salmonella and eggs, Salmonella and chocolate, Listeria and eggs, and Listeria and chocolate.

Not all search engines support Boolean logic but most academic resources (journals, bibliographic databases, reference works) will.

Some search engines will support phrase searching which looks for a specifc term. For example:

- "salmonella in eggs" will only find records with that exact term.

Proximity

Not all search engines recognise proximity operators but a few search engines will have advanced features where proximity searching can be deployed. The most common proximity operator is "NEAR" allowing you to specify two terms that can be found close together.

Wildcards

Wildcards are not supported by all search engines but can be used to represent a character or number of characters. They are useful when you are either not sure how to spell something or when you want to find records with different word endings. Different search engines use different symbols but the most common wildcards are "*" and "?". for example:

- poison* will retrieve all records that include poison, poisons, poisoned or poisoning

- col*r will retrieve all records that contain either colour or colour
- wom*n will retrieve all records that contain either woman or women

Field Searching

Electronic sources of information have a field structure. Not all sources use the same fields. You will therefore need adapt your search accordingly. Field searching is very precise and powerful but not all sources allow you to search in this way

Other Search Tools

Depending on the database or information resource you are using, you may be able to refine your search, save your search, set up search alerts which will run a search for you and email you the results on a regular basis. Search tools and user guides can be found either on your library website or may be made available by the resource provider. These are well worth using in order to get the most out of your searching.

CHAPTER 5

E-journal and Library Systems

INTRODUCTION

Invention of printing machine by Gutenberg in 1452 is one of the revolutions of human knowledge development. Since then all human knowledge and information are easily available through print media in the form of books, journals and other from of documents. But nowadays information generation is growing so fast in various new disciplines that print media can not be able to run so fast in respect of time and cost, place is also the vital problem to the library. At the same time information technology, computer and telecommunication developed tremendously which directly affects the publishing industry and now society are going to the paper less society.

With the rapid development of information technology and the emergence of Internet, multimedia the information sources is now easily available in electronic form. It reached to the people within very less time, less cost and occupied no space compared to today's so-called libraries. They include e-journal, and other e-publishing on data base, reference documents, newspaper, magazines. In addition to these online sources there are thousand of CDROM databases. The CDROM database and online source are collectively referred to as electronic sources of information. Here we will discuss about one item from the electronic publishing, *i.e.* Electronic Journal.

For more than three centuries journal played a central role in the creation and transmission of knowledge, especially in the field of science and technology. We can hardly imagine without the scholarly journal. Nowadays it is changing its shape, media, users and representation remarkably but the basic substance of a journal remains the same – to publish at regular interval the most recent communication notes queries and essays in order to enhance and expand the interchange and sharing the knowledge. But nowadays the paper journal have faced a huge criticism because of peer-review process, increasing cost, lack of selectivity and long publication delay. To overcome these problem journals are now available in electronic form and electronic media.

Definition

There is no standard definition of electronic journal. e-journal sometimes described as "virtual journal" or "paperless journal" or "online journal" etc. Consider first the definition of journal, according to ALA Glossary "a journal is a periodical especially one containing scholarly article and/or disseminating current information on research and development in a particular subject field." If this task is done by electronic media then it may call e-journal. If the content of a journal are produced and stored only in electronic form than it is called e-journal. When the content of a journal produced and stored and scanned in a database and then retrieved though online then same thing is called "online" journal. We may define e-journal in this angle that those journal which published and circulate through electronic media. Some specialist define e-journal as any serial, produced published and distributed nationally and internationally via electronic network such as BITNET, INTERNET.

Devid Pullinger and Brian Schakel wrote in 1990 that an e-journal is " one whose text input may be entered directly by file transfer from a computer or by other transfer mechanism in a machine readable form whose editorial processing is facilitated by a computer and whose articles are thus made available in electronic form to readers".

HISTORY AND DEVELOPMENT

Vannevar Bush first described the "e-Journal" in 1967 as a part of MEMAX proposal. Before that, as per UNESCO report published 1960 the first e-journal was created in the form of a project named "to test networking computers as a means of improving scientific communications". As a result of this project the first e-journal produced in 1980 in the name of MENTAL WORKLOAD. In 1976 the New Jersey Institute of Technology came out with the first prototype e-journal CHIMO-a weekly read only newsletter. PAPERFAIRE was an unreferred e-journal published by EIES (Electronic Information Exchange System). Most of the e-journal came into the picture in 90's decade, popular of them are PSYCOLOQUE edited by Stevan Harnad in 1989. E-JOURNAL published since 1991. By 1992 there was OJCCI (Online Journal of Current Clinical Trials), it was the first peer-reviewed science journal with graphics and completely searchable full text.

Probably Sondak and Schwarz were first published the electronic form of the scholarly journal. At present WWW and Internet help accelerated the activities of e-journal. According to Woodword and McKnight (1995) there are three steps of e-journal like ONLINE, CDROM, Networked journal. Online journal is available through online hosts like DIALOG, BRS etc. CDROM journal is usually full text of individual or collected journals of various subjects. Networked e-journal is based on mailing list-software server computing application including 'gopher' and 'www'. The other way of dissemination of research paper is now available by electronic page lay out. Hypertext and hypermedia formats enable linkages among sections within an article and among articles within the journals and other electronic resources.

How Does it Work? e-journal does the entire communication from authoring and submitting through referring and editing to publishing via computer. The various participants are communicated through a central main framed machine. The users accessed the system either through JANET (Joint Academic Network) or PSTN (Public Switched Telephone Network). Users can move different related articles at the same time using hypertext links and a 'pop-up' windows facilities. Which provides instant access to the bibliographical details of reference without leaving the text. By using CDROM drive, a high resolution (300 dpi) A4 screen and a laser printer a publisher earn a more profit without increasing the price. At least total 219 biochemical journal may digitally scanned and stored only in a single CDROM. Nowadays e-journal arises based on LISTSERV software. In this system a central computer holds a list of subscribers. When a new issue is available the system send a content page and abstracts via e-mail. If the subscriber then request for that article through e-mail article then automatically delivered by the software.

Advantages: An electronic journal provides following advantages:

1. A higher rate of acceptance of article.
2. Increased speed in peer-reviewed and publication process.
3. Possible more acceptance of articles by editors.
4. Lower production and delivery costs.
5. Use of sophisticated searching strategies.
6. Distribution and correspondence not limited by time and geographical boundary.

Future: Paper journal satisfied our need for a long time and till it providing its service to the people. But e-journal access is a new worldwide trend in information society. People enjoyed because of its instant satisfaction of being able to search and retrieve article to their desktop. Many organization offering to access through gateway system like by browsing or keyword etc. Some organization provides pay-per-view option. King (1991) predicts that by the year 2006 we will see a dramatic change in information society. He also feels that print media will continue to exits but will play a different role.

Ann Okerson (1991) also stated that if present trends continues through 1995 the likely result would be bibliographic confusion and chaos for utilities libraries and scholars. And at the end of the century the market for paper and e-journal will be divided equally.

Issues: Though e-journal gives a lot of facilities and it is time saver and least cost yet there are some problems. Till now it is not fully accepted by the scholar society as a pure substitute of printing media. Also they raise some questions about copyright, licensing etc. They raised some questions about if a library subscribes the e-journal do they get only current issues or he have to right to have backrun? Or he should have to pay for that? They raised another question about copyright, *i.e.*, anyone can easily download or manipulate the article which may against the author as well as the publisher interest. Can it be avoidable? The most vital challenges to the librarian are that as anyone can get any kind of information through online or Internet, then, do it any requirement for a library? These are all burning issues and challenges to today's librarian as well as the future library personnel.

Conclusion: On the basis of full text e-journal of 'American Chemical Society' we may conclude that it cannot replace the printed journal. It has to crossed a long way to compete the paper journal in developing countries like India due to a huge obstacle of socio-economic political problems. Also some scholar says that e-journal is a searching tool not a reading tool. At last we can say that libraries in no part of the world can afford to ignore these electronic source. Emergence of these new source has resulted into a change in traditional library. These include collection development, acquisition, cataloguing, users instruction etc. It is inevitable that in the next few years special libraries will be obliged to subscribe e-journal and other e-publishing.

BIBLIOMETRICS OF ELECTRONIC JOURNALS IN INFORMATION SCIENCE

The Internet has rapidly become a global publishing platform, and electronic journals covering a wide range of subject areas are now available. Information science is no exception, and we now find a significant portion of its literature appearing in e-journals. This article presents some bibliometric data on the currently available e-journals in the field and the articles appearing in them.

The first thing one must do in conducting a study of this type is to determine the corpus of journals and define what is meant by an "electronic journal". With the advent of the Internet and World Wide Web, anyone with a home page can be regarded as a publisher, and even simple newsletters published erratically and infrequently might be regarded as "e-journals." At the other end of the publishing spectrum are high quality, rigorously edited, peer-reviewed scholarly publications that are made available on the Web. Some of these electronic publications replicate existing print publications; others exist only in electronic form.

For the purposes of this study, e-journals were defined to be publications available in electronic form only and having an International Standard Serial Number (ISSN). The presence of an ISSN helps to lend an air of legitimacy to a publication and weed out more ephemeral publications such as newsletters and informal magazines, which tend not to apply for an ISSN. (Imposing a requirement that journals be peer reviewed serves the same purpose, but it is often difficult to ascertain whether a journal is peer reviewed or not.)

Two surveys of e-journals in information science have already been published. Joglekar and Sen (1999) identified 15 information science e-journals and presented some bibliometric data on them. According to their definition, an e-journal contains original work which is subject to a peer review process, and is published only on the Web at no cost. Jacso (2001) studied the coverage of e-journals (he prefers the term "digital journal") in databases covering library and information science. His definition of an e-journal is similar to that of Joglekar and Sen. Jacso chose 10 information science e-journals and reported on their coverage in six online databases.

Koehler et al. (2000) compared some of the bibliometric characteristics of three information science e-journals and a leading print journal, *Journal of the American Society for Information Science* (JASIS). They found that JASIS articles tended to have more citations, and its articles were typically longer than e-journal articles. They also observed that JASIS and Information Research (IR) seem to be perceived by authors as archival journals, while the other two e-journals they studied tended to publish reports of work in process.

In addition, they reported that JASIS authors were mostly from North America, and IR authors, originally mainly of UK origin, have become more geographically dispersed. Koehler et al. suggested that this means that IR was becoming a more mature journal.

Data Collection

Candidate e-journals for this study were obtained from the sources mentioned above, a directory of peer-reviewed scholarly e-journals published by the Association of Research Libraries (2000), and the excellent and comprehensive directory of information science e-journals maintained at the Thomas Parry Library at the University of Wales. Other Web-available directories were consulted, and the Goggle search engine was also used to identify likely e-journal sites.

As the e-journals were identified, they were processed for inclusion in the Information Science Abstracts (ISA) database. The entire run of each journal was examined, and articles relevant to the subject of information science, and published since 1995, were selected. Special efforts were made to ensure that ISA comprehensively covers all the relevant e-journals. A new Document Type (DT=E-Journal Article) was added to the database to facilitate retrieval of articles from these journals. Coverage of e-journals began in ISA Volume 35, Issue 8 (November 2000), which was a special issue devoted entirely to e-journal articles. That issue contained 557 articles from the first several e-journals that had been processed; since then, e-journals have been added to the ISA database on a regular basis.

Many e-journals offer an e-mail service to alert readers when new issues become available; these services are extremely helpful and have been used when offered to facilitate the timely updating of the database.

ISA is maintained and produced using the Microsoft Access platform. For this work, the records tagged as e-journal articles were extracted from the master ISA database and copied into a separate Access database (the "e-journal database"). Counts and analyses were then obtained by means of Access queries.

Data Analysis

In common with many other disciplines, information science has witnessed a flurry of activity in the e-journal area. The first information science e-journals appeared in the early 1990s; since 1995, three to four new journals, on average, have appeared each year. However, the number of articles appearing in information science e-journals is still only a small fraction of the total. The ISA database currently contains approximately 135,000 abstracts, so the 1,120 e-journal articles represent 0.8% of the total.

During the period in which e-journals have been published (since 1995), the ISA database contains approximately 24,000 abstracts, so the e-journals represent approximately 5% of the database for this period. If we limit these data to journal articles only (ISA contains approximately 73,000 abstracts with a Document Type of "Journal Article or "E-Journal Article"), the above percentages become 1.5% and 5.2%, respectively. As awareness of e-journals spreads and as authors begin to regard them as legitimate publication media, we can expect the number of e-journal articles to grow. (Recent research indicates that this is beginning to occur. Lawrence (2001) found that highly cited recent computer science articles are more likely to be online than in print.

e-journals differ from print journals in several significant aspects. They are disseminated completely in electronic form, and access to them is frequently free to the user. It is therefore simple to start a publication and just as simple to kill it.

When publication ceases, there are no subscription liabilities to concern the publisher because no funds have been collected from the users. There are therefore no subscriptions, and access to them all is freely available to anyone using the Internet.

CHAPTER 6

Electronic Access to Global Information

In addition with its library network programme, CALIBNET has added to itself under to information centre approach, a new dimension that of a purveyor of global information, a phenomenon that now pervades international information market.

With online access to Internet and in-house CD-ROM resources, CALIBNET can explore a wide spectrum of the knowledge base and cooperate and professional enterprises, and meet the information requirements of researchers, academics and other scholars, professional and any other practitioners engaged in a wide gamut of subject interest.

CALIBNET SERVICES/ACTIVITIES

- *On-demand Information Services*: CALIBNET has several attractive information packages:
  - *Confile Service:* CALIBNET's Confile service reaches at one's desk contents of any journal of one's choice out of over 20,000 high-impact journals. Libraries can now prune their journal subscription list or even forego subscribing to new ones, when budgetary constraints so demand, and still get expressed to their contents from ConFile. ConFile helps libraries in economizing on journal subscription and reducing the drain on precious foreign exchange resources.
  - *Caliborder:* On demand, caliborder offers the requisite back-up service by way of delivery of full text of any article and even patents.

  - *ConAlert:* Through ConAlert service CALIBNET gives current and tailored bibliographic information. One can leave with CALIBNET just keywords defining his subject interest and get at regular intervals, the current information related to his interest at his desk.
  - *RetroFile:* This service offers latest status and trend of research on any specific topic.

    ConFile, ConAlert and RetroFile, in combination, offers the latest information and advances in the entire spectrum of the subject interest.
- *CALIBLINK:* A special feature of CALIBNET is the Caliblink, a e-mail connectivity (from its ERNET hub) installed and working fine at four institutions.
- *Institutional Resources Development Services:* Some of the key institutional resources development services offered are:
  - Retrospective conversion of existing card catalogue in libraries into computerized local databases via electronic mode by down loading from international databases;
  - Consultative services on LIS automation;
  - Manpower development for operating and manning automated LIS environment through a wide range of graded training programmes, and customized courses for individuals or group at client's site.
- *SANJUKTA & PARAPAR Software.*

SANJUKTA

A multi-user storage and retrieval software has been developed in-house to support CALIBNET's Centralised Database and to provide online access from remote locations. SANJUKTA has been designed and implemented by A Mukhopadhyay, Technical Consultant, CALIBNET and his associates based on MOD+, a software he developed earlier to support management of small/medium-size libraries.The software has been developed, using 4 GL Code and designed to provide the user with options and flexibility in generating records, organizing and searching information viewing the search outputs, and interchanging data files with external databases with least manual interference.

PARAPAR

A conversion software package, PARAPAR has been developed in

CALIBNET to support interchange of bibliographic data between USMARC, UNIMARC and CCF files and also from non-standard formats to standard ones. Its primary objective is to convert data files, received from the participating libraries in variant formats, into a ISO-2709 compliant implementation through which the files are merged into the centralized Database of CALIBNET.

- *Guidelines for Implementation of UNIMARC:* It has been brought out by CALIBNET to provide the library professionals in India with a working tool for developing their databases in a mutually exchangeable format. The document has been prepared in 1994, based on UNIMARC Manual (1987), by A Mukhopadhyay, Technical Consultant, under a project sponsored by the National Information System for Science and Technology (NISSAT), Department of Scientific and Industrial Research, Government of India. The guidelines have made an attempt to take care of the special requirements of the Indian libraries. They are expected to serve the Indian libraries in upgrading their databases to the international standard.

Immediate Focus

- *Indian Resources Database:* Development of Indian Resources Database on historical value covering manuscripts and rare books, and personal collections, has already been initiated with porting on the CDB and index to serials published by Asiatic Society during the last two countries.
- *CALIBNET on INTERNET:* The design of CALIBNET web page is complete and is available on the Net. The web page(http://www.calibnet.org/) facilitates access to bibliographic information resources available through hosting of CALIBNET's centralized database. The CALIBNET website provides:

  a. Active link to access:

     — Indian Library and Network Resources.

     — Overseas Library Resources on India, including rare documents–printed and manuscripts.

     — Worldwide Library Catalogues.

     — National libraries of the world.

     — Newspapers and journals.

     — Electronic Reference tools.

- — Factual Information sources.
- — Book Trade Databases.

b. Varied CALIBNET programmes for:

- — On-demand Information services.
- — Electronic-mail connections.
- — Consultative services for Library Automation.
- — Manpower Development.
- — R&D in IT Application.

INFLIBNET

INFLIBNET is an autonomous Inter-University Centre of the University Grants Commission (UGC) of India. It is a major National Programme initiated by the UGC in 1991 with its headquarters at Gujarat University Campus, Ahmedabad. Initially started as a project under the IUCAA, it became an independent Inter-University Centre in 1996. INFLIBNET is involved in creating infrastructure, modernizing university libraries for sharing information among academic, information centres and R&D institutions in India and connecting them through a nation-wide high speed data network using the state-of-art technologies. INFLIBNET is set out to be a major player in promoting scholarly communication among academicians and researchers in India. Major activities include computerization and automation of libraries and information centres to support modern information service, creation and augmentation of databases to support academic and research work, establishment of a cooperative communication network for linking libraries, information centres and academicians to make optimum use of the resources available at the national level, up-skilling of existing library staff through regular training programmes, seminars, workshops and conventions.

Objectives

Objectives of INFLIBNET are:

- To promote and establish communication facilities to improve capability in information transfer and access, that provide support to scholarship, learning, research and academic pursuit through cooperation and involvement of agencies concerned;
- To establish INFORMATION AND LIBRARY NETWORK "INFLIBNET" – a computer communication network for linking

libraries and information centres in universities, deemed to be universities, colleges, UGC information centres, institutions of national importance and R&D institutions, etc. avoiding duplication of efforts.

Functions

In order to fulfil the broad objectives, INFLIBNET will :

- Promote and implement computerization of operations and services in the libraries and information centres of the country, following a uniform standard.
- Evolve standards and uniform guidelines in techniques, methods, procedures,computer hardware and software, services and promote their adoption in actual practice by all libraries, in order to facilitate pooling, sharing and exchange of information towards optimal use of resources and facilities
- Evolve a national network interconnecting various libraries and information centres in the country and to improve capability in information handling and service
- Provide reliable access to document collection of libraries by creating on-line union catalogue of serials, theses/dissertations, books, monographs and non-book materials (manuscripts, audio-visuals, computer data, multimedia, etc.) in various libraries in India.
- Provide access to bibliographic information sources with citations, abstracts etc. through indigenously created databases of the Sectoral Information Centres of NISSAT, UGC Information Centres, City Networks and such others and by establishing gateways for on-line accessing of national and international databases held by national and international information networks and centres respectively
- Develop new methods and techniques for archival of valuable information available as manuscripts and information documents in different Indian languages, optimize information resource utilization through shared cataloguing, inter-library loan service, catalogue production, collection development and thus avoiding duplication in acquisition to the extent possible
- Encourage cooperation among libraries, documentation centres and information centres in the country, so that the resources can be pooled for the benefit of helping the weaker resource centres by stronger ones.

- Enable the users dispersed all over the country, irrespective of location and distance, to have access to information regarding serials, theses/ dissertations, books, monographs and non-book materials by locating the sources wherefrom available and to obtain it through the facilities of INFLIBNET and union catalogue of documents.
- Create databases of projects, institutions, specialists, etc. for providing on-line information service
- Train and develop human resources in the field of computerized library operations and networking to establish, manage and sustain INFLIBNET.
- Facilitate academic communication amongst scientists, engineers, social scientists, academics, faculties, researchers and students through electronic mail, file transfer, computer/audio/video conferencing, etc.
- Undertake system design and studies in the field of communications, computer networking, information handling and data management.
- Establish appropriate control and monitoring system for the communication network and organize maintenance.
- Collaborate with institutions, libraries, information centres and other organizations in India and abroad in the field relevant to the objectives of the Centre.
- Create and promote R&D and other facilities and technical positions for realizing the objectives of the Centre.
- Generate revenue by providing consultancies and information services.

Major Activities

1. Library Automation
2. Database Development: INFLIBNET is involved in creation of union databases of books, theses, serials, experts and projects. These databases are available for online Access.
3. Software development
4. Information Services and Networking
   i) Bibliographic Information Services:
      — Online Database Access & Search
      — SEWAK

— CD ROM

— COPSAT

— OCLC's First Search

ii) Document Delivery Services

iii) University Information System

iv) Networking of University Libraries

5. Human Resources Development

6. Other Activities:

Library Automation

The automation of university libraries is a pre-requisite for networking and resource sharing. INFLIBNET Centre, through UGC, has been providing the required support to universities in phases. Till 1999-2000, 123 universities have been given initial grant of Rs. 6.5 lakh each to develop infrastructure for automation. By the end of 9th plan period, rest of the universities will also be included. After installation of the systems, further financial support is provided for the first five years to take care of recurring expenditure. These libraries on receipt of initial grant sign a Memorandum of Understanding with INFLIBNET. An integrated software for the automation of in-house functions called 'SOUL' has been developed. It has been well received by the university libraries. SOUL has been installed at 27 libraries. Many more libraries have shown desire to procure and install SOUL.

Database Development

Development of Union databases is one of the major activities of INFLIBNET. Eight databases have been developed and are continuously growing. They pertain to books, theses, serial holdings, current serials, experts, research projects, secondary serials/CD-ROMs and DDC serials. These are grouped under following two categories.

Bibliographic Databases	**Non-bibliographic Databases**
Serials Holdings	Research Projects
Current Serials	Experts
Secondary Serials Catalogue	University Information System
Theses	
Books	

The bibliographic databases represent the holdings of university libraries, for which the data is contributed by participating libraries. These databases provide an access to large pool of information available besides, serving as tool for resource sharing. Non bibliographic databases are created to promote the communication among the scholars.

Software Development

- *Library Management Software:* For the automation of in-house functions of participating university libraries, INFLIBNET Centre has developed a user-friendly state of the art GUI based software named ' SOUL' software for university libraries. This is based on Client/Server Architecture. It uses an robust RDBMS as back end tool. This works on Windows and Windows NT environment with a number of new features.
- *Utility Software:* Following utility software developed at the Centre are available to the universities on request.
- To search the data from union databases (OPAC).
- Catalogue card generation.
- Duplicate checking of records.
- Customised software for books, theses, serials.
- Data Conversion from Dbase, FoxPro and text file to ISO-2709 format.

SOUL: SOFTWARE FOR UNIVERSITY LIBRARIES

University libraries are complex entities, having large collections and serving a huge clientele. To carry out various operations in a library effectively, there is a need for automation. Computer and communication technologies have brought revolutionary changes in the information acquisition, processing, storage, retrieval and dissemination.

Keeping in view the latest trends in Information Technology (IT), INFLIBNET Centre has developed a Windows-based Library Management Software "SOUL", which provides total solution for Library Automation.

SOUL is designed using Client-Server Architecture which imparts extra strength to storage capacity, multiple access to single database, various levels of security, back up and storage facilities etc.

This software has been designed after a comprehensive study of different library related functions practiced in university libraries. It has MS-SQL Server

6.5 RDBMS as the back end. This user-friendly software is quite easy to work with. The software comprises following modules:

- Acquisition
- Catalogue
- Circulation
- OPAC
- Serial Control
- Administration

The in-built network feature of the software will allow multiple libraries of the same university to function together as well as access to the distributed databases installed at various university libraries and union catalogue mounted at INFLIBNET using VSAT network.

Information Services and Networking

Bibliographic Information Services

a) Online Database Access & Search

INFLIBNET is involved in creation of union databases of books, theses, serials, experts and projects. These databases are available for online Access:

- Books
- Theses
- Serials
- Experts
- Projects.

CHAPTER 7

The Digital and Online Cataloguing

Political posters are a vital form of cultural and political expression. However, their physical size and fragility makes them very difficult to store, they are often produced on archivally unstable paper, and because of the volatile and ephemeral nature of their content are rarely afforded the collecting and curatorial attention afforded other media such as books or records. These challenges are all powerful arguments for capturing their image, text, and relevant catalogue information in more archival and accessible formats.

As documents, they pose particular problems for digitization and cataloguing. Their physical size makes them relatively awkward to digitize, high resolution scans require enormous memory capacities, and they are an obscure enough document format that there are really no commonly-used standards for meaningful subject classification and metadata coding. As individuals and institutions begin to take on this formidable task, the need for practical standards and best practices emerges as a primary concern, especially considering the dramatically enhanced information sharing that digital media allows. Functional intercollection research depends on commonly accepted access points, keywords, and formats.

This *Study Guide* has been created to serve as a survey of the broad issues that need to be understood and considered before any organization begins to take on the task of creating a database of images. The decision to tackle this task should not be taken lightly. Even under the best of circumstances it will absorb huge amounts of time, cost more than you expected, and always draw you back for more. Here are some general questions that one should ask before starting:

1. What sort of materials are likely candidates for this approach?

   Most two-dimensional items, such as campaign buttons, posters, photos of murals, and t-shirts transfer well to digital format. Others may not.

2. Is the material unique enough to warrant the work?

   Cataloguing bottle caps found on the street may interest you, but is unlikely to draw much attention from researchers.

3. Has someone else already done it? Can you do it better?

   If there is already a complete archive of posters by the Cuban agency OSPAAAL available online, perhaps you should work on something else.

In addition, four key elements must be considered before assembling a digital collection: Method and quality of image capture and storage, Cataloguing software, Metadata content and structure, and Intellectual property protection.

Method and Quality of Image Capture and Storage

Posters are usually larger than 28×42 cms, the maximum size of most commercially available flatbed scanners. This leaves two options for digitally capturing the image: shooting it as a transparency and scanning that, or shooting directly with a digital camera. Either way involves understanding some of the technical issues of image documentation and file formats,.

The first option involves selecting an appropriate film emulsion, assembling a camera rig with lighting that is colour-balanced for that film, and making several shots of each image. Slides are then scanned, either with a dedicated slide scanner or by using a proprietary commercial system such as Kodak's Photo-CD system. A second approach is to digitize images directly. Because posters are so large and need high resolution to adequately capture relevant data, a professional-grade digital camera is usually needed.

In either case, a system for holding the posters flat, positioning the camera perfectly centred and squared on the image, and providing for balanced, even lighting are crucial to successful image capture. These are not minor tasks. Many images must be documented, demanding a Taylorist approach to streamlining the task in a manner that is safe for the documents. It is also important to evaluate if you will need to take your show on the road; some collections are too precious or protected to leave their repository, and documentation must be done on-site.

The final result must be a digital image that meets your needs and, ideally, is useful to others. The tradeoff is usually large files that are excellent for viewing fine details of the artifact (but take up lots of disk storage and transfer time) versus small files, which have the opposite characteristics. Resources for better understanding technical aspects of digital file formats, file sizes, resolution standards, and storage methodologies are listed at the end of this document.

Cataloguing Software

Once an image exists in digital form it must be catalogued. This is necessary for locating the original scan and linking the image to all the relevant catalogue information. Most modern database management programmes (such as Microsoft Access or Filemaker Pro) allow this basic process, allowing a displayed thumbnail image to appear along with selected entered data. Applications geared towards image management (such as Extensis Portfolio) offer advanced features for image display and retrieval. There are also specialized systems that include additional features particularly useful to archives and libraries.

The Getty Museum recently helped the Centre for the Study of Political Graphics (Los Angeles, CA) purchase MultiMIMSY 2000, designed by Willoughby, Inc. They use MIMSY to catalogue posters, and to track information about loans, exhibitions, conservation, etc. The software is designed for museums, rather than archives, and has many museum functions. It also has several authority files (for people, places, subjects, storage locations, etc.). The choice of software is largely determined by budget and anticipated needs. Cataloguing software should ideally offer the following characteristics:

1. Import and export of data from other systems.
2. Scalability (be able to handle as much data as you can throw at it).
3. Export to HTML and ability to access database through the www.
4. Cross-platform capability (Mac/PC).
5. Good customer support.

Metadata Content and Structure

Describing the image and the catalogued information that accompanies it is known as metadata, and is the cataloguing step that most dramatically cries for standardization. Some file fields will by necessity be purely internal, but most data accompanying a record must be seen as potentially valuable for research. This topic can be broken down into several elements: Subject Headings and Keywords, Style Protocols, and Format.

Subject Headings and Keywords: Documents need to be clearly described at the beginning if they are to be easily found later. The conventional approach to this process is to use what is known as a *controlled vocabulary*, where the terms available are consistent and comprehensive. Not only should these terms be obvious to the cataloger, they should make sense to "outsiders"-researchers, clients, and the public. Ideally, they should also mesh with terms used in other collections so that the end result is not so idiosyncratic that despite the compelling nature of its content it cannot be joined, filtered, and searched with material from other collections.

A useful start includes the Library of Congress Subject Headings (LCSH), the Library of Congress Thesaurus for Graphic Materials, and the Art and Architecture Thesaurus. However, many of the subjects dealt with in political posters are beyond the scope of standardized subject headings. This is one area where more collaborative work must be done.

Library of Congress Subject Headings are the standard for thousands of libraries as well as for a multitude of printed indexes. LCSH is the most comprehensive list of subject headings in print in the world. It provides an alphabetical list of all subject headings, cross-references and subdivisions in verified status in the LC subject authority file.

The Thesaurus for Graphic Materials I: Subject Terms (TGM I) provides a substantial body of terms for subject indexing of pictorial materials, particularly the large general collections of historical images which are found in many libraries, historical societies, archives, and museums. It was developed to support the cataloguing and retrieval needs of the Library of Congress Prints and Photographs Division, and is offered to other institutions in the hope that it will fill similar needs and will promote standardization in image cataloguing. TGM is primarily designed for automated cataloguing and indexing systems and is authorized for use in MARC records.

The Art and Architecture Thesaurus is a structured vocabulary that can be used to improve access to information about art, architecture, and material culture. It may be used as a data value standard at the point of documentation or cataloguing. In this context, it may be used as a "controlled vocabulary" or "authority." It provides "preferred" terms (or "descriptors") for concepts, as well as other synonyms that could be used by the cataloger or indexer. It also provides structure and classification schemes that can aid in documentation. It may be used as search assistants in database retrieval systems. It is a "knowledge base" that includes semantic networks that show links and paths between concepts, and these relationships can make retrieval more successful. The focus of each vocabulary is art, architecture and material culture.

Style Protocols: Catalogue data entry can be seen as a particular style of writing, with many rules regarding precision and consistency. An example- "If the artist's identity is not known, "Artist Unknown" will take the place of the artist's name. Note that "Artist Unknown" is always written in upper case. "Variation from standards may well result in lost data and imprecise recall. One authoritative source has been the Anglo American Cataloguing Rules (AACR2r), primarily designed for bibliographic material but also applicable to most archival materials. Other guidelines are available that may be more appropriate, but in this case existing standards are quite suitable for the task at hand.

Format: All document data must be entered into fields. The ultimate format of the data will ideally be one that is accessible to a wide range of institutions for research and display. One common format familiar in the library community is MARC (MAchine-Readable Cataloguing record). The MARC 21 formats are standards for the representation and communication of bibliographic and related information in machine-readable form. A MARC record involves three elements: the record structure, the content designation, and the data content of the record. The structure of MARC records is an implementation of national and international standards, *e.g.*, Information Interchange Format (ANSI Z39.2) and Format for Information Exchange (ISO 2709). Content designation, the codes and conventions established to identify explicitly and characterize further the data elements within a record and to support the manipulation of those data, is defined in the MARC 21 formats. The content of most data elements is defined by standards *outside* the formats, *e.g.*, Anglo-American Cataloguing Rules or the Library of Congress Subject Headings.

MARC records have their limitations, however, especially regarding non-bibliographic materials. One of the new standards to emerge is the Encoded Archival Description, or EAD. The EAD Document Type Definition (DTD) is a standard for encoding archival finding aids using the Standard Generalized Markup Language (SGML). The standard is maintained in the Network Development and MARC Standards Office of the Library of Congress (LC) in partnership with the Society of American Archivists. MARC records have been in use for many years, and are often the most readily available data structure. For example, the Library of Congress Yanker poster collection provides a MARC-format record of its holdings.

Development of the EAD DTD began with a project initiated by the University of California, Berkeley Library in 1993. The goal of the Berkeley project was to investigate the desirability and feasibility of developing a nonproprietary encoding standard for machine-readable finding aids such as inventories, registers, indexes, and other documents created by archives, libraries, museums, and manuscript repositories to support the use of their holdings. The project directors recognized the growing role of networks in accessing information about holdings, and they were keen to include information beyond that which was provided by traditional machine-readable cataloguing (MARC) records. The development of the EAD DTD included the following criteria: (1) ability to present extensive and interrelated descriptive information found in archival finding aids, (2) ability to preserve the hierarchical relationships existing between levels of description, (3) ability to represent descriptive information that is inherited by one hierarchical level from another, (4) ability to move within a hierarchical informational structure, and 5) support for element-specific indexing and retrieval.

Standard Generalized Markup Language was chosen over other possible solutions because of certain characteristics it possesses. SGML is a set of rules for defining and expressing the logical structure of documents thereby enabling software products to control the searching, retrieval, and structured display of those documents. The rules are applied in the form of markup (tags) that can be embedded in an electronic document to identify and establish relationships among structural parts. Because consistent markup of similarly structured documents is key to successful electronic processing of them, SGML encourages consistency by introducing the concept of a document type definition (or DTD). A DTD prescribes the ordered set of SGML markup tags available for encoding the parts of documents in a similar class. Archival finding aids, which share similar parts and structure, form a class of documents for which a DTD could be and was developed.

Although it is always preferable to design and enter data in the proper format to begin with, it is also possible to import data fields from one system into another, a process known as retrospective conversion. This is a much more complex task, given the great diversity of existing information in content and format. A recent document from the University of California Encoded Archival Description Project states that "Existing finding aids in typical repositories frequently vary in content in format that reflect both changing intellectual fashions in archival description, and changing technology used in the creation of finding aids.

Older finding aids in The Bancroft Library, for example, frequently have a minimum of identifying information, followed by a paragraph or two in which biographical or historical information is intermixed with administrative and scope and content information. This information may or may not be followed by a container list or lists of important correspondents. More recent finding aids generally have more detailed identifying information, and administrative and scope and content information is differentiated." The need for standardization in this area is crucial. A statement from the Planning Conference on UC Implementation of EAD held at UCLA on September 28-29, 1995, put it this way: "The UC Archivists' Council, UC Heads of Special Collections, several systems librarians, and representatives from the UC Division of Library Automation (DLA), Stanford, USC, The Getty Museum, and The Huntington libraries unanimously agreed that a pilot project to prototype a union database of finding aids using EAD would play a critical role in facilitating rapid implementation of the new standard by research libraries throughout California. "

Intellectual property protection

Any sharing or display of digital images poses a risk for inappropriate copying and use. In addition to standard textual warnings about protected material, several methods exist to help identify proprietary material and reduce abuse.

Without some level of protection, an organization exposes itself to litigation on behalf of the authorized agent, risks trampling the intellectual property rights of the original artist, and jeopardizes the expense of time and money that such a project requires.

The legal issues surface most prominently at three key points: *acquisition, presentation, and contractual use.*

Acquisition: The moment images are first gathered is usually the best time to establish authorized use. The artist and any other relevant parties that may have claim or consideration in the use of the image should sign a release form *before* the image is documented. In practice, many organizations may wish to use material for which no release (or an inadequate release) exists; in those cases direct follow up with the artist is the proper course of action.

Presentation: Images must be publicly displayed in a way that both properly credits the originating artist and also clearly describes legal limitations to image re-use by viewers. In addition, some technical and/or mechanical safeguards should be utilized that will limit unauthorized use. These safeguards usually include *limited-resolution images, watermarking,* and *advanced encryption protections.*

A common approach is simply to rely on displaying tiny thumbnail (~1x1.5" at 72 dpi) images that are adequate for getting a general impression of the item but are too low a resolution for any reasonable secondary use.

Watermarked images offer a higher degree of protection for images that are of sufficient resolution to be potentially abused. Various commercial systems are available that allow for some form of encoded identifier to permanently accompany an image and verify its source. Digimarc is popular one; it is easy to use because its code-embedding software is included in Adobe Photoshop, and it offers a web-spider searching feature that helps the owner learn of new web postings that contain images with the owner's user identification. Other forms of watermark embed a semi-ghosted visual logo across the image, making re-use impractical. It is important to note that these systems do not prevent image theft, they only help prove ownership once it has happened.

Advanced encryption protection systems such as Secure Image offer elegant methods to display material and still protect it from stealing. Unlike watermarks, these systems can actually block unauthorized downloading of images by web spiders, they can make screen capture impossible, and they can prevent direct linking of images from another site. They are also relatively expensive, with licenses costing as much as US $1500.

Contractual Use: Finally, any ultimate use of an image can be carefully described by contract. Generally, use contracts include specific language regarding the following subjects, if applicable:

1. Print reproduction conditions including print run, image size, colour or black and white, placement, length of use, and geographic distribution, sale/subscription price.
2. Web reproduction conditions, including restrictions on allowing direct links to the image from other sites and duration of use.
3. Image alteration, which can involve some restrictions (especially for fine artwork) that limit the end user's latitude in manipulating the image composition in any way, including flopping, cropping, and changing proportions.
4. Crediting; often there are specific guidelines as to the expected crediting of the artist, including name, date of creation, and title, as well as where that credit should reside and in what format. It is also not uncommon for supplementary information to be required, such as credit for documentary photographer, location of original artwork, image provider, participating artists, and original client.

5. Copyright protection is often specified, indicating exactly what copyright data must be displayed and where.
6. Political restrictions; some vendors go so far as to try and limit uses incompatible with their mission. For example one GettyOne image of Los Angeles graffiti includes the stated restriction "Cannot be used worldwide for political causes or issues".

One approach taken by a major institution (the Library of Congress) is to place responsibility on the patron for any misuse. This is their disclaimer:

"Division Responsibility:

As a publicly supported institution the Library generally does not own rights to material in its collections. Therefore, it does not charge permission fees for use of such material and cannot give or deny permission to publish or otherwise distribute material in its collections. It is the patron's obligation to determine and satisfy copyright or other use restrictions (such as donor restrictions, privacy rights, publicity rights, licensing and trademarks) when publishing or otherwise distributing materials found in the Division's collections.

It is the Division's responsibility to inform patrons of any donor restrictions, that is, restrictions on use stipulated by the donor when the collection was transferred to the Library. These agreements between the Library and the donor about use of the collection are separate from the legal rights of copyright, publicity, and privacy discussed in this document. For example, the terms of the gift of the Work of Charles and Ray Eames stipulates that works in the collection may not be published or used commercially without the permission of the Eames Office. This requirement is not a matter of copyright—it is possible that works in the collection may be subject to copyrights held by others—but is the result of the agreement made between the donor and the Library.

In addition, the Division's staff will attempt to inform patrons about other restrictions when information is readily available."

ONLINE CATALOGUING

TYPES OF CATALOGUING

- *Original Cataloguing:* For MARC records, you input a new master record catalogued according to current cataloguing practices and AACR2. If different rules for descriptive cataloguing are used to create the record (other than rules based on or consistent with AACR2,

AACR1, ALA 1949, ALA 1941, or ALA 1908), then code the 040 ‡e field with the appropriate MARC coding from the *MARC Code Lists for Relators, Sources, Description Conventions*. If you are using your own descriptive conventions, enter your OCLC symbol in subfield ‡e. Enter subfield ‡e immediately after subfield ‡a.

Dublin Core users apply various standards when creating Dublin Core records:

- The Dublin Core Metadata Initiative provides guidance on commonly-adopted best practices in *Using Dublin Core*: http://dublincore.org/documents/usageguide/
- In the library community, the DCMI-Libraries Working Group publishes the *DC-Library Application Profile* (DC-Lib): http://dublincore.org/documents/library-application-profile/
- Groups of libraries develop their own specific practices based on more general standards, such as those listed above. For example, see the Collaborative Digitization Program's *CDP Dublin Core Metadata Best Practices*: http://www.cdpheritage.org/cdp/ documents/CDPDCMBP.pdf
- *Copy Cataloguing:* A machine-readable record exists. You modify the record for local use and create a copy of the record with your modifications.
- *Transcribing Cataloguing Copy:* You create a master record using an existing nonmachine-readable catalogue record. Usually, you transcribe pre-AACR2 records, but you may also transcribe AACR2 records. Again, some records are created by other standards.

" When to Input a New Record," for more information on when to perform original and copy cataloguing.

LEVELS OF CATALOGUING

- Full-level cataloguing. Records that meet the requirements of second-level description (AACR2, rule 1.0D2).
- Core-level cataloguing. Records that meet the requirements of first-level description (AACR2, rule 1.0D1) and some of the requirements of second-level description (AACR2, rule 1.0D2).
- Minimal-level cataloguing. Records that meet the requirements of first-level description (AACR2, rule 1.0D1).
- Abbreviated-level cataloguing. Brief records that do not meet the

requirements of Minimal-level cataloguing specifications (*ELvl* code 3).

- Dublin Core. All records created in Dublin Core (*ELvl* code 3).

ORIGINAL CATALOGUING AND COPY CATALOGUING

Entering ISBD Punctuation

The General International Standard Bibliographic Description (ISBD) prescribes punctuation between elements or areas of bibliographic description for current cataloguing (*i.e.*, AACR2).

- Supply ISBD punctuation that occurs within variable fields. Enter punctuation and spaces between elements within a field as prescribed by AACR2.
- If punctuation separates data that occur in separate subfields, enter the punctuation at the end of the first subfield.
- Do not supply ISBD punctuation (space-dash-space) that occurs between variable fields, *e.g.*, between the 250 and 260 fields.
- Do not supply parentheses around transcribed series statements.

Space-dash-space

The OCLC catalogue card print programme supplies a space-dash-space (–) before the following fields:

- 250 Edition Statement
- 254 Musical Presentation Statement
- 255 Cartographic Mathematical Data
- 256 Computer File Characteristics
- 260 Publication, Distribution, Etc. (Imprint)
- 362 Dates of Publication and/or Volume Designation (First indicator value 0)
- 4xx Series Statements (First 4xx field)

If the field that precedes one of the listed fields ends with final punctuation (.? !), the print programme supplies a space-dash-space (–). If the preceding field does not end with final punctuation, the print programme supplies period-space-dash-space (. –).

Verifying Headings

You must use AACR2 or AACR2-compatible forms for all headings and uniform titles for current original cataloguing. Search the OCLC Authority File to verify forms of entry. Use current Library of Congress (LC) AACR2 or AACR2-compatible forms. If those forms are not in the OCLC Authority File, construct the heading or uniform title according to AACR2.

Including non-Roman Scripts

OCLC provides the capability to include Arabic, Chinese, Cyrillic, Greek, Hebrew, Japanese, and Korean scripts in bibliographic records. Include these scripts in your current original cataloguing if you have the knowledge and expertise to do so.

General Material Designations

Use General Material Designations (GMD) for current original cataloguing. GMDs are generic terms describing the medium of the item. OCLC defines subfield ‡h (Medium) in field 245 (Title Statement) for GMD information. Enter GMDs in lowercase letters enclosed in brackets. Example: ‡h [electronic resource].

GMDs and Library of Congress Rule Interpretations

Library of Congress Rule Interpretations (LCRIs), rule 1.1C, lists GMDs and provides standards for use. LC applies rule 1.1C for only certain types of materials. LCRI 21.29 limits the use of GMDs to the title area (field 245) only. Follow LC practice except:

If one of the following GMDs is applicable, it is mandatory for I-level, Core-level, and K-level records in field 245 subfield ‡h. Dublin Core users apply different codes.

‡h [art original]

‡h [microscope slides]

‡h [art reproduction]

‡h [model]

‡h [chart]

‡h [motion picture]

‡h [diorama]

‡h [picture]

‡h [electronic resource]

‡h [realia]

‡h [filmstrip]

‡h [slide]

‡h [flash card]

‡h [sound recording]

‡h [game]

‡h [technical drawing]

‡h [graphic] *

‡h [toy]

‡h [kit]

‡h [transparency]

‡h [microform]

‡h [videorecording]

* Use the "graphic" GMD only when applying the "Graphic Materials" descriptive conventions, indicated by the presence of the value "gihc" in subfield ‡e of field 040.

TRANSCRIBING PRE-AACR2 COPY

Master Record

When you create a master record from a nonmachine-readable record (often a paper record), you are transcribing cataloguing copy. Usually, the cataloguing copy is pre-AACR2. The National Union Catalogue, for example, has such records.

Guidelines in this section apply to all pre-AACR2 cataloguing copy whether part of a retrospective conversion project, reclassification project or part of normal acquisition and cataloguing workflow.

Latest Entry Cataloguing

Do not input latest entry cataloguing for serials. See the fixed-field element *S/L*

MRec

If you do not enter "dashed-on" information present in the paper copy, use code *d*.

For other modifications, follow the *MRec* guidelines for transcribing current (*i.e.*, AACR2) LC or NLM copy, listed in section 2.3, " Transcribing AACR2 Copy."

If more than one *MRec* code applies, enter the code in this order of preference: *s*, *d*, *r*, *o*.

Desc

Enter the code according to descriptive cataloguing rules:

Record is in non-ISBD form (pre-AACR1)

i Record is in ISBD form (AACR1)

040 ‡d

If you are transcribing LC copy, enter your OCLC symbol in subfield ‡d (Modifying agency) to indicate that you have made modifications (*e.g.*, changing a heading to an AACR2 form).

Verifying Name, Subject, Uniform Title Headings

Use AACR2 (or AACR2-compatible) forms for all name and uniform title headings (including the name and uniform title portions of name and name/uniform title subject headings) for retrospective cataloguing, even if the transcribed record is pre-AACR2.

You must search the OCLC Authority File to verify forms of entry. If the forms of name and uniform title entries are not in the OCLC Authority File, OCLC encourages you to construct the heading or uniform title according to AACR2, but you are not required to do so. If the subject headings are not in the OCLC Authority File, OCLC encourages you to construct the subject heading according to the Subject Cataloguing Manual, but you are not required to do so.

For entries in other 6xx fields, use the appropriate thesaurus. If the topical subject heading is not derived from a standard thesaurus but is compatible with the form of headings from that thesaurus and it has value to institutions other than yours, use either field 650 or field 651 with 2nd indicator 4 (Source not specified).

Many pre-AACR2 headings for personal names, corporate bodies, etc., are similar to corresponding AACR2 forms. However, some pre-AACR2 headings will never have corresponding AACR2 forms. Often, these headings include obsolete form subheadings. Their inclusion in WorldCat and in local catalogues usually results in split files of headings for similar materials because of different practices under AACR2 and older rules. Examples include:

OCLC encourages you to construct the heading or uniform title according to AACR2, but you are not required to do so. Change the heading or delete the heading in favour of an appropriate subject or genre heading.

If a heading appearing on retrospective cataloguing copy was incorrectly constructed under pre-AACR2, revise that heading to a valid pre-AACR2 or AACR2 form.

Series Headings

1. Fields 400, 410 and 411 Series Statement/Added Entry headings are obsolete as described in MARC 21, Appendix H. OCLC has invalidated and removed fields 400, 410 and 411. Enter such series statements as they appear in the retrospective cataloguing copy in field 490, correcting any obvious errors, and supply the series tracing in the appropriate 8xx field.
2. OCLC encourages you to construct an AACR2 form for the series but you are not required to do so. The form in the 4xx field should be compatible with the rules used for description. Trace the AACR2 form in an 8xx field.
3. If the name portion of a name/title series entry is verifiable online, enter the name portion to match the form in the name authority record.

Using GMDs (media qualifiers)

General Material Designators (GMD) are generic terms describing the medium of the item. Prior to AACR2, GMDs were known as media qualifiers. GMDs have also been called medium designators.Use subfield ‡h (Medium) for GMDs only in field 245 (Title Statement). Use only the current form of the appropriate GMD. Do not capitalize the first letter of the GMD. Enclose the GMD in brackets.

Guidelines and Exceptions

Use the cataloguing rules and conventions, including punctuation, applicable at the time of cataloguing with the following exceptions. These modifications do not require a *MRec* (Modified Record Code) code.

Guideline

Definition

Capitalization

Follow current practice

Diacritics

Enter "U.S." as "United States" and "Gt.Brit." as "Great Britain" for name headings used as the highest level of an official body of the country.

Spacing between Initials

In the descriptive cataloguing portion (2xx–5xx fields), close up spaces between single initials in accordance with current practice.

LC Control Number

See field 010 (Library of Congress Control Number) for guidelines for the input of special LC card numbers.

Main Entry, Added Entry

If the AACR2 form cannot be verified online and a single surname appears without a forename and is instead followed by a long dash, do not enter the long dash. Enter "Dezauche," as "Dezauche,".

If an asterisk precedes an added entry to indicate that the personal name has been revised, do not enter the asterisk.

Title Statement

- If the title portion has underlining, do not enter the underlining.
- Enter the same number of ellipses as appear on the LC copy.
- If ellipses occur within data, enter a space before and after the ellipses.
- If the ellipses are followed by a mark of punctuation (.,:; !?), do not enter a space following ellipses.
- If two vertical parallel lines (||) appear on the copy, enter space-slash-space (/) instead of these vertical lines. Such lines show that the title of a work is printed in verse or distinguish two editions or versions of a rare book.
- If the title has superscript and subscript alphabetic characters, enter the characters as regular lowercase characters, except in formulas.
- If the record (usually a non-English language record) has place and/or date of birth and death identified with an asterisk (*) for birth data and a single dagger (†) for death data, do not enter the symbol or the birth or death data.

Imprint Statement

- If the reprint statement has the appearance of a double imprint (*e.g.*, "Bonnae, Apud Henry & Cohen, 1856; Frankfurt/Main, Minerva, 1967"), separate the reprint statement from the imprint by a period. Enter the first (original) imprint as part of the preceding field (title or edition). Enter the reprint data in field 260 (Publication, Distribution, Etc. [Imprint]).
- In the following imprint, the place of publication appears to have a street address: "72-Souligne-sous-Ballon, l'auteur, 1968." But "72" is a postal code and "Souligne-sous-Ballon" is the name of the town. Enter both (as they appear on the card) as the place of publication.
- If a place name (*e.g.*, "Rio") is incomplete, enter the complete name with brackets around the data not appearing on LC copy (*e.g.*, "Rio [de Janeiro]").
- If two places of publication are separated by a conjunction (*and*, *und*, *u.*) or by a hyphen, enter a comma instead of the conjunction or hyphen and treat the two places as two separate places of publication.

German Imprint Statements

Separation of two place names by a hyphen usually (although not always) indicates that one place is located near a larger, better known place (*e.g.*, "Hamburg-Altona"). Treat such entries as a single place of publication. Two place names separated by "bei" or "b." (*e.g.*, "Ratingen b. Dusseldorf") constitute a single place. Treat two place names separated by *und* or *u.* as two separate places of publication.

Collation

Do not enter the statement *Cover title* in the collation. Enter *Cover title* in the first note field. When illustration information is given in the title paragraph or in a general note, but not in the collation, enter the collation as is. Do not add the illustration information to the collation. Do not enter illustration codes in the fixed field. If a statement of reprint is included, do not enter *reprint* in the 300 field. Use a 5xx note field for reprint information.

CHAPTER 8

Collection Development: Policy and Management

PURPOSE OR SCOPE OF COLLECTION

Curricular/Research/Programmatic Needs

British history, British studies, Great Britain, United Kingdom, Scotland, Ireland, Eire, Wales, Northern Ireland, British Isles, England, what's in a name? The two largest islands in Europe plus a host of small ones compose the British Isles. England, Scotland, Wales, and Northern Ireland compose the United Kingdom of Great Britain and Northern Ireland. Ireland, Eire, is an independent country. Scotland was an independent country until 1707.

Today, Scotland, Wales, and Northern Ireland once again have more authority over their internal affairs than in the previous centuries. The many smaller islands include the Isle of Wight, the Isle of Man, the Isles of Scilly, Lindisfarne, Jersey, Guernsey, Anglesey, Arran, Jura, and Islay islands, the Isle of Skye, the Shetlands, the Orkneys, and the Inner and Outer Hebrides. This policy encompasses collection building and maintenance for all of these places. History vs studies? While collecting primarily the discipline of history inclusion of "studies" in the policy title acknowledges and embraces the need to collect also material about the culture of the British Isles as well.

Specifically British history courses offered include the following: England and its Culture to 1688, Seminar in Modern European History (offered on various topics, including British ones), Historical Methods and Skills (offered on various topics, including British ones), Modern Britain since 1688,

Constitutional and Legal History of Medieval England, Constitutional and Legal History of England since 1400.

All of the general European history courses have content about the British Isles: World History to 1500, World History since 1500, European history to 1500, European History since 1500, Europe in the Middle Ages, 400-1000, Europe in the Middle Ages, 1000-1300, Later Medieval and Renaissance Europe, 1300-1500, Reformation Europe, 1500-1700, Europe in the Age of Revolution, 1700-1870, Contemporary Europe, 1870 to the Present, European Intellectual History: Natural Philosophy through Romanticism, European Intellectual History: Modernism and Post-Modernism, European Economic History, Families-Historic Perspective, History of Sexuality since the 18 Century, Seminar in Methodology and Historical Research, Historiography of Europe since 1870, Seminar in Medieval History, Seminar in International Labour and Working Class History, History of International Relations, History of Western Urbanization, World War II, and Special Topics in European History. British history is really foundational to comprehension of the histories of Africa, Asia, India, Canada, some parts of the Caribbean, and the United States. The department offers courses on the history of these countries and areas as well. Indeed, history of Africa is one of the great strengths of this department.

In addition to teaching, the Department's faculty publish books and articles, belong professional organizations, speak at national and international conferences, speak to the general public, create websites, and serve as consultants to schools and governmental units, all leading to dissemination of their research nationally and internationally. History faculty members either specializing in, or interested in, things British and Irish include the following:

- John Coogan, British and American foreign policy, ca. 1900-1950;
- William Schoenl, 20th century/contemporary;
- Gordon Stewart, British Empire, Britain and India, World history, Canada, 18th-20th centuries;
- J. Morgan Sweeney, Modern Britain, Ireland, and the Enlightenment;
- Jane Vieth, Modern Britain, World War II, Joseph Kennedy's ambassadorship, 19th century;
- Peter Vinten-Johansen, European and American health care, social and intellectual history of medicine, recently retired
- Emily Tabuteau, medieval England, cartularies, Anglo-Norman law.
- Christine Daniels, Early Modern, Colonial America

- Susan Sleeper-Smith, 18th and 19th Century. North America, gender, Native America

And, in addition to the History and English departments, many other units on campus offer courses and people do research in which British or Irish history and culture might figure in the content.

Examples: art history, philosophy, religious studies, theater, music, criminal justice, political science and pre-law, James Madison College, ethics in the life sciences, African studies, Asian studies, Canadian studies, Latin American and Caribbean studies, American studies, American Indian studies, apparel and textile/design, comparative literature, critical studies in the teaching of English, film studies, interdisciplinary humanities, interdisciplinary studies in the social sciences, museum studies, horticulture, landscape architecture, postcolonial and Diaspora literature; global cultural and literary studies, Western European studies, women, gender, and social justice, and women's studies.

The number of English department faculty with British and Irish culture interests are particularly numerous. In order to do our best to collect historical material supporting their teaching and research interests we take space here to list some of their interests related to history:

- For the earliest and medieval period: cultural history, medieval medicine, sex, aging and death in medieval medical compendiums, medieval devotional literature, medieval marriage and family, death and dissent, King Arthur, the Chronicles (early histories of England), Chaucer, *Prose Brut*, Langland, Henry of Lancaster.
- For the 16th and 17th centuries: cultural history, scientific and medical discourse, historiography, social formation, early modern travel and travel writings, economies of exchange (colonial gifts and formation of English nationalism), coronation of Queen Elizabeth I, Shakespeare, Shakespeare performance and reviews of performances, including those in the Colonies, "nabob" texts, East India Company petitions, colonial narratives, colonialism, Hardt, Negri, Gibbons, Thomas More, Machiavelli, William Harvey, Francis Bacon, Rene Descartes, Thomas Hobbes, Cavendish, John Locke, Robert Boyle, Sir William Jones.
- For the 18th century: cultural history 1660-1832, travel writing, manhood, physiognomics, Enlightenment racial science, incest and sexuality, gender issues, transatlantic modernism, Mary Wollstonecraft, Samuel Stanhope Smith, William Godwin, Lavater,

Mary Shelley, Alexander Pope, Jonathan Swift, Lady Mary Wortley Montagu.

- For the 19th century: cultural history, medicine, science and technology, liberalism, sentimentalism, print, mass markets, authorship, commerce, visual studies, travel writing, the Grand Tour, romanticism, Samuel Taylor Coleridge, Thomas Coryate, Mary Louise Pratt.
- For the 20th century and forward: both British and Irish cultural history, film in the United Kingdom, modernism and the *avant garde*, sexuality, Gay and Lesbian studies and sexuality, images of reproduction, literature of Empire, cultural periodicals post-1945, colonial conquest, decolonization, third world imperialism, Irish Renaissance, violence and modernism, criticism and religion, World War I, Henry James, Virginia Woolf, James Joyce, Marsden Hartley.

At present there are 70 names on the private e-mail list for faculty and graduate students on campus with interests in the British Isles.

History of the Collection/Existing Strengths and Emphases

British history collection is extensive and deep, one of the M.S.U. Libraries' particular strength is in the humanities. It compares very favourably in both quantity and quality with the other major university library collections in the United States on this subject. Within the C.I.C. institutions (Big Ten schools plus University of Chicago), local history collection for England, Scotland, and Wales is outstanding in both size and uniqueness, according to graphs using the OCLC WorldCat Collection Analysis programme.

What about our collecting proclivities today? Despite our distinctive local history holdings compared to those of other nearby university libraries, at present little local history is being collected beyond the record society publications, and monographs on places written from the vantage point of modern socio/economic history and published by standard trade and university presses. This is because local history is not a focus of research on campus at this time. We continue to collect 15th-18th century printed books on microfilm in order to complete large set orders begun decades ago in which we have substantial investment. We own and offer both EEBO and ECCO, the full-text online products corresponding to the pertinent microform sets; however, these electronic resources contain only a small portion of the works available in the corresponding film sets. We continue to collect secondary monographs and texts of primary works from standard trade and university presses covering all the periods of British history, giving special attention to known areas of faculty interest.

In 2002, the monies in the British Studies fund, which were being used primarily to collect works on the 1970 to present period were combined back into the British history fund as part of a desire on the part of the higher management to reduce the number of collection funds. By including the word "studies" in the policy title here we acknowledge our need and desire to collect more interdisciplinary and cultural material. We collect some antiquarian items from the 18th Century to help develop the British Studies collection in Special Collections, utilizing the Library Memorial Endowment funds in memory of Professor Thomas Bushell and Kathleen D. Kennedy.

FACTORS INFLUENCING COLLECTION POLICY

Anticipated Future Trends

We anticipate that usage of the collection will remain steady. Though money is tight, we will continue to purchase quality monographs and maintain numerous periodical subscriptions to support our range of faculty teaching and research interests as well as we can, covering all periods from the medieval to the present. While methods by which scholars study history change somewhat over time, the older approaches do not disappear. Now that the History department has moved to the College of Social Science we must support social science methodological approaches as well as the more traditional narrative and textual ones. The emphases on Migration studies, Labour and Working Class History, and Gender dictate this. We also support the cultural and interdisciplinary approaches favoured by some of our literature scholars.

We expect some impact upon this collection and its usage from the proposed New Residential College in the humanities. The appointment of a new Dean for the College of Arts and letters may affect directions too.

In terms of primary sources, we already have a significant investment in full-text electronic resources, with the subscription to the Oxford English Dictionary and purchases of LION, EEBO and ECCO. We look forward to adding Parliamentary Papers online, Early British Periodicals online, and the Empire Online. We want to attract scholars of "things British" and in order to do that we must offer suitable electronic products.

We will continue to support Special Collections' 18th-Century Studies Collection by funding purchases with the Bushell and Kennedy funds, mentioned above.

Regional or Network Resources, if Any

According to the National Shelflist Count and the OCLC WorldCat Collection Analysis system, the M.S.U. Libraries' collection of British history is among the dozen or so largest in the country. Compared to other collections ours is particularly strong in local history for England, Scotland, and Wales. The other similarly sized collections include: Library of Congress, University of Wisconsin, Columbia University, University of California-Berkeley and Los Angeles campuses, University of Michigan, Indiana University, Ohio State University, University of Washington, University of Virginia, University of Texas-Austin, and University of North Carolina.

The Centre for Research Libraries (CRL) is a significant resource for us to draw upon. They own many newspapers, dissertations, and primary materials on microform which we borrow for patrons on interlibrary loan.

We often purchase or subscribe to electronic resources cooperatively with other CIC institutions and the Michigan Library Consortium.

Relationships to Resources Treated in Other Policy Statements

In the starred (*) areas, above, the British history/studies bibliographer may recommend, purchase, or jointly purchase titles. The British history/studies bibliographer tends to handle periods not covered, historical aspects of the topics, sometimes biography, and works originating in the British Isles.

COOPERATIVE COLLECTIONN MANAGEMENT

The history of cooperative collection development is a tapestry interwoven with the strong fibres of a shared belief in the theoretical value and promise of cooperation and a rather ragged record of achieving that promise.

Dominguez and Swindler open their insightful analysis of cooperative collection development at the Research Libraries Triangle University Libraries with the statement that, "[c]ooperative collection development is the flag, motherhood, and apple pie of librarianship." Using one of these three icons as a metaphor, one might observe that it is easier to salute the flag than to put into practice the beliefs and values that it symbolizes.

Dominguez and Swindler go on to note that despite extensive literature on the topic, there are few "critical analyses based on long-term case studies that document what has worked and why." Others have also observed the scarcity of critical analyses of cooperative collection development ventures (Bennett, Branin, Weber).

This article offers a descriptive account and critical analysis of three cooperative collection development projects undertaken by the Virtual Library of Virginia (VIVA)—a consortium of the academic libraries in Virginia. We begin with a review of the current state of cooperative collection development efforts among academic libraries and a synopsis of the collective work undertaken by VIVA librarians, who, with the help of a consultant, planned and conducted the pilot projects.

BACKGROUND ON COOPERATIVE COLLECTION DEVELOPMENT

Libraries have a long, successful tradition of cooperation in many areas. At least one writer traces the tradition back to "the great library at Alexandria's lending materials to Pergamum in approximately 200 B.C." (Sohn) Cooperation in the functions of acquisitions and collection development is a more recent phenomenon. Most of the extensive literature on its history cites Walter Lichtenstein's South American buying trip in 1913-14 as the first joint acquisitions programme and the Farmington Plan of 1948 as the initial cooperative collection development programme. (Sohn)

The fifty-year chronicle of cooperative collection development programmes is summed up by many authors as filled with only modest successes (Atkinson, Bennett, Hewitt and Shipman, Shreeves, Weber). Our collective sense of having achieved only limited success may itself constrain our potential. Branin concluded that, "[t]his lack of significant, ongoing achievement is certainly one force blocking more cooperative activity in the field of collection development, for momentum has never been established."

The chronicle is not entirely bleak. Articles abound that describe the promise of cooperative collection development ventures-particularly in the early years of such ventures. (Dannelly, Dowd, Farrell and Reed-Scott, Ferguson, Forcier and Powell, Gwinn and Mosher, Hacken, Pettas and Bates, Sohn) In general, these more optimistic articles describe only one specific project, rather than a cumulative record of success in multiple projects, or describe the onset rather than the culmination of-or several years of experience with-a project. Dismal notes are more often struck usually in the articles that essay to evaluate the cumulative record of cooperative collection development nationwide. In these writings, there is consensus that the greatest successes have been achieved either at the local level (where geographic proximity is a critical success factor) or among libraries with similar missions and of similar size. (Branin, Hewitt and Shipman, Keller, Rutstein)

Most recently, some writers have begun to question the value of cooperative efforts to develop print collections. Shreeves makes a strong case for focusing cooperative ventures on the acquisition or creation of digital collections and for sharing expertise rather than print collections. He states that, "[t]he changes being experienced during the present transition to a largely digital environment offer new opportunities for cooperative collection development efforts but also call into question the value of investing in models based on a predominantly print environment. Collection development librarians may find that, in the future, their expertise may be the most important resource they have to share rather than the collections they are building."

COOPERATIVE COLLECTION MANAGEMENT PROJECTS

Mindful of the uneven track record of such ventures, the VIVA Collection Development Committee nonetheless set forth in 1995 to explore the potential for the academic libraries in Virginia to build their print collections cooperatively. Our success in the cooperative acquisition of digital collections emboldened us and the success of the VIVA Interlibrary Loan Committee in speeding up the lending of materials among our libraries gave us the certainty needed to rely on one another's collections. We shared a firm goal of increasing the number of unique titles within Virginia, aware, as De Gennaro has stated that, "[b]y itself, the network creates no new resources."

Before describing and analyzing the three cooperative collection management projects that VIVA undertook, a short description of VIVA itself may be helpful. VIVA was in the vanguard of the current trend to establish statewide consortia for purchasing electronic collections and enhancing the sharing of existing collections. Created in 2004, VIVA includes the libraries of the thirty-nine public colleges and universities in Virginia, which are located on fifty-two campuses. In addition, twenty-eight independent colleges participate in many VIVA activities. The impetus for creating VIVA came from the State Council of Higher Education for Virginia (SCHEV) and the initial funding proposal was developed by a subcommittee of the SCHEV Library Advisory Committee. VIVA's mission "is to provide, in an equitable, cooperative and cost effective manner, enhanced access to library and information resources for the Commonwealth of Virginia's academic libraries serving the higher education community." (Hurt, Perry)

The strong commitment to cooperation among the VIVA libraries has resulted in shared projects in nearly all aspects of library operations, including interlibrary lending, cataloguing, special collections, user training, and collection development. The continued improvement of interlibrary lending has been a central goal throughout VIVA's history. In fact, VIVA developed as a partial successor to VALC (the Virginia Academic Library Consortium), whose focus was primarily on enhanced interlibrary lending. The VIVA Resource Sharing Committee (initially the ILL Enhancement Committee) oversaw the purchase of Ariel software for all the libraries (and training in its use), developed new ILL protocols, manages a financial subsidy for "returnables," and facilitates shared information and training toward the goal of fast, efficient ILL operations in all of our libraries.

The cataloguers from the VIVA libraries have collaborated on a number of initiatives, most notably the development of shared guidelines for the description of electronic resources. The VIVA reference and instructional librarians have teamed up to develop efficient and effective staff training not only in the electronic collections that VIVA has purchased but also in other areas of shared training needs. The special collections librarians and archivists in Virginia's academic libraries have also initiated several cooperative projects, including shared training in putting finding aids online, joint development of a web-based timeline of Virginia history with links to special collections, and coordinated projects to digitize materials from the special collections of the six largest libraries. The work of the Technical Issues Committee undergirded all other VIVA initiatives and branched into other areas such as exploring a shared, dedicated line to OCLC for FirstSearch, ILL, and technical services support before it was disbanded as no longer needed in the current technology environment.

While the commitment to cooperation pervades all aspects of library operations and has resulted in benefits throughout our libraries, the central focus of VIVA has been on the cooperative acquisition of digital collections. The list of shared purchases and subscriptions is extensive. A current inventory is available at www.viva.lib.va.us

The benefits to Virginia's students and faculty of the cooperative acquisition of digital collections have been substantial. VIVA tracks the financial benefits in several ways, most notably by estimating the savings that have accrued through joint purchases compared to what the same digital materials would have cost had each member library purchased them separately. From July 1994 to September 1999, VIVA estimates these savings at $30.4 million. The greatest benefit realized from our cooperative acquisitions is the vastly expanded access to resources for the students and faculty throughout Virginia. For many of the member libraries, it would otherwise have been impossible to acquire these resources.

There are other, less tangible benefits that VIVA's members have received as well. All of the librarians who have had first-hand participation on VIVA's committees and workshops agree that one of the greatest rewards has been learning from each other. Shreeves suggests that in the future one of the most fruitful types of resource sharing among librarians will be sharing of our own expertise. VIVA librarians would readily endorse that concept. Another less tangible benefit for the members of the VIVA Resources for Users Committee (initially the Collections Committee) is that we gained hands-on experience in cooperative decision-making and selection. We have even gained experience in cooperative deselection decision-making, as we have needed to cancel several subscriptions.

Encouraged by our success, the benefits already realized, and a strong framework of cooperative decision-making, what was at that time the Collections Committee accepted the challenge when, in 2005, the VIVA Steering Committee charged the group with exploring the potential for cooperative development of our printed collections.

PROCESS FOR COOPERATIVE COLLECTION DEVELOPMENT

Prior to VIVA, there had been several other initiatives within Virginia to explore cooperative collection development. Most of the earlier initiatives were undertaken by the libraries of the six doctoral institutions in the Commonwealth-the College of William and Mary, George Mason University, Old Dominion University, University of Virginia, Virginia Commonwealth University, and Virginia Polytechnic and State University. There had also been several successful ventures in cooperative collection development among small numbers of academic libraries located within specific geographic regions.

The most recent previous attempt at statewide cooperative collection development took place in 2011. The chief collection development officers shared information on serials cancellation projects that were underway at most of the libraries at that time (or planned for the near future). The group agreed, in principle, to continue to share information about anticipated cancellation or acquisition of expensive serial titles-defined as over $500 in the case of cancellation and over $250 for new purchases. However, after an initial flurry of activity, the ongoing sharing of information was only sporadic.

During the late 1980s and the early 1990s, efforts at cooperative collection development were hampered by a shared sense that interlibrary lending did not work well enough to allow extensive reliance on external collections; the scarcity of detailed serials holdings data; the absence of a shared union catalogue; slow methods of communication; geographic separation over large distances; and the moderate amount of overlap among doctoral programmes.

By 2005, the landscape had changed considerably. Through new protocols for lending, widespread use of the Ariel software, subsidized express delivery of "returnables," and a firm commitment to fast service, Virginia's academic libraries had substantially improved the lending of materials among ourselves. Most of the libraries fulfiled and maintained commitments to input their detailed serials holdings on OCLC. E-mail revolutionized our communication processes. Geographic distances, moderate overlap among doctoral programmes, and the lack of a shared catalogue remained obstacles. The chief underlying obstacle-the difficulty of persuading faculty to rely on off-site collections-also remained, but its force had lessened as a result of movement from ownership to access that had occurred nationally. The terrain was also changed by the fact that this venture was intended to include all thirty-nine public colleges and universities, as well as any interested independent colleges, rather than being limited to the six doctoral institutions.

Ready to explore new possibilities, but mindful of the limited success of past efforts within Virginia and nationally to build collections cooperatively, the VIVA Collections Committee recognized the need to bring in an outside expert to assist us in making a new start at cooperative collection development. We invited George Soete, a well-known expert on cooperative collection development and a skilled facilitator, to lead two workshops on cooperative collection management. We planned to hold the two workshops at eighteen-month intervals. The initial two-day workshop was held in November 2005.

The agenda for the initial workshop included:

- A review by Soete of the key points about collaborative collection management, based on his experience as a practitioner and consultant;
- Identification of threats and opportunities in the internal and external environments both pushing libraries toward a collaborative approach and pulling them away;

- Identification of key success factors for the collaborative programme and specific projects; development of guidelines for the projects;
- Identification of key initiative areas: where would it make sense to mount further collaborative projects? Where not?
- Identification of potential projects: analysis of project ideas using the EASE/IMPACT model;
- Identification of strategies for implementation, including development of incentives for libraries to develop and implement projects, and development of ways of working with key library stakeholders (especially faculty) to interpret collaborative programmes to them.

The participants at the 2005 workshop included the thirteen members of the VIVA Collections Committee, the chairpersons of the other VIVA Committees (at that time: Interlibrary Loan, Technical Issues, User Services), some other members of the VIVA Steering Committee, and the VIVA Project Coordinator.

The workshop proved a valuable way to pool and expand our shared knowledge about cooperative collection development and, in particular, to enhance our understanding of why cooperative projects succeed or fail. It provided a framework for a systematic analysis of VIVA's existing accomplishments, a review of needs and opportunities for collaboration, and a frank discussion of obstacles as well as opportunities. Perhaps most importantly, the workshop energized participants and reduced existing skepticism about the potential for success in an undertaking in which so many others (including ourselves and our local predecessors) had previously achieved only limited results.

The VIVA Collections Committee and Steering Committee agreed that the appropriate steps for VIVA to take at that time toward cooperative collection development would be to launch several pilot projects. We deliberately planned to have pilot projects that would differ from each other in significant ways, so that we might learn as much as possible from these varied experiences. The expectation was that the projects would test whether or not our libraries could or should attempt the coordinated development of print collections on any broad scale.

In typical workshop "brainstorming" fashion, participants generated a list of twenty-six possible projects. From that list, four high-priority, potentially successful areas were identified. The initial four areas were:

1. Nursing and Allied Health
2. Scientific, Technical, and Medical Literature
3. Business
4. Preservation

Subsequently, when the project areas were presented to the VIVA Steering Committee, which coordinates all major decisions for the consortium, preservation was vetoed as an area in which to set up a pilot project.

Before describing the next steps in developing the three pilot projects, it may be useful to record some of the chief points from the workshop deliberations about what works and what does not work in cooperative collection development ventures.

Soete identified for workshop participants the following key assumptions, derived from his extensive experience in cooperative projects:

- Technical systems are typically ahead of human systems. The chief difficulties in undertaking cooperative projects are human, not technical.
- The next frontiers in the cumulative development and refinement of cooperative collection development are:
- Cooperative Collection Management (CCM) contracts that define objectives in a meaningful, clear way, and
- Systems for measuring the effectiveness of CCM.
- Print will be around for a while and there is still benefit in developing shared collections.
- New formats also offer opportunities for sharing.
- Collection dollars will continue to decline.
- Saving money is a worthwhile objective and benefit of cooperation.
- Resource-sharing is only successful when all participants perceive that their institutions gain from the cooperation.
- We need to examine our assumptions and mental models about what every library "must" have and what users "must" have on site. Too often, these assumptions are taken as self-evident without adequate review and reflection.
- Pilot projects allow valuable experimentation.

- Nothing is "forever." In setting up cooperative collection development agreements, it makes sense to plan carefully and try to anticipate the future, but it is also important to monitor and review agreements and to adjust or end them when necessary.

At the time, the workshop participants agreed with these planning assumptions. Four years later, it is less likely that all participants would still agree with all of these assumptions.

Participants also endorsed the following project guidelines:

- Projects need not involve all members as active participants, but some benefits should accrue to all members as a result of the projects. Outsiders may also be involved.
- Agreements generated by the projects should be positive and enabling rather than negative and forbidding (that is, they should describe what the libraries will collect rather than what they will not collect).
- Incentives are important. Increased access to broader collections for faculty and students is one sort of incentive.
- Selectors themselves, rather than administrators, are in the best position to craft and implement agreements-with the help of liaisons from central VIVA committees such as the Collections and Steering Committees.

We would seek projects that auger success and are:

1. Comprehensible;
2. Innovative and interesting;
3. "Do-able;" and
4. Allow for wide participation and wide benefit.

The next step in developing the pilot projects was to appoint subcommittees of subject specialists who would develop specific projects within the identified area. Three Coordinated Collection Management (CCM) subcommittees were appointed: Allied Health and Nursing (AHN); Business; and Science/Technology/Medicine (STM). Each committee was charged with the following objectives and suggested strategies:

As indicated above, the CCM subcommittees were asked to participate in the process of deciding on shared purchases of electronic collections in addition to their charge to develop pilot projects that dealt with print collections. The rationale for giving both assignments to the subcommittees was twofold. First, we believed that it might be desirable to develop electronic and print resources in unison.

For example, the shared purchase of a specific indexing and abstract database might make it more feasible for the participating libraries to then shape their collective print journal collections in that subject area based, partially, on the titles indexed. Second, we felt it would be beneficial for the groups of subject specialists to develop a shared process of decision-making and selection by first tackling the shared expenditure of new, incremental funds from the shared, central VIVA budget. After a framework for these decisions was developed, it might be easier to tackle the more difficult work of shaping shared printed collections-an effort that might entail changes in the expenditure of existing, local institutional funds.

In retrospect, this decision may have resulted in some loss of the momentum that was generated at the workshop led by Soete. It took several months to appoint the subcommittees and for them to plan and hold initial meetings. Their initial focus was on recommending expenditures from shared funds prior to a fast-approaching fiscal year cutoff. Thus, the groups were not able to direct significant attention to planning pilot projects for the cooperative development of print collections until nearly a year after the initial workshop had been held. By that time, not surprisingly, a good deal of the original momentum had dissipated, as had the sense of a shared vision of the possibilities. Furthermore, some of the subcommittee members had not participated in the 2006 workshop.

To rekindle a sense of shared vision and commitment and to assist the CCM subcommittees in planning their pilot projects we invited George Soete to return earlier than initially envisioned for the second, planned workshop. The workshop was held in November 2006. The workshop agenda included:

- An opportunity for all CCM subcommittee members to hear directly from the VIVA Steering Committee about the importance of cooperative collection management to VIVA;
- A review of the material from the November 1995 workshop, including re-visiting the reasons for choosing these subject areas for pilot projects;
- A discussion of questions and concerns that the CCM subcommittee members had about how to carry out their charge;

- An opportunity for the CCM subcommittee members to seek advice from a national expert, the VIVA Steering Committee and Collections Committee members, and from each other on how to move their projects forward; and,
- A cross-institution dialogue about the politics at each of our institutions with regard to local autonomy, faculty readiness to rely on collections at other institutions, ability to gain "buy-in" from individual selectors, and so on.

The workshop provided an excellent opportunity for all those directly involved in the cooperative collection development pilot projects to be reinvigorated by a sense of the importance of their responsibilities, to learn more about cooperative collection development projects carried out elsewhere, to share information with each other, and to discuss frankly and openly the sometimes formidable obstacles to such resource-sharing.

Charlene Hurt, then chair of the VIVA Steering Committee, conveyed an inspirational message to the workshop participants through Katherine Perry, the VIVA Project Director. Hurt urged us to see that we can not only accept, but celebrate, the concept of collective ownership of the totality of the state's academic library resources. She recommended that we think in terms not of doing "more with less," but rather of doing "more with more"-since the shared VIVA acquisitions budget had greatly expanded our collective resources.

By the end of the two-day workshop, the three CCM subcommittees had each developed a clearer sense of purpose and direction, as well as the nucleus of a plan for their pilot project. In addition, the members of the VIVA Collections Committee who did not serve on one of the CCM subcommittees (otherwise known as the "Wallflower Group") developed a plan for a fourth pilot project. The projects were as follows:

1. *Allied Health and Nursing:* Using the titles indexed in CINAHL as a core journal list, build a shared statewide collection of journals in allied health and nursing. Categorize each title as either tier 1 (must have at the local institution), tier 2 (want to have in state), or tier 3 (can rely on ILL from out of state). Seek agreements among in-state institutions to ensure coverage of all titles in tiers 1 and 2.
2. *Business:* Using the same 3-tier categorization described above, seek coordinated agreements about subscriptions to or cancellations of economics journals titles that cost over $200.

3. *Science/Technology/Medicine:* Develop a cost-sharing model for the shared VIVA subscription to the Academic Press IDEAL database that would go into effect in 1997/98, when the terms of the AP contract require such cost-sharing and shared decisions about subscription cancellations. Attempt to develop a model that would be applicable to other, future contracts

4. *Project Confidence:* Identify a core collection of an online full-text journal service that VIVA will commit to provide for at least three years in order to facilitate the review of local journal subscription in VIVA libraries and increase the potential for cancellation of local print or microform subscriptions in favour of reliance on the VIVA shared electronic subscription. This project would compare the full-text coverage of the standard services such as IAC, UMI, and Wilson for overlapping titles that VIVA would be likely to continue to provide whether by extending our shared subscription to the IAC *Expanded Academic Index* or by choosing an alternate provider in future years.

A description of the goals, methods and outcomes of three of the four projects described above follows. While the cost-sharing model developed by the STM Subcommittee was very important, we do not include it since its focus was not on cooperative collection management.

Bibliography

Abdul, A.M. Hug and Mohammed, M. Aman: *Librarianship and the Third World: An Annotated Bibliography of Selected Literature on Developing Nations, 1960–1975*,Garland Publishing, New York, 1977.

Amoroso, E.: *Fundamentals of Computer Security Technology*, Prentice Hall, Englewood Cliffs, 1994.

Berard, R.: *International Encyclopedia of Information and Library Science*, John Feather & Paul Sturges, Routledge, London, 2003.

Brichford, Maynard J.: *Archives and Manuscripts: Appraisal and Accessioning*, Chicago, Society of American Archivists, 1977.

Buchanan, B.: *Theory of Library Classification*, London, Bingley, 1979.

Carroll, Frances Laverne & Harvey, John F.: *Internationalizing Library and Information Science Education,* Connecticut, Greenwood Press, 1987.

Chan, L.M.: *Library of Congress Subject Headings: Principles and Application*, Colo, Libraries Unlimited, 1995.

Chepesiuk, Ron: *Winthrop College Archives and Special Collections: A Manual of Policies and Procedures,* South Carolina: Winthrop College, 1978.

Choudhary: "Library Networks in India: An Overview," *in New Vistas in Library and Information Science*, Delhi: Vikas, 1995.

Dasgupta, A.K.: *An Essay in Personal Bibliography: A Bibliography of Writings on and by S.R. Ranganathan,* Asia, Bombay, 1967.

Devi, Savitri and Johri, Nutan: *Bibliographic Reprints: Library Science and Informatics,* NASSDOC, New Delhi, 1986.

Duckett, Kenneth W.: *Modern Manuscripts: A Practical Manual for Their Management, Care, and Use*, Nashville, American Association for State and Local History, 1975.

Gentle, James E.: *Random Number Generation and Monte Carlo Methods*, Springer-Verlag New York, 1998.

Gupta, B.M.: *Libraries, Archives and Information Technology: An Annotated Bibliography, 1970–1990*,Aditya Prakashan, New Delhi, 1991.

Harry Gidney Aldis: *The Printed Book,* Cambridge University Press, Cambridge, 1916.

Hopcroft, John and Jeffrey Ullman: *Data Structures and Algorithms*, Addison-Wesley, 1983.

K.K.: *Documentation on Acquisition in Libraries,* Janaki Prakashan, Patna, 1982.

Kahan, W.: *Accurate Eigenvalues of a Symmetric Tridiagonal Matrix*, Computer Science Dept., Stanford University, 1966.

Kahn, Miriam B.: *Disaster Response and Planning for Libraries,* Chicago, American Library Association, 1998.

Kapur, Shabad: *Classification and Cataloguing: A Select Bibliography*, Harman Publishing House, New Delhi, 1988.

Kaur, Baljit: *Human Development and Family Studies in India: An Agenda for Research and Policy*, New Delhi, Sage, 1993.

Kearfott, R.B.: *Rigorous Global Search: Continuous Problems,* Dordrecht, Kluwer, 1996.

Koul, R.K.: *Indic Names: A Documentation List,* Seemant Prakashan, New Delhi, 1980.

Kruckeberg, Dean & Starck, Kenneth: *Public Relations & Community: A Reconstructured Theory*, Greenwood, 1988.

Kumar, P.S.G., A. Tejomurty, and H.R. Chopra: Research in Library and Information Science in India: a Bibliography of Ph.D., M.Phil., and M.L.I.Sc. Dissertations, Concept, New Delhi, 1987.

Lammle, Todd: *CCNA* Cisco Certified Network Associate Study Guide, Sybex, London, 2005.

Malhan, I.V. and Kapur, Shabad: *Library Education: A Select Bibliography*, Metropolitan, New Delhi, 1982.

Markey, K.: *The Online Catalogue: Developments and Directions*, London, Library Association, 1989.

Mitchell, J.: *Dewey Decimal Classification and Relative Index: Devised by Melvil Dewey*, Albany, Forest Press, 1996.

Neumaier, A.: *Interval Methods for Systems of Equations,* Cambridge, Cambridge University Press, 1990.

Pathak, Vijay and Ramiah, L.S.: *Bibliography of Research in Library and Information Science in India,* Indian Documentation Service, Gurgaon, 1986.

Prasher, Ram Gopal : *Indian Library Literature: An Annotated Bibliography,* Today and Tomorrow's, New Delhi, 1971.

Ranganathan, S.R.: *The Five Laws of Library Science,* Bangalore, Sarada Ranganathan Endowment for Library Science, 1988.

Raymond, Godfrey Nunn: *Asian Libraries and Librarianship: An Annotated Bibliography of Selected Books and Periodicals, and Draft Syllabus,* Scarecrow Press, Metuchen, N.J., 1973.

Rowley, J.E.: *Organising Knowledge: An Introduction to Information Retrieval,* Aldershot, Gower, 1987.

Satija, M.P. and Amrik Singh: *Bibliography of Colon Classification, 1930–1993,* MD Publications, New Delhi, 1994.

Seitel, Fraser P.: *The Practice of Public Relations,* Macmillan, 1994.

Singh, Sewa and Singh, Sukhbir: *Colon Classification: A Select Bibliography,* Ess Ess Publications, Delhi, 1992.

Stoll, E.: "A Very Fast Shift-Register Sequence Random Number Generator", *Journal of Computational Physics,* 1981.

Taylor, Arlene G.: *Wynar's Introduction to Cataloging and Classification,* Westport, Libraries Unlimited, 2000.

Taylor, Sue: Building Libraries for the Information Age: Based on the Proceedings of a Symposium on The Future of Higher Educational Libraries at the King's Manor, Institute of Advanced Architectural Studies, University of York, York, 1998.

Tejomurty, A. and Shukla, K.H.: *Thirty-three Years of Annals of Library Science and Documentation,* RBSA Publishers, Jaipur, 1988.

Venkat Reddy, K.: "Libraries as Intellectual Workshops," in *New Horizons in Library and Information Sciences, Festschrift*, T.R. Publications, Madras, 1994.

Vickery; B. C.: *Information Systems*, Butterworth, London, 1973.

Wexelblat, Richard: *History of Programming Languages*, Academic Press, New York, 1981.

Wilson, Leslie B. and Clark, Robert G.: *Comparative Programming Languages*, Addison-Wesley, England, 1988.

Index